"This book belongs on the shelf of every public supply chain professional. The text is interesting, readable, and equally relevant to students, new buyers, and seasoned professionals. The many examples bring clarity and are often entertaining."

—John Adler,
CPPO, Vice President of Procurement, Dallas Area Rapid Transit

"In professional procurement we must continually add value to the procurement process. This revised book, designed to complement NIGP's Public Procurement Competency Framework, will show you how to add that value."

—Edward J. Pabor,
CPPO, CDT, C.P.M.

"This third edition of *Legal Aspects of Public Procurement* enhances earlier editions by adding real life scenarios, allowing students to relate the text to the procurement world they work in. The authors' expansion of critical topics such as invitations for bid and requests for proposals makes this text more relevant to today's procurement workload. These experts in procurement legal matters establish a solid foundation that should be a standard desktop reference for all emerging procurement leaders."

—Kristy D. Varda,
CPPO, CPPB

LEGAL ASPECTS OF PUBLIC PROCUREMENT

Legal Aspects of Public Procurement, Third Edition provides a glimpse into the relationships between the legal, ethical, and professional standards of public procurement, outlining not only the interconnections of federal, state, and local law but also best practice under comprehensive judicial standards. The book addresses the ever-changing legal structures that work in conjunction and define the public procurement profession, providing recommended guidance for how practitioners can engage in the function while staying ethically aligned. Instead of trying to address every issue at the heart of public procurement, however, the book seeks to establish the history and spirit of the law, outlining how practitioners can engage proactively and willingly to not only perform their function, but to also become advocates for procurement law modernization.

This third edition features new chapters on competitive sealed proposals and contract administration, as well as a thoroughly revised and updated chapter on procurement of information technology to better relate to an increasingly digital world. Promoting a start-to-finish guidance of the procurement process, *Legal Aspects of Public Procurement* explores the relationships between solicitations, offers, contract administration, and the cutting-edge aspects of technology procurements, providing a theoretical and case-study driven foundation for novice and veteran practitioners alike.

Michael Flynn, Esq., is a professor of law at the Nova Southeastern University Shepard Broad Law Center in Fort Lauderdale, FL. Professor Flynn received his undergraduate, magna cum laude, and his law degree, cum laude, from Gonzaga University in Washington. He was a trial lawyer and litigator in private practice and the Assistant Attorney General in the Washington State Attorney General's Office. He served as the Chief of the Consumer Protection and Antitrust Division of the Washington State Attorney General's Office in Eastern Washington. He has taught at the University of Washington, the University of Miami, and Stanford University; has authored over 35 articles; and has conducted or presented at seminars and conferences for various professional groups.

Kirk W. Buffington, CPPO, C.P.M., is the Director, Procurement Services for the City of Fort Lauderdale, FL. Prior to public service, he was employed in the private sector. He holds a bachelor's degree from Florida State University and earned his masters of business administration degree from Webster University. A strong supporter of the profession, He has served numerous positions of leadership in procurement associations on the local and national level. He sits on the NIGP Board of Directors. By invitation, he presented a paper at the first International Symposium on Supply and Public Procurement in Budapest, Hungary in 2003. He is a well-known speaker on government eProcurement topics.

Richard Pennington, CPPO, was General Counsel to NASPO ValuePoint from 2013 until 2018. He is a retired Air Force colonel who specialized in government contract law as a judge advocate. With the State of Colorado, he served as an assistant attorney general, state purchasing director, and director of the Division of Finance and Procurement. He was also of counsel in the Denver government contracts practice of McKenna, Long & Aldridge LLP. He received his Air Force commission from the U.S. Air Force Academy, a J.D. from the University of Denver, and an LL.M. (Government Procurement Law) from The George Washington University. His articles appear in NIGP's *Government Procurement* and NCMA's *Contract Management* magazines. He is the author of *Seeing Excellence: Learning from Great Procurement Teams.*

Cornerstones of Public Procurement

NIGP—The Institute for Public Procurement, USA
Content Editor

Recently Published Books

Legal Aspects of Public Procurement, Third Edition
Michael Flynn, Kirk W. Buffington and Richard Pennington

LEGAL ASPECTS OF PUBLIC PROCUREMENT

Third Edition

MICHAEL FLYNN,
KIRK W. BUFFINGTON
AND RICHARD PENNINGTON

Routledge
Taylor & Francis Group
NEW YORK AND LONDON

Third edition published 2020
by Routledge
52 Vanderbilt Avenue, New York, NY 10017

and by Routledge
2 Park Square, Milton Park, Abingdon, Oxon, OX14 4RN

Routledge is an imprint of the Taylor & Francis Group, an informa business

First edition published by the National Institute of Governmental Purchasing 2004
Second edition published by the National Institute of Governmental Purchasing 2007

Library of Congress Cataloging-in-Publication Data
A catalog record for this book has been requested

ISBN: 978-0-367-47172-9 (hbk)
ISBN: 978-1-003-04116-0 (ebk)

Typeset in Galliard
by Apex CoVantage, LLC

Contents

Preface

Few tasks are as daunting as assimilating and explaining the legal aspects of public procurement. Still, that is the purpose of this book, which contains an amalgam of instructional text, statutory provisions, and relevant case studies—real and hypothetical. While the basic structure of this revised edition remains the same, new chapters have been added to cover the legal aspects of competitive sealed proposals and contract administration. In addition, we revised the chapter on procurement of information technology to better relate to our increasingly digitalized world.

The vast amount of law available and applicable to procurement contracts requires that the book focuses on some of the most critical and applicable portions of the law of contracts with an emphasis on United States law. It has been used to teach Canadian procurement practitioners for many years, however. Because both U.S. and Canadian contract law have evolved from a common origin—English common law—the principles taught in this book are very similar in both countries.

Chapter 1 contains the essential principles and structure of the United States legal system. It includes the foundations of statutory, common, and administrative law. It also provides a brief, but relevant, history of statutory law relating to public procurement, including an updated review of legal precedents affecting the protection of market competition. The chapter also includes a short discussion of laws governing public records and intellectual property rights, including patents, copyrights, and trademarks, and closes with some suggested guidelines for performing legal research.

Chapter 2 discusses the legal framework for procurement law and highlights the sources and types of contracts in public law. Within the framework of public procurement, the chapter reviews the general principles for applying and interpreting public contract law and describes its relationship to civil and public law, criminal law, and tort law. Of particular importance to the public procurement professional, this chapter also discusses the government's authority to contract, the law of agency, and the relationship between the principal (typically, the government) and its agents (typically, the public procurement professional). As statutory law defines the operational parameters of public procurement, this chapter also discusses the framework and key concepts of ABA's Model Procurement Code for State and Local Governments while introducing other statutes and regulations, such as the Uniform Guidance regulations that govern federally funded procurement, that impact the public procurement function. In addition, a brief introduction to cooperative procurement law is included in this edition. At the end of the chapter, the importance of developing enabling legislation is emphasized.

Chapter 3 focuses on the basic components of contracting, including the six essential elements needed to form a legal contract. In several cases, these contractual elements are parallel to the Uniform Commercial Code and public procurement practices. The chapter addresses conditions that could lead to a voidable contract, including mistakes, misrepresentations, trade constraints, and remedies for contract breach. The chapter reviews the conditions for oral and written contracts and contrasts some of the differences between private and public contracting.

Chapter 4 provides a comprehensive review of Article 2 of the Uniform Commercial Code, which serves as the template of laws governing the sale of goods in the United States. Within the chapter, the reader will learn about the range of contract warranties, from warranty of title and express warranties to two essential types of implied warranties. The chapter also offers a good understanding of contractual performance requirements under the Code, which include both the buyer's and seller's rights when performance is not consistent with contractual provisions, the concepts of acceptance and rejection of goods, and the remedies that are available if one of the parties breaches the contract. The chapter addresses special remedies, such as liquidated damages, as well as incidental and consequential damages. Finally, the chapter highlights four key concepts within Article 2 of the Code: the statute of frauds, the parol evidence rule, assessing conflicts on the use of different contract forms, and the principle of unconscionability.

Chapter 5 emphasizes the legal issues in solicitations for competitive sealed bidding. Solicitations require development of specifications and contract terms and conditions. Then, there are formalities that have to be followed in public bidding, including responsiveness of bids. One unique aspect of public procurement is the requirement that the contractor be responsible, along with procedures for suspending and debarring contractors from doing business with the government when they have recurring issues with integrity and performance. Preserving the integrity of the bidding process also involves providing remedies for resolving allegations of bidding irregularities.

With this edition, a new Chapter 6 was added to introduce the legal issues in competitive sealed proposals (RFPs). The chapter discusses pre-solicitation issues, such as confidentiality of information, organizational conflicts of interest, and the impact of international law on procurement practices. The chapter covers cost and price analysis, a topic not as relevant to competitive sealed bidding, while also exploring legal issues that can arise between the time of proposal receipt and contractor award, especially the discussions or negotiations that occur between a public entity and the proposer.

The new Chapter 7 looks at the legal context for contract administration. While Chapter 5 has a useful checklist for terms and conditions, Chapter 7 highlights key legal principles that illustrate the operation of those terms and conditions. The chapter discusses changes during contract performance, a differing site conditions clause of particular importance to construction, and theories of constructive change that often arise out of contract administration activities. The chapter covers issues of time and scope in government contracts in addition to the terminations of contracts. The chapter treats the topic of waiver separately because of its importance. The discussion includes liability allocation clauses—some of the most negotiated provisions—and how they operate. The chapter closes with a discussion of common approaches to the resolution of contract controversies during performance.

With the phenomenal growth and impact of technology in the public sector, Chapter 8 provides an opportunity to explore legal issues in evolving developments in IT procurement. The original chapter, much of it retained in this revision, provided a good framework for understanding the "small print" in contracts and issues to consider when negotiating software licenses. This revised chapter invites analysis of legal issues in new developments in information technology. Software is often not hosted on government sites, but is in the "cloud," requiring analysis that is not license-based. In addition, the high number of failures in large software integrations, so-called "waterfall" implementations, has spawned new project delivery methods, such as Agile and modular procurement. Chapter 8 looks at these developments from the perspective of legal issues introduced earlier in the book.

Chapter 9 provides an excellent discussion of the ethics and professionalism in public procurement. The chapter discusses ethics within public procurement with respect to obligations to employers, suppliers, the profession, the field of public administration, and the general public. Chapter 9 ends with a summary of attorney rules of professional conduct that are especially relevant to procurement practitioners.

Chapter 10 concludes the text by providing both actual case law and hypothetical situations for consideration. The case law explores legal decisions on the acceptance and rejection of goods and cases involving the rights of both parties in contract awards. New cases have been added regarding contract administration topics. The hypothetical studies parallel issues related to Article 2 of the Uniform Commercial Code with respect to liquidated damages, the unenforceable terms of a purchase order, applying implied warranties to a contract breach, the implications of law of agency, and volume purchase commitments.

In the intervening decade since the last edition was published, full-text judicial opinions have been published online. Almost all of the cases cited in this book can be found without a legal research database subscription, and these cases can provide excellent discussion topics in classrooms and office meetings. Another innovation with this edition is NIGP's promotion of call-out boxes. These are short, textual "asides" that illustrate points, return to an application of previous materials, or show how concepts are applied.

This book covers a lot of legal ground, and yet it provides only a glimpse of the legal framework that governs public contracting. Hopefully, the reader will gain a true appreciation and understanding of the breadth and depth of the legal aspects of public procurement.

Note

We acknowledge that many legal references use the terms "offer" and "offeror" when referring, respectively, to the response to a Request for Proposals and the person or entity that responds. While the law may be slow to change, public procurement continues to evolve, resulting in a changing and expanding language. NIGP has taken a proactive approach, assembling a community of procurement professionals from the United States and Canada to discuss, review, and update terms and definitions. To maintain consistency through its educational products, NIGP has updated the language in this textbook. Specifically, the terms "offer" and "offerors" used in the manuscript when discussing the response and responder, respectively, to a Request for Proposals have been changed, when appropriate. The term "offer" has been revised to "proposal" and the term "offeror" to "proposer" when discussing Requests for Proposals. Similarly, the term "Bid Protest" is no longer used in every context. Rather, it has been revised to "Protest against the Solicitation" or "Protest against Award."

Acknowledgments

This is the third time that I have had the privilege of being a co-author of the NIGP text, *The Legal Aspects of Public Procurement*. Each time the adventure of writing this book has been a pleasure because of the support and expertise provided by NIGP. With this edition, I had the pleasure of working with Bradley Davis as the editor. Bradley's energy and skillful editing makes my writing better than it probably is, and I am so grateful for his patience and guidance. I also want to thank Carol Ann Ivory (again!) and Laura Shelters at NIGP for making my task easy!

This edition introduced me to a new co-author, Richard Pennington, a skillful lawyer, writer, and teacher. On the previous two editions, Kirk W. Buffington was my co-author and trusted colleague. I regret that Kirk could not participate in this revision of the text and wish him well. However, there has been no better partner in the revision of this text than Richard. Thank you, Richard, for teaching me and for your expertise.

I cannot begin to thank all of the people who have guided, supported, and inspired me in the writing of my portion of this book. As a litigator and trial lawyer turned law professor, I did not envision that I would ever actually write a book. I first must acknowledge Professor Robert Whaley of The Ohio State University Law School. Professor Whaley is, in my estimation, the preeminent educator and textbook author concerning the Uniform Commercial Code. I hope that my modeling of this book in part on his work is a tribute. I also cannot leave out Professor Thomas Crandall, who taught me the Uniform Commercial Code at the Gonzaga University School of Law. Professor Crandall was a treat to have as a teacher!

I also thank my support group at the Nova Southeastern University Shepard Broad College of Law, especially my "West Wing" colleagues Professors Mike Dale, Joseph Hynlka, Amanda Foster, and Professor Emirates Joel Mintz. I also thank Professor Michael Masinter, who is my "go-to" teammate when it comes to sticky Uniform Commercial Code and other legal questions. These colleagues not only represent a standard of excellence for law teachers and scholars, but make coming to work fun.

I also want to thank my wife, RoseAnn Flynn, a better lawyer and person than I, and my two talented daughters, Kelsey the actor and Mallory the high school teacher and coach, for their unending support.

I know I have left out people to thank, and I thank them all now. It almost goes without saying that any mistakes or inaccuracies in this book should be blamed on me, and anything that is good about this book is a credit to others.

Mike Flynn

The decision to assist in this portion of the LEAP Text Writing Project was not taken lightly when I was first approached by NIGP. But, even so, I had no idea of the amount of work, time, and effort that would ultimately be expended in completing this text. As a full-time working professional with more than 15 years into his working life, I would never have thought I would actually write a textbook. Completing this project has been a true exercise in realizing the potential that is in all of us.

This book and many other accomplishments in my personal and professional life would not be possible without the support, patience, and encouragement of my husband, Glenn Voeltner. His belief in my abilities was greater than my own. Thank you, Glenn, for all you have done to make me a success.

I must thank the staff of NIGP, and especially Carol Hodes, who first approached me and believed in me enough to think I could complete this task. Carol became a true sounding board throughout this project. Her humor and good sense kept me going when I thought I couldn't. I must also thank and acknowledge the contribution of my co-author, Michael Flynn, who stepped in at the last minute and said, "Yes, we can do this." Without his encouragement and very competent editing, this book would have never been completed.

I must also acknowledge the support of both my former employer, the City of Fort Lauderdale, and the staff of the Procurement Division, including Patty Oliveira, who assisted in typing and support of my efforts; Leroy Harvey, my research assistant and contributor of one of the book's chapters; and, of course, the rest of the staff: Linda Wilson, who always told me what she thought; James Hemphill, my able number two, who provided assistance at work; Carrie LeBlanc, Frankie Faison, Richard Ewell, Marsha Perri Bennett, and David Nash, all of whom never thought I was crazy for this endeavor, or at least didn't tell me so to my face. They all made it possible for me to complete this project. In addition, I must acknowledge the support and patience of Mr. Bruce Larkin, my director, who encouraged me and has mentored me throughout my career at the city.

Obviously, I have left out some who contributed to the completion of this text. I must agree with my co-author that all inaccuracies and mistakes are my responsibility, and what is good about this book is a credit to those mentioned here and to many others in my life.

My thanks to all.

Kirk W. Buffington

I was a late-comer to this book. I've taught using the previous edition for 10 years. It was a terrific textbook for the classroom. Many thanks to Kirk W. Buffington and Mike Flynn for their creative insight. I've heard that co-authoring can be a challenge, but Mike made it very easy on this third edition. Thanks, Mike!

I was honored to be asked to contribute. My journey to here started with the government contracts program at The George Washington University, where Ralph Nash and the late John Cibinic introduced me to government contracting in a way that has sustained my learning as I moved from Air Force JAG into state procurement. My colleagues at the Colorado attorney general office took a chance on a retired Air Force colonel, and my fellow procurement professionals at the Colorado State Purchasing Office put up with my "federalism." After my state service, the Denver Government Contracts Office of McKenna, Long & Aldridge LLP scratched my private law practice itch and helped with my first book, the *Colorado Procurement Handbook*. For five years, I was part of an exceptional team, NASPO ValuePoint, supporting states in cooperative procurement. They let me practice my craft and stay connected to two great associations, NIGP and the National Association of State Procurement Officials.

NIGP spurred my teaching transformation and introduced me to this book. I want to thank some NASPO and NIGP colleagues in particular. Barb Johnson was my NIGP training mentor and provided valuable practitioner insight into the RFP chapter. Keith McCook has been an attorney colleague for years in my NASPO affiliation; Keith is one of the smartest government procurement attorneys I know and contributed immensely to my revisions. Richard Goldberg helped sharpen my understanding of Agile. John Adler, a NASPO colleague who pushes the envelope on best practices and teaching, improved all three new chapters. Dugan Petty, who has spanned leadership in procurement and information technology in two states and two national associations, brought his special competence to the information technology chapter.

Bill McAvoy, NASPO's lead author on the request for proposals chapter of *State and Local Government Procurement: A Practical Guide*, offered invaluable suggestions. NIGP instructor colleagues Ed Pabor and Jon

Walton spent considerable time doing a final review of the book and offering valuable suggestions. And, finally, I echo Mike's praise of Brad Davis, and I'd add Lisa Frank. They are exceptional editors who made this book much better. Thanks for the help, everyone!

Richard Pennington

Chapter 1

The Essential Principles and Structure of the United States Legal System

The center of every public procurement professional's responsibility is a contract—that document that creates a legally binding obligation for the seller to deliver the goods or services and for the buyer to pay for them. Whether you call this agreement a purchase order, a letter agreement, a procurement contract, or any other name, the contract is the core of the procurement professional's responsibility.

Within this area of responsibility, the public procurement professional must know and understand the law of contracts within the context of public procurement. Though not expected to be a lawyer, it is imperative that the procurement official has a sense about the principles of contract law and the legal consequences of their actions. Additionally, being able to talk intelligently with legal counsel regarding strategy, methodology, and legal justifications will go a long way in giving the public procurement professional greater credibility. There may be times that the public procurement professional finds a specific court case regarding a procurement issue that legal counsel was not previously aware of.

Contracts operate within a broad context of law and regulations. This chapter focuses on the essential principles and structure of the United

States legal system. The discussion introduces statutes broadly applicable to commercial practices in the market economy, the Sherman and Clayton Anti-Trust Acts, as well as their impact on the protection of market competition. The chapter includes two other statutory schemes broadly applicable to both public procurement and other government and commercial operations: open records statutes and intellectual property rights. The chapter concludes with an overview of the United States judicial structure and suggested guidelines for performing legal research.

The Foundation: Sources and Types of Law

The American legal system is founded upon English tradition with a singularly American twist. The American legal system looks to statutory law, administrative law, and common law for its guidance.

Statutory Law

Statutory law includes the Constitution of the United States in addition to the constitutions of the various states and the charters of local government entities. The United States Constitution is the primary source of law in our country. Among other things, it establishes the relationship between the federal government and the states. The Constitution authorizes the U.S. Congress to enact laws within the powers granted by the Constitution. The authority not specifically granted to Congress or other parts of the federal government are then reserved for the states. As the predominant source of law, public entity legislation, administrative rules, and contract provisions can be invalidated if they violate constitutional protections. For example, the United States Supreme Court has invalidated government contract provisions establishing submission of offers and participation preferences based on the ethnic status of company owners where not supported by adequate factual evidence of past discrimination.

Statutory law also includes the legislative enactments by the U.S. Congress, the various states' legislative bodies, and the legislative actions of local government entities. The primary source of law and authority for public procurement professionals is legislatively enacted statutes and ordinances. This legislation not only grants contracting authority to a government official or entity, but also may set out the specific policies and procedures for purchasing goods and services. For example, most state statutes contain a specific section concerning public works projects that include the requirements for the construction of public buildings and facilities.

Once legislation is signed into law by the president of the United States at the federal level, or the governor of a state at the state level, it is called a "public law." Public laws are organized by subject matter in both the United States Code and the corresponding state statutory codes.

Administrative Law

Administrative law includes the rules and regulations formally promulgated by federal, state, and local government entities. Administrative law divides into two different but connected kinds of processes: rule making and rule enforcement. The rule-making function of administrative law refers to the process of government entities at the federal, state, and local level enacting rules for the implementation of legislative policy. This is a formal process in which government entities, armed with the authority granted by a legislative act, craft rules and regulations that reflect the intent of the legislative body in enacting a law. For example, a state or local government entity may choose to enact a law that requires a contractor to obtain a particular kind of license to engage in a specific type of business activity.

As part of legislative enactment, the government entity may delegate and task an entity to set up the procedure to obtain a license, including the qualifications and fee for such a license. The government entity must then create a licensing scheme within the parameters of the delegation of authority given to it by the legislative enactment. This rule-making function permits the governmental entity to interpret the legislative enactment and effectively carry out the intent of legislative enactment. Once the entity crafts the rules and regulations, these proposed rules and regulations are then announced, signaling the ability of the public to provide written comments concerning the proposed rules and regulations. In addition, in most cases, the entity will be required to hold public hearings to accept comments from the public. This process of written comments and public hearings ensures all parties have adequate notice and an opportunity to be heard before the rules and regulations are formally adopted and implemented. This is due process in action.

In addition to the rule-making function, and perhaps even as part of the rule-making function, administrative law may also include a quasi-judicial process in which the entity can now enforce the rules and regulations. These "administrative" hearings are usually less formal than a court proceeding but still afford basic due process rights for the participants. These due process rights are both procedural, a full and fair opportunity to be heard in a public hearing, and substantive, the right to fair and reasonable determination of the contested issue. For example, when a contractor is denied a license based on the application of administrative rules and regulations, the contractor will be afforded due process rights—they will have a right to appeal that decision to a hearing officer or panel to review the denial. Many states have administrative law processes and hearing officers for resolving challenges to awards of contracts and claims arising during contract performance.

Common Law

In contrast to statutory law, common law is created by judicial decisions through the court systems. The collection of judicial opinions from both the federal court system and the various state court systems makes up the common law, which is the body of courts' opinions interpreting the statutory law and the rights of the parties to a lawsuit. As such, the judicial opinions represent the case law that is aggregated into the common law. This case law has value because it sets a precedent for what a public procurement professional should and should not do in particular circumstances.

When lawyers, judges, and others refer to the common law, they are citing the collection of court decisions regarding a particular legal subject. It is from this collection that a legal rule of general application can be extracted. Once extracted, this rule would then apply as precedent in similar situations. For example, the concept that a person who acts in bad faith—lies—when entering into a contract will not be entitled to receive the benefit of that contract is a legal principle based on the common law. With the exception of the State of Louisiana, which follows the French "civil code" model rather than the English "common law" model, judicial decisions that make up the common law establish legal parameters for public procurement professionals. The Canadian province of Quebec is likewise a civil law jurisdiction that does not follow the English common law tradition and relies more on statutory and administrative law.

Hierarchy of the Sources of Law

It is important to understand the interrelationship of all three sources of law. Simply stated, no statute can go beyond what the federal or state constitution permits, no administrative rule or regulation can go beyond the grant of authority provided in a statute, and no common law or case law can go beyond what is allowed by federal or state constitution or statute. That being said, a federal or state court is empowered to determine the meaning and coverage of a constitutional provision, a statutory directive, or an administrative rule or regulation. The court's function in this regard is to determine if a statute or administrative rule falls within the grant of authority provided by a constitution or a statute. In this regard, the courts make sure that a statute or administrative rule or regulation is valid; falls within the specific grant of authority; and in this process will interpret the language of a constitutional provision, a statutory provision, and an administrative rule or regulation. This means that the court, where a statute or administrative rule is silent on a particular topic, will look to the common law for guidance in determining the validity and breath of a statutory or administrative rule or regulation provision. While this can be a complex balance for the courts, it is an essential part of the separation of powers built into the governing structure of the United States.

A Note About International Law

Although most public procurement professionals may never read a treaty, international law can affect procurement practice in both the United States and Canada. Canada's procurement laws and practices are largely informed by the United Nations Commission on International Trade Law (UNCITRAL) Model Law on Public Procurement, originally adopted in 1994 and modernized in 2011. The procurement practices in the United States had already evolved over two centuries of legislation in public works and contracting support for the military—then extended to state and local governments with laws similar to those in the federal sector—accounting for different terminology but largely synonymous concepts in the UN Model Law. One example is the use of the term "bid" in U.S. procurement law and practice; Canada and UNCITRAL, on the other hand, use the equivalent term "tender." Still, while the Model Law may use different terminology, the procurement principles are essentially the same as those in the American Bar Association Model Procurement Code for State and Local Government, discussed in Chapter 2.

Model laws aside, both countries are parties to binding treaties affecting state and local government procurement. The World Trade Organization Agreement on Government Procurement was negotiated at the federal level in both countries and has procurement requirements for large acquisitions when companies in other WTO-covered countries submit an offer. Canadian provinces and some U.S. states (as well as a handful of large municipalities) are bound by its provisions. Minimum solicitation publication times for large acquisitions are among the rules in the WTO agreement; the topic is discussed in some detail in Chapter 6.

Other treaties like the WTO often include advertisement, competition, offer award review, and other requirements for large procurements as defined in the agreements. Failure to satisfy the requirements by covered public entities can be a basis for legal challenges of awards. Ideally, entities covered by treaties have laws and policies that conform their procurement practices to those requirements. Public procurement professionals need to know which international agreements apply to their practice.

History of Statutory Law Affecting Public Procurement

The first purchasing-related action for the new American nation occurred in 1778, when the Continental Congress approved the appointment of purchasing commissaries. They were paid two percent of the value of their disbursements in support of the Continental Army. It was not until 1792, however, that the U.S. Congress passed its first statute addressing purchasing. That statute authorized the Departments of War and Treasury to contract on the nation's behalf. The first large acquisition was six frigates for the Navy. The Department of War, under political pressure, awarded contracts for the ships to six different contractors in six different states. Congress later canceled three of the contracts because of delays and cost overruns, yet two of the ships were still built—the U.S.S. Constellation and the U.S.S. Constitution.

The Purveyor of Public Supplies Act, which Congress passed in 1795, was the first comprehensive legislation dealing with procurement. Procurement abuses (such as contracting with friends and relatives) led Congress to pass the Procurement Act in 1809, which established a general requirement to conduct purchases through the use of formal advertising. It also permitted other procurement options, such as open purchases and advertising for proposals.

The Civil Sundry Appropriations Act, passed in 1861, was the first law to create a statutory preference for formal advertising, now more commonly known as competitive bidding. It mandated the use of that selection method, except for the purchase of personal services and procurements, to meet public exigencies.

During World War II, Congress suspended that 1861 Act and, by executive order, President Franklin Roosevelt created the War Production Board. The executive order gave the board extraordinary powers over procurement. Ultimately, Congress reinstated the 1861 Act after the end of the war.

The 1861 Act governed federal procurement until the passage of the Armed Services Procurement Act in 1947 and the Federal Property and Administrative Services Act in 1949. Those laws generally applied to military and civilian agencies, respectively, and maintained a preference for formal advertising.

In the meantime, the Council of State Governments commissioned a study in 1975 of procurement practices at the state and local government levels. That study, originally entitled *State and Local Government Purchasing*, is updated and republished periodically by the National Association of State Procurement Officials (NASPO) in its surveys of state procurement practices and as *State and Local Government Procurement: A Practical Guide*. The original study became the foundation of a groundbreaking project undertaken by the American Bar Association (ABA), funded in large part by the U.S. Department of Justice, to draft model procurement legislation for state and local governments. The result of the project was the creation of the Model Procurement Code for State and Local Governments, approved by the ABA's House of Delegates in 1979.

In 1984, Congress passed the Competition in Contracting Act, significantly changing the manner in which the federal government conducted its procurements. That Act amended the Armed Services Procurement Act and the Federal Property and Administrative Services Act. Among the most important changes were the abolishment of the traditional bias toward formal advertising and the authorization of the use of a variety of competitive procurement procedures.

More recently, Congress passed other major reforms of the federal procurement system. The Federal Acquisition Streamlining Act of 1994, among other things, eased the procedures for buying commercial products, raised the small-dollar-purchasing limit to $100,000, enabled electronic procurement, and encouraged consideration of past performance in selecting contractors. The Federal Acquisition Reform Act of 1995 further refined the procurement process, simplifying the purchase of commercial items between $100,000 and $5 million and authorizing certain design-build selection procedures. In 2000, the American Bar Association published a revised Model Procurement Code for State and Local Governments that also modernized public procurement.

Statutory Law Affecting Market Competition

While Chapter 2 deals with statutes having primary application to procurement, some federal and state laws warrant discussion as part of the essential principles and structures of the legal system. The first of those are the legal principles that govern market competition. Federal and state antitrust laws and federal and state unfair and deceptive trade practice laws seek to control commercial behavior by prohibiting unfair competition, preventing the concentration of economic power, and proscribing deceptive and unfair business practices. A comprehensive discussion of the various federal and state antitrust and unfair and deceptive trade practice statutes is beyond the scope of this text; however, public procurement professionals need to be familiar with key laws in order to recognize and report potential violations to legal counsel.

The Sherman Antitrust Act

The U.S. Congress enacted the Sherman Antitrust Act in 1890, which makes antitrust violations a crime. Section 1 of the statute prohibits any contract, combination, or conspiracy that results in a restraint of trade that impacts interstate commerce. The key to a Section 1 violation of the Sherman Antitrust Act is proof of collective action by two or more entities. Section 2 of the statute prohibits every person from monopolizing any part of interstate trade or commerce. In contrast to a Section 1 violation, a Section 2 violation of the Sherman Antitrust Act is primarily concerned with unilateral conduct and requires a showing that the targeted entity possesses substantial control over the market for a commodity.

Section 1 violations of the Sherman Antitrust Act can be categorized into horizontal restraints of trade and vertical restraints of trade. Horizontal restraints of trade in violation of Section 1 of the Sherman Antitrust Act concern agreements among rival competitors to restrict output, fix prices, divide markets, and exclude other competitors. For example, when all of the manufacturers, all of the wholesalers, or all of the retailers of a product agree to raise the price of the product, then such action by the manufacturers, wholesalers, or retailers would violate Section 1 of the Sherman Antitrust Act. Perhaps one of the best examples of this kind of violation can be found in an examination of oil companies and the price of gas. The crucial proof problem in this kind of antitrust case is proof of an agreement among competitors. Although proof of an actual written or oral agreement between competitors is possible, an agreement in violation of Section 1 of the Sherman Act can also be proven by circumstantial evidence. For example, proof that on a particular day every month for a certain period of time, the price of gas sold to gas stations went up by $.02 per gallon is some proof that the oil companies may have an agreement to fix the price of gas.

Another customary practice that may result in a violation of Section 1 of the Sherman Act occurs when two or more competitors agree to allocate geographic markets. For example, if one group of onion growers agree with another group of onion growers to only sell onions in a particular number of states in the western part of the United States, and the other onion growers agree to only sell onions in other particular states in the western part of the

United States, then this kind of "horizontal" agreement to divide market territories would be illegal.

Finally, another kind of Section 1 violation involves a group boycott by rival competitors. For example, when a group of dentists in Indiana collectively refused to provide x-rays of patients to insurance companies who wanted to use the x-rays to reassess the dentists' charges for services and implement cost containment measures, such an agreement violates the prohibitions of Section 1 of the Sherman Antitrust Act.

From the perspective of the public procurement professional, one of the most common violations of Section 1 of the Sherman Antitrust Act is bid rigging—an agreement by two competitors to not bid against one another for a public works job. There are four basic bid rigging schemes:

1. **Bid Suppression.** A situation where one or more competitor(s) agree not to bid or withdraw a submitted bid or inflate a bid so that a specific bidder will win the contract. In return, the non-bidders receive reciprocation in a subsequent contract bid, kickback, payoff, or a lucrative subcontract.
2. **Complementary Bid.** A situation where all but one bidder submits, per agreement of the bidders, token bids that are either intentionally inflated or non-responsive to the requirements of the bid to lose the contract so that only one bidder satisfies the bid requirements and wins the contract. These complementary bids give the appearance of competitive bidding when in fact they are not.
3. **Bid Rotation.** A situation where, by agreement, all bidders submit bids but arrange to take turns being the lowest qualified bidder for a series of related or unrelated contracts.
4. **Customer or Market Allocation.** A situation where businesses providing the same goods or services divide up geographic territory or customers per agreement, which results in only one bidder for certain contracts in a particular location or only one bid submitted to a particular customer. This customer or market allocation and complementary bidding occur together many times and can be found not only in bid contracts but also in a quoted price type of contract for services.

Some of the signs that bid rigging may be involved in a project include:

- Different companies submit identical bids as individual line items or lump sum bids;
- Bids come in way above the entity's estimate for the value of the contract or way above comparable bids by the same companies in other areas;

- A winning bidder subcontracts part of the business to one or more of the losing bidders;
- There is some indication of a physical alteration of bids, particularly at the last minute;
- Particular line items for some bidders are much higher than for others (no relation to cost);
- The range of bids shows a clear gap between the winner and all others;
- The bids of all companies are very close (an indicator that bidders knew each other's prices);
- Bids have the same increment between the prices of each supplier;
- All companies submit high bids when work is known to be scarce;
- The supplier submits different bids for the same line item on different contracts that are close in time;
- The suppliers appear to have engineered a split of the contract by each bidding low on some aspect of it and inexplicably high on other parts;
- There is physical evidence of collusion, such as different companies submitting bids with the same handwriting, in the same envelopes, with the same mathematical or spelling errors, or from the same fax number;
- Qualified bidders do not bid, especially if they initially took steps to bid;
- If a contract is re-bid because all initial bids are unacceptable, the bidders come back in the same order or some bidders fail to re-bid;
- There are significant increases by most bidders over previous prices when there have been no substantial cost increases;
- Prices mysteriously drop when a new bidder appears on the scene; or
- There is evidence that competitors met before or after the bidding.

Some signs that a payback or other kickback may be occurring in a contract include the following:

- Any kind of territorial pattern;
- A supplier always bids for a contract but never, or always, wins it;
- All of the suppliers in the group win an equal volume of business over time;
- All of the suppliers win an equal number of contracts over time; and
- Any additional pattern that may present or present itself among suppliers.

Additionally, situations in which the same supplier seems to win business repeatedly or situations where competitors never come around to solicit business might be signs of market or customer allocation. If attempts are made to get other competitors interested, they may refuse to quote or show reluctance in some way. If they do quote, it may be ridiculously high to discourage the public entity from changing suppliers. Other behavior may make it obvious that companies that should want the entity's business are not interested in it.

While these indicators may arouse suspicion of collusion, they are not proof of collusion. For example, bids that come in well above the estimate may indicate collusion or simply an incorrect estimate. In addition, a bidder can lawfully submit an intentionally high bid that it does not think will be successful for its own independent business reasons, such as being too busy to handle the work but wanting to stay on the entity's list. Only when a supplier submits an intentionally high bid because of an agreement with a competitor does an antitrust violation exist. As such, indicators of collusion merely call for further investigation to determine whether collusion exists or whether there is an innocent explanation for the events in question.

While collusion can occur in almost any industry, it is more likely to occur in some industries than in others. An indicator of collusion may be more meaningful when industry conditions are already favorable to collusion.

- Collusion is more likely to occur if there are few sellers. The fewer the number of sellers, the easier it is for them to get together and agree on prices, offers, customers, or territories. Collusion may also occur when the number of firms is large, but there is a small group of major sellers and the rest are "fringe" sellers who control only a small fraction of the market.
- The probability of collusion increases if there is no substitute product for the product in question or if there are restrictive specifications for the product being procured.
- The more standardized a product is, the easier it is for competing suppliers to reach agreement on a common price structure. It is much harder to agree on other forms of competition, such as design, features, quality, or service.
- Repetitive purchases may increase the chance of collusion, as the suppliers may become familiar with other bidders, and future contracts provide the opportunity for competitors to share the work.
- Collusion is more likely if the competitors know each other well through social connections, trade associations, legitimate business contacts, or shifting employment from one company to another.
- Bidders who congregate in the same building or town to submit their bids have an easier opportunity for last-minute communications.

Antitrust violations are serious crimes that can cost a supplier hundreds of millions of dollars in fines and can send an executive to jail for up to ten years. These conspiracies are, by their nature, secret and difficult to detect.

If suppliers are conspiring to collude on prices, the procurement professional is the last person in the world that they want to know about the scheme. Even the most conscientious professional can be victimized. Nonetheless, here are some procedures that can discourage anticompetitive activity:

1. Expand the list of bidders to make it more difficult for bidders to collude. Buyers should solicit bids from as many suppliers as economically possible. As the number of bidders increases, the probability of successful collusive bidding decreases. While there is no magic number of bidders above which collusion cannot occur, experience suggests that collusion is more likely to arise where there are five or fewer competitors.
2. Require bidders to sign and submit a non-collusion affidavit, stating that the bidder has not colluded and informing bidders of the penalties both for violating the Sherman Act and for signing a false non-collusion affidavit.
3. Ensure that all procurement professionals are familiar with the indicators of bid rigging, price fixing, and other types of collusion.
4. Maintain procurement records, e.g., bid lists, abstracts, and awards. When collusion is suspected, it may be necessary for procurement professionals to review the procurement history of a product—ideally with the assistance of legal counsel—to determine if a pattern of bid allocation or rotation is present.
5. Ask questions—if the bids submitted do not make sense, press the suppliers to explain and justify their prices.
6. Know and understand the dynamics of the markets and industry in which major purchases are made. A knowledgeable buyer may suspect collusion from market behavior that may not arouse suspicions in an uninformed buyer.

Aside from horizontal restraints of trade, Section 1 of the Sherman Antitrust Act also prohibits vertical restraints of trade, that is, for example, an agreement between a manufacturer of a product and its wholesale sellers of the product that sets the minimum price at which the product may be sold. This kind of "vertical" agreement is labeled resale price maintenance. Such agreements imposed by a manufacturer on a wholesaler or by a wholesaler on a retailer have occurred in many industries. For example, when the manufacturer of automobile parts and the wholesaler of those automobile parts agree not to sell the parts for less than a certain dollar amount to a car dealership or parts store, then the price of the parts may be inflated above the market value of the part. This kind of agreement ensures an inflated profit for both the parts manufacturer and wholesaler, inflating the cost of the automobile parts to the consumer.

The Federal Trade Commission has noted that some manufacturer-imposed requirements in the supply chain may be acceptable. Some floor prices or limitation of geographical coverage can encourage dealers to provide a level of service that manufacturers want to offer the consumer when they buy the product. The benefits must be weighed against any reduction in competition from the restrictions, and they have in recent years been evaluated using the "rule of reason."

Another example of a vertical restraint of trade that may be a violation of Section 1 of the Sherman Antitrust Act is a tying arrangement. In this scenario, a seller of a good or product requires a buyer to agree to purchase one particular item in order to purchase another particular item. For example, if the seller or lessor of mobile home park land for placement of a mobile home conditions the purchase or lease of such land to the purchase of a mobile home from that same seller or another designated seller of mobile homes, this kind of "conditioned" agreement can be an illegal tying arrangement. But the law on tying also has been changing, with some lower courts applying the "rule of reason" to assess the competitive aspects of tied products.

Although this review of Sherman Antitrust Act violations is by no means comprehensive, the public procurement professional needs to be aware of the application of the principles and concepts contained in the prohibitions of the Act that will apply to public works and other projects.

The Clayton Antitrust Act and the Robinson-Patman Act

In 1914, the U.S. Congress enacted the Clayton Antitrust Act to strengthen and expand the prohibitions contained in the Sherman Antitrust Act. The key differences between a violation of the Sherman Antitrust Act and the Clayton Antitrust Act are:

1. A violation of the Clayton Antitrust Act does not require proof of an agreement, conspiracy, or concerted action among commercial entities to make out a violation;
2. The penalties under the Clayton Antitrust Act include a civil remedy, which means that private citizens do have the right to initiate a lawsuit and recover money damages for a violation; and
3. The activities complained of as a violation must be in, not just affect, interstate commerce.

The Clayton Antitrust Act, and its amendments contained in the Robinson-Patman Act, passed in 1936, prohibit price discrimination, certain kinds of mergers, interlocking directorships between competing companies, certain kinds of exclusive dealing, and refusal-to-deal arrangements that substantially lessen competition.

The courts and legal scholars have struggled with the application of both the Clayton Antitrust Act and, most notably, the Robinson-Patman Act. The legal nuances in applying these statutory provisions stem from the varying economic perspectives that a court may adopt. However, the purpose behind both statutory provisions is to protect small businesses and consumers from the predatory practices of other larger businesses who wield monopoly power.

Perhaps the best way to understand the thrust of both the Clayton Antitrust Act and the Robinson-Patman Act is through case studies. For example, let's say that one manufacturer of pre-packaged pies controls over three-fourths of the pre-packaged pie market in a particular state and makes a high profit on its sales. A national manufacturer of pre-packaged pies notes the high profit margin of this other essentially local and state-confined pre-packaged pie manufacturer and is attracted to enter that market. In entering this market, the national pre-packaged pie maker offers its product at a price well below the existing supplier of the product. In fact, the national pre-packaged pie supplier offers to sell its pies below its actual cost to produce the pies and well below the price it offers its pies in any other state. The thinking and planning of the national pre-packaged pie supplier is that because of its market power it can offer its pies below cost in one state and make up for its loss in the volume of sales of its pies in other states. Furthermore, the national pre-packaged pie manufacturer figures that such "below cost" pricing will eventually force the local, pre-packaged pie supplier to go out of business. Once this occurs, the national pre-packaged pie supplier can raise prices above the market price level to recoup, if not exceed, its temporary loss from selling below cost. This kind of "predatory pricing" amounts to geographic price discrimination in violation of the Robinson-Patman Act.

From this example, one can see that the key to prohibitions contained in the Clayton Antitrust Act and the Robinson-Patman Act is proof of market power in the offending business. This is precisely the intended effect of the Clayton Act—to prevent monopolies and the use of monopoly power to lessen competition and injure consumers. The controversy surrounding the enforcement of these Acts centers on the notion that certain kinds of monopolies may be more economically efficient and benefit consumers. This debate is still ongoing and will be the subject of more extensive academic, judicial, and political discussion.

From the perspective of the public procurement professional, the prohibitions of the Clayton and Robinson-Patman Act apply equally to public works and other contracts, and are additional enforcement tools available for use.

The Federal Trade Commission Act

The U.S. Congress passed the Federal Trade Commission Act in 1914, establishing the Federal Trade Commission as an independent regulatory agency of the federal government and empowering it to enforce the Clayton Antitrust Act and the Robinson-Patman Act. With the passage of the Wheeler-Lea Amendment to the Federal Trade Commission Act in 1938, the Federal Trade Commission's power was extended to cover any business practice that results in unfair competition and any deceptive or unfair business practice.

State Antitrust Laws

State antitrust laws largely mirror the prohibitions contained in the Sherman and Clayton Antitrust statutes and provide for private, public, civil, and criminal enforcement. In addition, state unfair and deceptive trade practice statutes borrow the proscriptions of the Federal Trade Commission Act. However, unlike their federal counterparts, state unfair and deceptive trade practice statutes sometimes permit private enforcement. Also, some states' laws treat supply chain practices like dealer floor prices and tying arrangements differently.

State attorneys general have a role in enforcement of the federal Sherman and Clayton Antitrust statutes also. Their consumer protection or unfair trade practice offices have expertise with regard to enforcement of these kinds of statutes. They also typically have established relationships with local United States attorneys and federal law enforcement organizations. These cases are very factually intensive and require specialized expertise in investigation and prosecution. In cases where unfair trade practices or collusion are suspected, the state attorney general can be a resource for the legal counsel of local governments.

What Should a Procurement Professional Do?

Here are two different scenarios that procurement professionals may face.

PROBLEM #1: The county's Emergency Department needed to purchase propane fuel for the emergency generators used by the county in case of a power outage. There are five suppliers of propane fuel in the state. The county began its pre-bid preparation by pricing out the cost of a gallon of propane fuel in the area and found that the prices ranged from $1.90 per gallon to $2.00 per gallon among the five suppliers. Upon sending out the invitation for bids, the county received back four bids from suppliers from various parts of the state ranging from $3.00 per gallon to $3.10 per gallon, and only one bid from a local supplier at $2.50 per gallon.

Does this raise any concerns for the county? What key factors must the procurement professional be concerned about? What should the county do?

PROBLEM #2: The county's Emergency Department hired an emergency management consultant to help work out a plan so that in the event of the next emergency, the county will not run out of propane fuel for emergency generators. The county administrator had lunch with the consultant to discuss the plans. The county administrator advised the consultant that the county was getting ready to purchase propane fuel and asked for the consultant's opinion as to how much to buy. Two days later, the price of propane fuel for all five suppliers in the area jumped from $2.35 per gallon to $3.00 per gallon. The county sent out an invitation for bids and only two suppliers submitted bids—one bid for $3.50 per gallon and the other bid for $3.80 per gallon.

Does this raise any concerns for the county? What key factors must the procurement professional be concerned about? What should the county do?

Statutory Law Governing Public Records

At the federal, state, and local government levels, there are a variety of public record, open record, and Freedom of Information Act statutes. These statutes provide the guidelines under which the public is entitled to review the work and records of government. This means that procurement files and other records, as well as meetings where procurement and other kinds of purchasing contracts are discussed, may be accessible to the public. These statutes are often known as Sunshine Laws. Florida's Sunshine Law is notable in that its public meeting provisions have been interpreted by at least one court as covering evaluation committee deliberations.

Statutes vary by locality and jurisdiction, so it is impossible to discuss the various scenarios within the context of this text. Nevertheless, it is critical for the public procurement professional to clearly understand and operate under these statutory laws. It is also critical to understand the breadth of the applicable law in terms of the inclusion or exclusion of working documents, handwritten notes, emails, and drafts. For example, in some jurisdictions, a proposal submitted by a supplier in response to a Request for Proposals (RFP) is subject to the public records laws; while in other jurisdictions, the submittal is considered a working or draft document and is not subject to the public records laws until such time as the proposal is negotiated and finalized via a contract.

Within the context of public records, the public procurement professional must have a full understanding of the conditions under which a potential supplier submits proprietary and trade secret information to the public entity for evaluative purposes. Typically, this information is submitted as a confidential document by the potential supplier in a segregated part of the proposal, consistent with instructions in the solicitation. These practices rely on potential application of an exemption under most open records or Freedom of Information laws. Approaches to exemptions from disclosure vary, however. A common analysis exempts from disclosure trade secrets, privileged information, confidential commercial, and financial data where disclosure would be likely either to (1) impair the government's future ability to gain necessary information or (2) harm the competitive position of the person providing the information.

Usually, the contractor bears the burden of overcoming the presumption in favor of disclosure. In Florida and Colorado, for example, data that includes significant commercial/financial information, supplier lists, and customer lists may qualify as trade secrets exempt from disclosure.

Information is not protected simply because a bid or proposal is submitted. Under Montana constitution, all records held by a public entity are presumed to be open for inspection to the public, including trade secrets that may have been provided to a government entity. The reach of the presumption has been judicially extended to proposals submitted in response to a request for proposals (RFP). Procurement professionals must work closely with legal counsel in determining how their laws affect the disclosure of information submitted in response to solicitations.

Statutory Law Governing Intellectual Property Rights

Intellectual property refers to the creations of the mind; that is inventions, literary and artistic works and symbols, names, and images used in commercial settings. Ordinarily, intellectual property divides into three common categories: patents for inventions; copyrights for literary works, such as novels, music and movies, drawings, such as architectural designs, paintings, photographs; and trademarks symbols or logos. While the nuances of patent, copyright, and trademark law are well beyond the reach of public procurement officers, public procurement officers should be generally aware of the parameters of the protections afforded to the holder of intellectual property rights.

In procurement of technology, copyrights and patents may limit the use of products and some services. These rights must be defined in underlying contracts. Apart from the well-known importance of intellectual property rights to procurement of software, in higher education, sources of revenue like sports programs use logos that must be protected by trademark laws, and contracts permitting their use must be carefully drafted.

Patent Law

Patent law is designed to protect the original inventor's rights in a product or process. Patents must be registered with the U.S. Patent Office. Upon submitting an application for a patent, the patent holder is entitled to protection for a period of 20 years.

While ideas are not subject to patent protection, the product or process generated as a result of an idea may be patented. For example, the idea of intermittent automobile window wipers cannot be patented; however, the design for and the actual physical components of intermittent automobile window wipers can be patented. In addition, a process may be patented. For example, the chemical process used to produce a particular drug as well as the drug itself can be patented both as a process and a product.

That being said, not all products and processes can be patented. The product or process must be "new;" that is, the product or process must be novel, or at least a new and improved version of an existing product or process and not obvious to one skilled in the art. For example, a company that creates a "new and better" mousetrap can seek the protection of patent law.

The purpose of obtaining a patent is to prevent the use of a patented product or process without the holder's permission. The unauthorized use of a patented product or process would constitute patent infringement and subject the violator to legal liability, including monetary damages. These damages can be substantial and include lost profits; payment of a fee for the past, present, and future use of the patented item; and an injunction prohibiting the violator from using the patented item without permission.

Copyright Law

Copyright protection is granted in favor of an author of any original work that is produced in a medium from which the work can be reproduced.

What is not protected by copyright is the actual content of the original work. Consequently, an oral presentation or speech cannot be copyrighted because it is not reduced to a tangible medium; however, the tape recording or printed pages of a speech can be copyrighted as it is an actual product. Likewise, a compact disc of music can be copyrighted, but actual music notes that make up the music cannot be.

Copyright protection is provided for the life of the author plus 70 years. The employer, absent some kind of contrary agreement, owns the copyright of works produced by an employee. So, too, are works "made for hire"—that is, works produced by independent contractors at the request of another. In this instance, the copyright protection is provided for 120 years from the date of creation or 95 years from the date of publication of the work, whichever is shorter.

The major exception to copyright protection is "fair use." The fair use doctrine permits the reproduction and use of copyrighted material for the purpose of teaching, scholarship, research, reporting, comment, and criticism. For example, this exception permits a literary critic for a newspaper to reprint excerpts from a copyrighted book in a book review. However, the fair use doctrine has limits based on the amount of copyrighted material that is being fairly used and whether the fair use of the copyrighted material is for profit. Additionally, the type of work that is copyrighted and the market effect of the fair use are all factors that limit the application of the fair use doctrine. For example, the fair use doctrine exception to copyright protection would not apply to a teacher who photocopies a 500-page book for the students and then sells the photocopied book at a profit.

For the public procurement professional, the copyright protection of computer software is a good case study and an important issue because governments may need to put the same software on many computers. Most, if not all, software is copyrighted. Consequently, the holder of the copyright has the authority to limit the use of the copyrighted material. On the other hand, the copyright holder may also permit the use of copyrighted material. In the context of software, the holder of the copyright may enter into a contract that grants a prospective end user a license to use the software. These software licenses come in many shapes and forms.

An individual software license would permit one person to load and use software on one computer. Copying or loading the software into another computer would constitute a copyright violation. A "machine" software license would permit the software to be used on a specific computer. This would require the purchase of a license for every computer that uses the software.

A "site" software license usually permits the software to be used at a single location on a specified maximum number of computers and provides for a discounted price on multiple copies of software. The various terms and conditions in these kinds of software licenses differ based on the particular needs and circumstances of both the copyright holder and the licensee. However, a "site" software license is usually restricted to a specific organization, a single geographic area, a specific department within a location, or a particular school. For example, the latest version of accounting software may be covered by a site license that is restricted to the business office of a corporation.

The "enterprise" software license is similar to the site license, but it permits the standardized use of a software program for an entire organization. This type of license usually runs for a limited time and may be subject to renewal. The most visible example of this type of enterprise license is a multinational corporation's license to use Microsoft Word.

A "suite" license allows a single end user to purchase permission to use a group of many applications of the software. The license to use a "suite" of software applications is sold as one unit, and the various applications of the software covered by this license cannot be separated and given to other end users. In short, a suite license permits a software package that has a number of different applications to be loaded into a single computer. For example, an in-home educational software package may require a suite license.

Finally, a "concurrent" license permits a maximum number of end users to simultaneously connect to a software application within a network. For example, if the concurrent license allows 10 simultaneous applications for an entity staff of 25 employees, up to 10 of the 25 employees can connect to that particular software program at the same time. The concurrent licensee in this example would need a license for 10, not 25, copies of the software program.

The unauthorized use of any type of copyrighted material would amount to copyright infringement. The penalties for copyright infringement can be severe. In some instances, copyright infringement has led to criminal prosecution of the violators. Regardless, every person who participates in copyright infringement is subject to legal liability. This means that any individual as well as any organization and its employees involved in copyright infringement will be liable for the violation. The legal remedy afforded a copyright holder includes money damages for lost profits; injury to reputation; lost business opportunities; payment of a copyright fee for past, present, and future use of the copyright material; and an injunction prohibiting the use of the copyrighted material by the violator without permission.

Trademark Law

Trademark law protects distinctive marks or other symbols by which an author seeks to specially identify a product, good, or service. The original purpose of trademark protection was to not only protect the trademark holder's rights to a distinctive mark or symbol, but to also prevent consumer confusion or deception regarding similar products, goods, or services. For example, the Nike "swoosh" is a trademark as was the RCA gramophone with the perched dog. Trademarks should, but are not required, to be registered with the federal government. Some of the advantages of registering a trademark include:

- A presumption that the trademark belongs to the person or entity that registered the mark;
- Notice to other persons of the mark; and
- Ease in registering the mark in foreign countries.

A trademark's registration extends for ten years and may be renewed.

The penalty for trademark infringement is substantial. The violator of a trademark will be subject to an injunction that will prohibit the violator from using a mark or symbol. In addition, a violator may be liable to pay for the trademark holder's attorney's fees and lost profits including treble damages.

An Overview of the United States Judicial Structure

The United States has one of the most complex, yet simple, legal systems in the world. Most geographically large nations with a federal system only have a few regional courts from which cases may be appealed to one national court. In the United States, each of the 50 states has a separate court system, each composed of trial, intermediate appellate, and supreme courts. That being said, there is some variation across states in how courts are structured and named. In Florida, for example, there is a county court in each of Florida's 67 counties, a circuit court in each of Florida's 20 judicial circuits, a district court of appeals in each of Florida's five appellate districts, and one Florida Supreme Court.

In addition, the United States has a federal court system consisting of trial courts, intermediate appellate courts, and the Supreme Court. Currently, there are nearly 100 federal trial courts (called District Courts), with at least one in every state in addition to the District of Columbia (DC) and the territories of Guam, Puerto Rico, the Northern Marianas, and the U.S. Virgin Islands. There are presently 12 federal intermediate appellate courts known as the Circuit Courts of Appeal. One of the Courts of Appeal is in Washington, DC, and the others are spread regionally across the 50 states. In 1982, the U.S. Congress created a Court of Appeals for the Federal Circuit that has nationwide appellate jurisdiction over specific kinds of lawsuits.

Both state and federal court systems have specialized courts of limited jurisdiction. At the state level, examples include juvenile, probate, small claims, and traffic courts. At the federal level, examples include international trade, military appeals, tax, and bankruptcy courts, as well as the U.S. Court of Federal Claims that hears federal bid protests and contract claims against the United States. It's important to note that the United States Court of Appeals for the Federal Circuit is the only appellate court with the power to hear patent case appeals.

Courts at the same level in either the federal or state court structure generally perform the same function. Trial courts are where most criminal and civil cases begin. There are two parties to each trial court case: the plaintiff (the individual or government that brings a civil complaint) and the defendant (against whom the complaint or charge is brought). In criminal cases, the plaintiff is known as the prosecution. When a party loses at the trial court level and appeals, that party is referred to in the subsequent written opinion as an "appellant" in civil cases. The party defending the appeal and trial court decision is the appellee.

Appellate courts do not hear witnesses or take evidence. They review trial court records for errors of law. For example, in the cases summarized in Chapter 10, the factual descriptions written by the appellate courts would have been taken from the record in the trial court. Only rarely does an appellate court resolve the dispute at its level. More often, they return the case to the trial court, often for a new trial.

Case law creates judicial precedent. When a state supreme court, for example, decides a case, it becomes binding precedent for courts within that state; however, it is not binding outside that jurisdiction. This is an application of the principle of *stare decisis*, meaning that once a decision (a precedent) on a certain set of facts has been made, the courts will apply that decision in cases that subsequently come before it with the same set of facts. Federal courts and some states have intermediate courts of appeals organized by geographical district, so the opinions in one district are not binding on courts in another district.

States' appellate or trial courts may consider decisions in other jurisdictions as persuasive authority, however. For example, some state courts consider federal opinions on government contract issues as persuasive authority in state and local government cases where the underlying policies are similar.

Legal Research

Procurement professionals will rarely conduct legal research with the sophisticated techniques that attorneys learn to find and research relevant law. Nonetheless, statutes, ordinances, regulations, and full-text judicial opinions are widely available online, and an understanding of the essential elements of legal research can be useful to public procurement professionals.

Two Types of Legal Sources: Primary and Secondary Sources

As with other forms of library research, legal research requires locating and using primary and secondary sources. In legal research, primary sources are publications that present the law itself, i.e., the actual text of constitutions, statutes, regulations, court decisions, or treaties. Secondary sources are those publications that describe, summarize, and analyze the conflicts and consequences resulting from the application of those laws. It also includes finding aids for legal research in the form of indexes to court decisions and treaties.

Two Types of Primary Legal Sources: Chronological Series and Codes

Within all three areas of legal research, one finds that primary legal sources fall into two basic types of publications: (1) chronological series that compile the full text of statutes, regulations, and court decisions in the order they were adopted; and (2) codes that collect or arrange the law according to topics or subjects.

Since statutory, case, and administrative law are all continuously being adopted or modified, their respective chronological legal series are frequently updated. The most up-to-date published sources of federal and state law will usually be issued as a chronological series.

Secondary Sources: Court Digests and Legal Encyclopedias

There are at least two characteristics of secondary sources that are useful when researching case law. First, they provide interpretative material to assist the reader in understanding the cause, nature, and consequence of case law on a specific topic. Second, they aid the reader in a more thorough search of the primary sources for relevant cases.

A series of case digests may be in libraries. They can be described as an index that classifies reported case decisions by subject and presents a brief abstract for each decision. Citations in the digested cases point to full opinions that are in the chronological reporters or available online.

The two major legal encyclopedias are *American Jurisprudence 2d* (*Am Jur 2d*) and *Corpus Juris Secundum* (*CJS*). The "2d" in *Am Jur* and "secundum" in *CJS* refer to the second edition. Like more generalized encyclopedias, both *American Jurisprudence 2d* and *Corpus Juris Secundum* are multi-volume works that present hundreds of articles written in narrative form that are arranged alphabetically by topic title. Both use extensive footnotes to cite federal and state court decisions relevant to the article's topic. Pocket parts and replacement volumes to reflect the current law update both. McQuillen's *The Law of Municipal Corporations* is another well-regarded treatise that has comprehensive discussions of government fiscal and procurement law.

Virtually all of the judicial opinions or statutes cited in this book can be found online. The resources briefly described in this section illustrate the additional research capabilities that legal counsel have in determining what law is current.

Conclusion

This chapter introduced the overall structure of law in the United States and three topics of special importance in a market economy and transparent government—unfair trade, intellectual property, and open records. The next chapter builds on legislation and regulation focused more specifically on public procurement.

From this brief overview, it is clear that the legal context for procurement and contracts is complicated, comprehensive, and copious. The task for the public procurement officer is to successfully navigate through the legal maze of public procurement contracts by understanding and applying statutory, common, and administrative laws to each legal situation. As public procurement professionals gain an understanding and appreciation of the legal structure, they add substantial value to the procurement function as a source of authority.

References

American Bar Association. *The 2000 Model Procurement Code for State and Local Governments*. Chicago: American Bar Association, 2000.

Calmari, J. D., and J. M. Perrillo. *The Law of Contracts*. 4th ed. Hornbook Series. St. Paul, MN: West Publishing, 1998.

Council of State Governments. *The Book of States, 2018 Edition*. Lexington, KY: Council of State Governments, 2018.

Dolan, J. F. *Uniform Commercial Code: Terms and Transactions in Commercial Law*. Boston: Little Brown Publishing, 1991.

Federal Trade Commission. "The Antitrust Laws." www.ftc.gov/tips-advice/competition-guidance/guide-antitrust-laws/antitrust-laws.

Gavil, Andrew. *An Antitrust Anthology*. Ottawa, ON: Anderson Publishing, 2003.

Gellhorn, Ernest, and William Kovacic. *Antitrust Law and Economics in a Nutshell*. 5th ed. Stephen. St. Paul, MN: West Publishing, 2004.

Ginsberg, Jane, Jessica Litman, and Mary Kevlin. *Trademark and Unfair Competition Law: Cases and Materials*. Durham, NC: Carolina Academic Press, 2017.

Hynes, J., and Mark Loeswenstein. *Agency, Partnership, and the LLC in a Nutshell*. 5th ed. St. Paul, MN: West Publishing, 2011.

Kempin, F. G. *Historical Introduction to Anglo-American Law in a Nutshell*. St. Paul, MN: West Publishing, 1990.

Keyes, W. N. *Government Contracts in a Nutshell*. St. Paul, MN: West Publishing, 2000.

Miller, Arthur R., and Michael H. Davis. *Intellectual Property: Patents, Trademarks, and Copyright in a Nutshell*. 5th ed. West Nutshell Series. St. Paul, MN: Thomson/West, 2012.

NASPO. *State and Local Government: A Practical Guide*. Lexington, KY: NASPO, 2019.

———. *State and Local Government Purchasing Principles and Practices*. Lexington, KY: NASPO, 1997.

Pierce, Richard J., and Ernest Gellhorn. *Regulated Industries in a Nutshell*. 4th ed. West Nutshell Series. St. Paul, MN: West Group, 1999.

Weston, Glen E., Peter B. Maggs, and Roger E. Schechter. *Unfair Trade Practices and Consumer Protection: Cases and Comments*. 5th ed. American Casebook Series. St. Paul, MN: West Pub. Co, 1992.

White, James J., and Robert S. Summers. *Handbook of the Law Under the Uniform Commercial Code*. 2nd ed. Hornbook Series. St. Paul, MN: West Pub. Co, 1980.

Chapter 2

The Fundamentals of Procurement Law and Procurement Authority

Despite popular belief, government is not all-powerful. The power of a government to act is strictly limited to the authority granted to the government by the federal, state, or local constitution or charter; federal, state, or local statute or ordinance; and administrative rule. Therefore, absent a specific grant of power from one of these sources, a government will not have the authority to enter into a purchase contract. In most instances, the power of a government comes from a legislative enactment authorizing specific state and federal officials and entities to enter into purchase contracts.

A key to public procurement is the scope of the purchasing authority granted to a government official or entity. For example, if a county ordinance does not permit human resource personnel to enter into any kind of contract on behalf of the county, then those county employees must stay within that restriction. In contrast, many federal, state, and county laws grant the general power to enter into contracts to a specific official or entity, including the ability to establish general parameters and to set up a system for the administration and management of this power to contract. Over time, these legislative authorizations to contract have become more centralized within particular government officials and entities. In short, the authority of a government official or entity to enter into a contract is only that authority granted to that official or entity by law.

This chapter explores the concepts of authority. It also provides an overview of legislation, regulations, and common law principles of particular relevance to the practice of public procurement.

Public Contracting

Within the context of public contracting, the most important sources of the power to contract are statutory law and administrative rules and regulations. The genesis for public contract law is a statute or ordinance setting forth specific procedures that the government must follow in purchasing any commodities that it needs. In many instances, statutes and administrative regulations will even incorporate the common law of contracts by reference; however, absent a specific statute or administrative rule, the common law of contracts will apply to public contracts.

Common Law Sources of Public Contract Law

Like the general law of contracts, the law of public contracts has its own body of common law. Decisions of courts on legal challenges to contract awards and on claims filed under contracts form much of that common law, but there are other important sources for it, as well. Certain governmental administrative entities, particularly within the federal government, have a responsibility to decide protests against solicitations, protests against awards, and contract claims, and the abundance of those administrative decisions is an important source of government contract law principles.

For instance, the U.S. Government Accountability Office, formerly named the U.S. General Accounting Office, has decided protests against solicitations and against awards for the federal government since 1926. The legal principles of public procurement announced in its written decisions over the years have been the basis for many of the essential concepts that drive the practice of public contracting at the federal, state, and local government levels. Many of those concepts have now found their way into the language of statutes and ordinances.

Likewise, the decisions of the federal government's boards of contract appeals, responsible for deciding claims filed under contracts, are key sources of direction on federal contract interpretation and administration. While these administrative sources of public contract law do not have the same legal effect as do decisions of courts and, thus, do not meet a narrow definition of "common law," they are, nonetheless, important and often provide guidance to state courts on issues relating to public contracts.

Applying Contract Law to Public Procurement

As a general rule, the principles of general contract law apply to the government procurement process, except where the law of public contracts specifically displaces them. If statutes and rules that establish procedures for the award of public contracts are prescribed, such as those in the Federal Acquisition Regulation (FAR) that regulates federal government contracts, there is a broad displacement of general contract law and the requirements of public contract law apply. On the other hand, the public contract laws of most state and local governments are not as specific as those of the federal government; and, thus, general contract law will play a greater role in the procurement processes of those entities.

Other Law Applicable to Public Procurement

While procurement statutes or ordinances explicitly authorize a government official to contract for the government, it is the law of agency that prescribes the extent of that authority and whether and how that official may delegate it. Following is a short summary of some types of law that apply.

Criminal Law

A crime is an act for which the law imposes punishment, such as imprisonment or fines. For the most part, criminal laws that affect public procurement may apply to any public procurement professional or purchasing contract. Criminal law prohibits certain kinds of activities, such as kickbacks, bribery, false claims, false statements, mail or wire fraud, misuse of government property, and anti-competitive practices. Statutes set out what is a crime and then judicial opinions establish case law precedent interpreting the specific requirements of a crime.

Tort Law

Tort law is the counterpart to criminal law in that it permits parties to sue each other for damage to a person or property. This is civil as distinguished from criminal liability. Tort law is becoming increasingly more defined by statutory law but is still mostly a product of common law. Under tort law, one person becomes obligated to another not based on a contractual relationship, but due to various duties that the law creates. If a person runs a red light and crashes into another car, that person is financially liable to the owner of the damaged car and to any injured individuals because that person's actions were negligent, i.e., they fell below the standard of care that the law creates for someone driving a car.

For public procurement professionals, tort law most likely comes into play during the administration of a contract or after a product has been purchased. For instance, a contractor constructing a public building discovers an error in the plans and specifications that will cost it more money to perform the contract. If the procurement professional and the contractor do not resolve the dispute amicably, the contractor may file a claim for those additional costs. One of the legal theories that the contractor may include in its claim, in addition to the government's violation of the contract itself, is that the government negligently misrepresented the work to be performed.

Likewise, the government may wish to file a claim against a contractor and the engineer or architect hired to design a building where the roof of the new building leaks every time it rains. One of the legal bases that the government may assert, beyond simple breach of contract, is that the contractor negligently constructed, or the design professional negligently designed, the building.

By law, the time limits within which someone must bring a lawsuit against someone else for a negligent act are generally shorter than those set for bringing a lawsuit for a breach of contract. If the time has run out for pursuing a claim for breach of contract against a government contractor, there may not be time to pursue that contractor on the basis of negligence.

The potential for tort liability accounts for contract terms and conditions that shift or limit potential liability and litigation costs associated with contract performance. Some of those are discussed in Chapter 7.

The Government's Authority to Contract

A government's power to contract is generally inherent in the powers that its constitution or charter grants it to govern. While a government has that inherent power, government officials do not. For purposes of public procurement, the legislative branch of government—a legislature, board, or council—must specifically authorize officials in the executive branch of government to enter into contracts. Without that authority, those officials may not do so. Thus, the existence of that authority is the foundation of any public procurement system.

State legislatures and county, district, or municipal boards or councils define the scope of that authority and identify who may exercise it by passing legislation that becomes statutes or by passing ordinances, respectively. The most effective procurement statutes and ordinances are those that establish the general parameters of an official's contracting or procurement authority and authorize that official to enact rules, regulations, or policies to implement it.

States vary regarding how broadly government powers to act are viewed; for example, whether government entities can engage in revenue-generating activities. Counsel would assist procurement professionals in close questions of authority where it is not expressly granted. In some local jurisdictions, the Dillon Rule frames the authority of local governments. Named after an Iowa judge who created the analytic framework in 1868, the rule adopts a narrow interpretation of local government authority, permitting it to engage only in activities explicitly authorized by the state and resolving ambiguities about the existence of a power against a local government's having it. The rule only permits powers necessary, fairly implied in or incident to, expressly granted, or those that are indispensable to the declared purposes of the public entity. States have gradually expanded the outlook on local government power, however.

The concept of delegation is a power that procurement professionals need to understand in the context of their jurisdiction's law. Procurement authority often is conferred by appointment to a statutory position (e.g., "chief procurement officer") or by delegation from central authorities. Contracting authority may be independently conferred. Sometimes the government's financial officer controls the form of commitment documents like contracts and purchase orders, and contracting authority is delegated by that officer. Expenditure authority commonly remains with an entity who receives the appropriation, but contracting authority may or not be fully delegated to that entity. Procurement professionals need to be intimately familiar with their entity's scheme for delegation of procurement-related authority.

The authority to contract and commit public funds may be further constrained by internal approvals. In Colorado, for example, the state controller approves all state contracts, and legal review may be required. In states having concerns over outsourcing, the human resources department may have a role in approving service contracts. Information technology and facilities departments must often approve contracts by other entities even if they otherwise have delegated procurement authority. While state judicial opinions may differ in this regard, failure to obtain a required statutory or regulatory approval may make the underlying contract void, although courts are hesitant to permit a government to obtain the contractual benefits and avoid payment on an absence-of-authority theory (*Adams County Community Center for Retarded and Seriously Handicapped, Inc. v. State of Colorado*, 594 P. 2d 1046 (Colo. 1979)).

The Law of Agency

Any entity, such as a corporation, partnership, or any level of government, must employ individuals to act on its behalf as it conducts business. These individuals are called "agents," and their roles and responsibilities are a set of legal principles referred to as the law of agency. The law of agency, which is essentially a product of common law, focuses not only on the creation of agent relationships but also the liability for losses suffered by others who deal with agents. Comprehensive coverage of the law of agency is beyond the reach of this book; however, every public procurement professional needs to be familiar with some of the basic principles of the law of agency.

An agent is someone who acts on behalf of the principal. For example, the CEO of a corporation may act as an agent of that corporation. Further, a procurement officer may act as the procurement agent for the public entity that employs that professional. Within the context of public procurement, a local, state, or federal law will usually grant the power to contract to a government official or entity. In turn, where authorized, the government official or entity will delegate, either by law, administrative rule, or some other writing, the authority to enter into contracts to a public procurement officer. While such delegation of authority to an agent could be oral, it is highly recommended that the authority be provided in writing to clarify what the agent has been specifically authorized to do.

There are essentially two ways to create an agency relationship—by agreement between the principal and agent or by law. An agency relationship created by agreement requires the principal to perform an overt act as evidence of the principal's intent for the agent to act on behalf of the principal. In addition, the agent must also accept the principal's offer to be an agent. In most instances, the principal and the proposed agent execute a written document in which the principal offers and the agent accepts appointment as the principal's agent.

An agency relationship created by operation of law can occur in two circumstances. First, a local, state, or federal statute may grant authority to another person. Second, a court of law may rule that an agency relationship exists as a matter of law, even though there is no agreement between a principal and an agent and there is no local, state, or federal law that creates an agency relationship.

The creation of an agency relationship by common law usually occurs in the context of some dispute. In this case, the court rules that despite the lack of a formal agreement or other legal basis for the relationship, a person is acting on behalf of another person in relation to a third party. By way of illustration, if a government entity knows that one of its employees, who is not an agent by agreement or law, is entering into purchase contracts with suppliers and fails to take steps to stop that employee from so acting, it may find that a court of law will rule that this employee was an agent. In this instance, the court ruling is based on the premise that the principal is obligated to know who its agents are, what those agents are doing, and must accept the consequences—both good and bad—of its agents' acts. This is sometimes called "agency by estoppel."

Types of Authority

Once an agency relationship is established, the agent's authority to act may be expressed, implied, or apparent.

Express authority means that the principal expressly confers, in writing, the authority of an agent to act on behalf of the principal. This express authority can be very specific. For example, the procurement agent may only have limited authority to enter into purchase contracts for less than $5,000. Express authority can also be generalized where the procurement agent has the authority to enter into all purchase contracts according to the needs of the principal.

Implied authority is also actual authority, and is a companion to any express authority conferred upon an agent. It permits an agent to do whatever incidental or customary actions are necessary to perform the expressly authorized acts. For example, an agent who has express authority to enter into a purchase contract will also have the implied authority to enter into a shipping and storage contract, if that is necessary, as well as the authority to reject goods that do not conform to specifications.

Apparent authority is a trickier concept because it only applies when an individual does not have actual authority (express or implied) to act on behalf of a principal. Rather, the principal, through some overt act, cloaks a person with the apparent authority in the eyes of a third party to act on behalf of the principal. For example, many businesses issue identification badges for all of their procurement office employees; however, some of these employees do not possess the express authority to enter into contracts on behalf of the business. If a commercial procurement office employee wearing the procurement office badge enters into a contract with a supplier to bind the principal, the supplier may argue that this employee had the apparent authority to act as an agent for the principal. The key requirement for applying the concept of apparent agency is that the principal does some act to create a reasonable impression that a specific person is the principal's agent even though that person has not been granted express authority. Additionally, apparent agency can be created when the principal knowingly permits a person without express authority to act as an agent on the principal's behalf.

Generally, the principles of apparent authority do not apply to bind governments as a matter of public policy. The idea is that government operations are too large and varied to risk holding them responsible for the acts of unauthorized persons. That being said, courts are whittling away at that exclusion for governments and finding instances that, in fairness, hold the government responsible for the acts of its "apparent" agents, especially where goods or services have been accepted.

In certain instances, a person without actual authority may bind the government to an otherwise unauthorized purchase by the government's ratifying it. For ratification to occur, an authorized person must know, either actually or constructively, about the unauthorized purchase and approve it directly or by implication, such as by actions.

Public entities are strongly encouraged to avoid the legal consequences of alleged apparent authority by maintaining vigilant supervision of their employees and providing clear and conspicuous disclosure of who has the express authority to act on their behalf.

Liability of a Principal

In general, a principal will be bound by the acts of an agent performed within the course and scope of the agent's work. For example, a person may be a procurement agent for a public entity; however, when the person enters into a contract outside of business hours for personal goods or services, and without any indication of authority to act on the principal's behalf, the person is acting outside of the course and scope of the agent's work. Consequently, such a contract will not bind the principal to pay for the goods or services.

On the other hand, some unauthorized acts performed by an agent within the course and scope of an agent's work may bind the principal even if they technically violated policy limitations. For example, many government entities circulate lists of approved and unapproved suppliers. If a procurement agent, during the course and scope of the agent's work, enters into a purchase contract with an unapproved supplier, the principal (i.e., the government entity) will be bound to that contract. The fact that the agent's act in entering into this purchase contract may be against policy or be "unauthorized" does not diminish the binding effect on the principal because the agent did act within the course and scope of the agent's work.

It is important to remember that a principal-agent relationship is different from an employer-independent contractor relationship. An independent contractor is not an employee of the principal but may still be an agent of the principal. Some architect contracts with public entities are examples. An independent contractor is a person contracted by an employer to provide goods, services, or work for that employer. In this capacity, the employer does not have control over the details of how the independent contractor will perform the task but, rather, just pays for the goods, services, or work. Yet they can be made agents contractually.

On the other hand, an employer has control over all the details and the work to be performed by an employee. In this context, an employer could easily invest agent authority in an employee. This relationship between employer and employee is called respondeat superior. This classic agency relationship would directly apply to a public procurement professional employed by a government entity, although an employment relationship does not automatically create procurement authority. On the other hand, torts like automobile accidents can create liability of the employer under the doctrine of respondeat superior.

In contrast, an employer is not ordinarily held accountable for the acts of an independent contractor. Further, it is unlikely that an employer will confer agent authority on an independent contractor simply be virtue of the relationship. For example, it is unlikely that a plumber hired by an entity to do plumbing work would also be given the power to act as an agent for the employer.

The Impact of State Statutory Laws

The constitutions and state laws of the 50 U.S. states describe the relationship between state government and the various county and municipal governments as well as special taxing districts, including public school districts. Additionally, these state statutes empower or restrict the authority of local governments.

This relationship varies dramatically from state to state. In some situations, municipalities, special districts, or public school districts are an instrumentality of the state government and bound totally or partially by state statutes and laws. In other situations, the state statutes give wide latitude on the passage of local ordinances and regulations by providing an overarching framework of laws. In states following *home rule* principles, largely in the western United States, municipalities claiming home rule status are given wide latitude to legislate in areas where the state does not have statewide impact or interests. Because of the complexity of these legal relationships, it is important that public procurement professionals be fully aware of the relationship between their public entity and state statutes.

Public Works and Architect-Engineer Selection

There is a long history of public works (i.e., construction) being treated separately in statutes. Even with a general procurement code covering goods and services, public works contracting often has its own statutory scheme that must be followed by all governments and public entities in the state.

Until relatively recently, all large construction had to be procured by competitive sealed bidding. The definition of "public works" may differ, however, among states. For example, the point at which maintenance crosses over into a public work is a question resolved differently by the states. Job order contracting, a blanket contracting arrangement where multiple, prequalified contractors submit informal quotes as individual construction projects are identified, may be considered "public works" in states that require use of competitive sealed bidding in construction.

The distinction between public works and other service contracts is important because of the other statutory requirements that apply. Certain preferences, like residency and other geographical preferences, might only apply to public works projects. Some states have "little Davis-Bacon" statutes that mirror the federal government Davis-Bacon Act requiring payment of prevailing wages on construction projects. Some states' public works statutes require that a percentage of work in certain trades be performed by local labor. Domestic content requirements for materials, similar to the U.S. Buy American Act, can attach to public works projects in some states under their laws.

Public works statutes might restrict permissible contract clauses, like no-damage-for-delay provisions, for example. Other statutes may explicitly permit post-award negotiation of construction contracts (without a re-solicitation) where all bids are over budget.

Public works statutes often require that progress payments be made to prime contractors. Sovereign immunity principles prevent contractors from filing liens on public property for nonpayment. This principle restricts the use of liens by subcontractors as well—an important protection in private construction contracts. In lieu of the availability of liens, statutes may require a public entity to obtain payment and performance bonds. They often prescribe a process for the release of retained funds, requiring notice to subcontractors before final payment and permitting them to file claims for nonpayment.

Over the past decade, integrated project delivery has been statutorily authorized by more states and local governments. Design-build and sophisticated fast-track delivery methods that are not amenable to competitive sealed bidding and low-bid awards are permitted and procured using competitive sealed proposals (RFPs). Revisions to the ABA Model Procurement Code for State and Local Governments added provisions for procurement of infrastructure facilities and services.

Many states have statutes prescribing the use of qualification-based selections of architects and engineers. Sometimes referred to as "little Brooks acts" (named for the analogous federal statute), these selections do not consider cost. Negotiations are conducted in order of the best qualified firms, and negotiations with the most qualified firm are abandoned only if a fair and reasonable cost cannot be achieved.

Even though the legal concepts in this book apply, construction procurement is a specialty that must be handled with care. Procurement professionals must have a clear understanding of the contours of authority and legal requirements when moving into public works procurement.

Key Components of the ABA Model Procurement Code

While each state and local government establishes its own statutes, ordinances, and regulations governing the public procurement function, it is important to note that there have been efforts to create a standardized template of rules and policies that can serve as a model for the development of state and local government legislation.

In 1975, the Council of State Governments commissioned a study of procurement practices at the state and local levels. The result of the project was the creation of The Model Procurement Code for State and Local Governments by the American Bar Association in 1979. The Code has helped to create transparent, competitive, and reliable processes by which billions of dollars in public funds are expended through contracts with private sector businesses.

In 1997, the ABA Sections of Public Contract Law and State and Local Government Law initiated its sponsorship of the Model Procurement Code Revision Project in collaboration with leading organizations including the National Institute of Governmental Purchasing, Inc. (NIGP), the National Association of State Procurement Officials (NASPO), Public Technology, Inc. (PTI), the Construction Industry Roundtable (CIRT), the American Consulting Engineers Council, and the Council on Federal Procurement of Architectural and Engineering Services. There were several reasons cited for updating the Code, including:

- A rapid increase in the volume of public procurement spending;
- Technological advances in the way that public procurement transactions are processed via personal computers, email, and the Internet; and
- The need to purchase proprietary technology for public entities.

The goals of the revision project were to:

- Reduce transaction costs for all governmental entities at the state and local levels;
- Reduce transaction costs for private sector suppliers of goods and services;
- Substantially increase available levels and ranges of competition through modern methods of electronic communications; and
- Encourage the competitive use of new technologies, new methods of performing, and new forms of project delivery in public procurement, particularly in the field of construction.

With assistance from the Massachusetts Institute of Technology (MIT), proposed revisions were circulated to interested parties. In July 2000, the revised Code was released as The 2000 Model Procurement Code for State and Local Governments. The 2000 Code remains a statute that provides the fundamentals of sound procurement that should be implemented by regulations consistent with the statutory framework (ABA 2000). The ABA has also published Model Procurement Code Recommended Regulations for State and Local Governments.

The key modifications to the 2000 Code are as follows:

- **Electronic Commerce.** The 2000 Code modified definitions and added new definitions to Articles 1 and 3 that allow procurement processes to adapt to the electronic age.
- **Cooperative Purchasing.** The 2000 Code modified definitions and language in Article 10 to extend the benefits of cooperative procurement of supplies and services among state and local governments.
- **Flexibility in Purchasing Methods.** The 2000 Code provided badly needed flexibility to senior procurement professionals to adapt procurement procedures to unusual circumstances.
- **Processes for Delivery of Infrastructure Facilities and Services.** The 2000 Code provided more explicit guidance on the use of construction delivery methods.

The ABA developed the Model Procurement Code as a "model" rather than a "uniform" code so that state and local governments adopting the code could adapt it to their own entity and political constraints. About half of the states and many local governments have adopted a version of it. While implementation of the Code has fallen short of the vision of the initial supporters, an ever-increasing number of jurisdictions consider it for enactment.

The Model Procurement Code contains 12 articles that cover broad categories of the contracting process. Articles 1 through 10 cover basic policies for the procurement of supplies, services, and construction; management and disposal of supplies; and legal remedies. Article 11 provides socioeconomic policies that a state or local government may wish to amplify. Article 12 establishes ethical standards for public officials and contractors relating to procurement. The following is a synopsis of the scope of each Article.

Article 1: *General Provisions.* Article 1 describes the general purposes of the Code, specifies its applicability, provides guidance for interpretations, and contains definitions of terms used in more than one Article.

Article 2: *Procurement Organization.* Article 2 sets forth the basic organizational concepts for establishing procurement policy and conducting procurement operations. It also contains several alternative proposals for establishing the policy-making office. In addition, Article 2 provides for certain exemptions from central procurement and authorizes the creation of a Procurement Advisory Council to suggest reforms and improvements and a Procurement Institute to train procurement personnel.

Article 3: *Source Selection and Contract Formation.* Article 3 describes the selection and contract formation methods authorized by the Code and authorizes procurement professionals to select and apply these methods. With the 2000 edition, Article 3 provides greater flexibility in the extent to which competitive sealed proposals may be used as a source selection method. Additionally, the modified edition requires that Request for Proposals (RFP) specify the relative importance of price and other factors and sub-factors that will be separately evaluated and scored by the procuring entity. Finally, Section 3–207, added in the 2000 revision, allows chief procurement officers, with prior notice, to initiate procurements above the small purchase threshold where the officer determines that unusual or unique situations exist that make application of all the requirements for competitive sealed bidding or competitive sealed proposals contrary to the public interest.

Article 4: *Specifications.* Article 4 contains requirements for developing, monitoring, and using specifications. It requires that specifications be written in a manner to maximize competition to the extent possible.

Article 5: *Procurement of Construction, Architect-Engineer and Land Surveying Services.* Article 5 was substantially rewritten in 2000 and now establishes five project delivery methods that may be applied by the procuring entity to procure infrastructure projects and services: design-bid-build, design-build, design-build-operate-maintain, design-build-finance-operate-maintain, and operations and maintenance.

Article 6: *Modification and Termination of Contracts for Supplies and Services.* Article 6 authorizes the use of clauses in contracts for supplies and services covering changes and variations in estimated quantities and sets forth the criteria for making price adjustments pursuant to such clauses. It also authorizes the inclusion of other clauses, including liquidated damages, excusable delay, and termination.

Article 7: *Cost Principles.* Article 7 provides for the promulgation of regulations establishing cost principles to be used to determine types of costs reimbursable under cost-type contracts.

Article 8: *Supply Management.* Article 8 establishes requirements for control over the life cycle of procured supplies and establishes criteria for the management, transfer, and disposal of surplus property.

Article 9: *Legal and Contractual Remedies.* Article 9 provides mechanisms for the resolution of protests relating to solicitations and awards, contract performance, and debarment or suspension determinations. In addition, this Article provides procedures for handling contracts awarded in violation of law.

Article 10: *Intergovernmental Relations.* Article 10 contains provisions designated to facilitate cooperative procurement among the various units of government. It permits standardization of specifications for use by several jurisdictions, joint use of real and personal property, and sharing of personnel among local governments and between a state and its political subdivisions. The Article also provides that a state, at the request of other jurisdictions, may provide procurement information and technical services to those jurisdictions.

Article 11: *Assistance to Small and Disadvantaged Businesses; Federal Assistance or Contract Procurement Requirements.* Article 11 provides administrative procedures for assisting small and disadvantaged business in learning how to do business with the public entity. This Article can also be used to incorporate additional state socioeconomic policies that are to be implemented through the procurement process. Article 11 requires compliance with federal law and regulations not presently reflected in the Code when procurement involves the expenditure of federal assistance or contract funds.

Article 12: *Ethics in Public Contracting.* Article 12 contains ethical standards with accompanying sanctions that are applicable to all participants in the public procurement process. The proposed ethical standards cover conflicts of interest, gratuities and kickbacks, contingent fees, and misuse of confidential information. Additionally, this Article authorizes establishment of an Ethics Commission with authority to render advisory opinions to participants in the procurement process.

Cooperative Procurement

Over the last several years, procurement professionals have seen increased workloads, often reduced staffing, and additional pressures to achieve organization financial goals with reduced resources. Cooperative procurement, the aggregation of requirements, and other cooperation among public entities has grown in popularity. NIGP's development of a Global Best Practice on cooperative procurement illustrates its importance.

Cooperative Procurement Authority

It's important that procurement professionals fully understand the limits of cooperative procurement authority in their jurisdiction. A threshold question is whether a public entity can participate and the formal requirements to do so.

There is no generalized name for authority to conduct cooperative procurement, and the authority can be granted in various sections of statutes. States having adopted the ABA Model Procurement Code for State and Local Governments have a comprehensive article on cooperative purchasing. Other state statutes treat cooperative purchasing under names such as "joint powers" or "interlocal cooperation." Moreover, the authority sometimes resides in separate statutes governing specific entities, such as municipal and county governments and higher education.

Generally, the cooperative contract must be awarded by a public entity to permit participation by others. The 2000 Model Procurement Code extended cooperative procurement authority to more not-for-profit entities.

Legally Sufficient Solicitation Practices

The cooperative procurement authority granted to governments sometimes requires the underlying contract to have been competitively awarded by a lead government entity in accordance with the participating government's law. Those requirements often include publication of the solicitation.

Section 10–201(2) of The 2000 Model Procurement Code added a new provision regarding competition:

> All Cooperative Purchasing conducted under this Article shall be through contracts awarded through full and open competition, including use of source selection methods substantially equivalent to those specified in Article 3 (Source Selection and Contract Formation) of this Code.

Public entities who have adopted the "substantially equivalent" standard to measure compliance with competition requirements may have an easier time harmonizing other entities' cooperative procurements with their own state law or ordinance requirements.

Later Participation: "Piggybacking"

Virtually all states' statutes authorize at least true cooperatives, that is, a joint procurement where requirements are established cooperatively and the parties each participate in the procurement. Statutes that authorize "piggybacking" may impose limitations.

Piggybacking is defined in the NIGP Dictionary of Terms as a form of intergovernmental cooperative purchasing in which an entity will be extended the pricing and terms of a contract entered into by another entity. Often, a larger entity competitively awards a contract that includes language allowing other public entities to utilize the contract and achieve more favorable pricing. But some jurisdictions have legal requirements before they can use a cooperative; South Carolina, for example, requires the public posting of the state's intent to participate.

Moreover, courts may review whether the participating entity's contract is substantially the same as the cooperative contract as awarded (*Accela, Inc. v. Sarasota County*, 993 So.2d 1035 (Fla. Dist. Ct. App. 2008)). In *Accela*, the court held the contract was not a proper exercise of cooperative authority. The software system purchased though piggybacking more than doubled the number of modules bought along with the cost, when compared to the underlying contract. This consideration is closely akin to the issue of impermissible scope of a contract amendment as discussed in Chapter 7.

Other Impacts of Statutory and Administrative Laws

There are too many ancillary statutory or administrative laws that impact the procurement function on the federal, state, and local level to mention specifically in this text. Nevertheless, the public procurement professional must remain vigilant regarding these ancillary laws and their impact on their operations. There are some key laws that are worth noting here.

Budget/Finance Laws

These laws are critical in public procurement. Budget statutes prohibit a governmental entity from spending funds beyond those that the legislative body appropriates for it. They are the impetus for encumbrance accounting that requires a purchase requisition or other form to be used that certifies the entity has the funds. Additionally, finance laws address issues, such as the manner of paying suppliers, whether the government will pay interest on late payments, and whether the government will make payments to suppliers in advance of contract performance.

Fiscal law is derived from governments' constitutions and charters, statutes and ordinances, and administrative rules and regulations. Conway (2012) devotes an entire chapter to fiscal law. The non-appropriation clause common in government contracts is a means of conditioning government contractual obligations on availability of funds necessary to discharge them.

Governments' resistance to suppliers' requests that they indemnify them against claims and liability arising from government acts in part is grounded in fiscal law. Generally, governments are unable to agree to contingent liabilities: 1) in an uncertain amount, 2) not merely incidental to the transaction (as might be the case of an adjustment authorized by the changes clause), and 3) without legislative authorization. Colorado statutes, for example, authorize a limited "hold harmless" provision for state leases when approved by the state risk manager. Otherwise, the state's fiscal rules prohibit indemnification of contractors by the state.

Electronic and Digital Signature Laws

The other emerging area affecting procurement is the use of electronic signatures. One of the most widely adopted laws is the Uniform Electronic Transactions Act (UETA), passed in 47 states and the District of Columbia. The states who have not enacted UETA have their own statutes dealing with electronic signatures. There are companion statutes, including the Electronic Signatures in Global and National Commerce Act (ESIGN).

These statutes impact much more than contract signatures. But the primary effect on procurement has been in two areas: helping resolve any lingering doubt that contracts can be enforced though electronic signatures are used and prompting development of new policies regarding the legal requirements for contract approval and signatures. Government controllers and chief financial officers often lead or play a key role in developing the policies. Even in governments having electronic signature laws, it is not uncommon for financial rules to still require manual signatures on contracts.

Electronic signatures can be as simple as adding a scanned signature to a document to more sophisticated systems with encryption and keys to decode the documents. Digital signature statutes authorize infrastructure for secure electronic signatures. With the advent of cloud information technology solutions, procurement of digital signature protocols and infrastructure involve important collateral policies like the storage of electronically executed documents.

State and Federal False Claim Statutes

These statutes prohibit filing a false claim or statement with the government. In the context of procurement, state and federal false claim statutes prohibit a supplier or other provider of goods or services from falsifying or inflating in any way a request for payment. These statutes provide for both public and private enforcement and civil and criminal penalties. These statutes often contain generous "whistleblower" provisions. In the federal and some state false claims statutes, if the government is successful in a subsequent lawsuit involving a person who reports a false claim to the government, the person reporting the violation will receive a percentage of the money recovered in the lawsuit.

Federal Laws and Their Relationship to Federal Funding

In 2014, revisions were made to the governing regulations in federally funded programs. Known as Uniform Guidance, the intent was to streamline government by integrating a variety of Office of Management and Budget (OMB) Circulars and entity regulations known as the Common Rule.

The new Uniform Guidance of 2 Code of Federal Regulations (CFR) Part 200 integrates pre- and post-award policies, such as publication of award opportunities, cost principles, financial management, and auditing, into a single policy. Its provisions include procurement standards and rules governing tangible and intangible property (including intellectual property). In addition, while an appendix of contract provisions identifies minimum required contractual terms and conditions, it may not cover all the contractual language that is required by federal-funding entities in their policies.

When procuring property and services under a federal award, a state must follow the same policies and procedures it uses for procurements from its non-federal funds. All other non-federal entities, including subrecipients of a state, must satisfy the Uniform Guidance's procurement standards.

Notably, for other than state recipients, the procurement standards incorporate the federal government's simplified acquisition threshold and micro-purchase limits. A micro-purchase is defined as a purchase of supplies or services using simplified acquisition procedures, the aggregate amount of which does not exceed the micro-purchase threshold in the Federal Acquisition Regulation. Micro-purchase procedures (akin to state and local government discretionary purchases where no competition is required) comprise a subset of a non-federal entity's small purchase procedures. The simplified acquisition threshold—akin to state and local government small purchase thresholds—is a dollar amount below which federal entities use simplified quote procedures.

Under the Uniform Guidance's procurement standards, procurements by micro-purchase (currently purchases up to $10,000) do not require the use of any prescribed process. However, the non-federal entity must consider the price to be reasonable, and "to the extent practicable, the non-Federal entity must distribute micro-purchases equitably among qualified suppliers." Procurements under the simplified acquisition threshold (currently $250,000) and above the micro-purchase threshold can be conducted informally using price or rate quotations from an adequate number of qualified sources.

One notable change for non-state entities is the requirement to prepare cost estimates for all procurements and cost or price analysis in connection with every procurement action greater than the simplified acquisition threshold, including contract modifications. Moreover, profit must be negotiated as a separate element of price for each contract where there is no price competition. As had been the case before the Uniform Guidance, cost-plus-a-percentage-of-cost methods of contracting are prohibited; a prohibition already in many public entity procurement laws or ordinances.

Federal entities may prescribe additional policies and regulatory requirements in the Code of Federal Regulations.

Cooperative Procurement Meets Federal Law

In 2013, the Federal Transit Administration (FTA) disapproved of the purchase of buses from the Minnesota Cooperative Purchasing Venture contract where the transit agencies were out-of-state entities not parties to the original Minnesota contract.

According to the FTA, "joint procurements" are permitted where quantities reflect "current and reasonably expected needs" advertised in the original contract. The FTA publishes a Best Practices Procurement Manual that explains the permissible use of "piggybacking." Piggybacking is permissible when the original contract includes an "assignability clause" that permits assignment of all or part of the specified deliverable items. The original ordering quantities—or at least minimum and maximum quantities that represent the reasonably foreseeable needs of the parties—must have been specified in the solicitation.

This view of piggybacking permits the originally ordered/evaluated quantities to be partially or wholly assigned, as, for example, where the original procuring entity unexpectedly finds that it does not need the entire quantity that was estimated in good faith. But the FTA guidance does not allow originally procured amounts to be increased, a practice the FTA characterizes as "tag-ons" and impermissible non-competitive procurement. These limitations are not generally satisfied under widely adopted cooperative purchasing practices.

In the case of use of state contracts by in-state local governments, on the other hand, the FTA policy permits the traditional use of state contracts, what the FTA calls "schedules." However, with respect to use of federal transit funds to piggyback across state borders, the FTA guidance imposes limitations. There are other FTA policies that reflect this restrictive view of the permissibility of local government use of other public entity contracts. For example, the FTA limits the ability of a transit agency to amend a piggybacked contract to add federal terms and conditions that were not in the original solicitation.

Until 2014, there was uncertainty about how the FTA viewed state contracts and whether they considered permissible "schedules." Then, a supplier under the State of Washington's vehicle lift contract requested the FTA to clarify the FTA guidance as applied to their contract. The vehicle lift contract was sourced as a Western States Contracting Alliance (WSCA) cooperative master agreement by the State of Washington as lead state. Estimates of expected usage likely did not meet the FTA's criteria for reasonable estimates, and FTA terms and conditions were not in the original solicitation. The FTA concluded, however, that "[e]ligble states and their subordinate entities that are able to order from this contract . . . are listed on the contract website. . . . Eligible grantees ordering from this contract still would have to ensure that other FTA requirements such as Buy America are met as the complete the procurement process." The letter approved of local governments in Washington using federal funds ordering from the state contract.

In 2016, the FTA revised its policy based on changes in the law and permits eligible public entities to purchase from any state's cooperative contract or schedule. FTA (2016) section 3.3.5.

The Federal Transit Administration publishes a Best Practices Procurement Manual to provide information on procurement requirements for grant recipients. Some funds under the auspices of the Federal Transit Administration come with Buy American Act requirements.

Other federal funding entities may have additional requirements, and it is important to be intimately familiar with the relevant federal agency policies, generally available on the agency websites or the Code of Federal Regulations.

Reform of Public Procurement Laws, Administrative Law, and Enabling Legislation

Public procurement professionals are strongly encouraged to influence changes in statutory and administrative laws to adopt best practices for the profession.

There are several key issues for public procurement professionals to consider when advocating changes to legislative and administrative laws:

- Statutes and ordinances fall within the purview of statutory law and reflect the highest level of authority for the public procurement function. Accordingly, statutes and ordinances should provide the overarching rules of conduct for public procurement.
- Statutes and ordinances are adopted by the legislative governing body (the state legislature, the city council, the county commissioners, etc.). As such, they are extremely difficult to change. In contrast, administrative laws (regulations, policies, and procedures) are typically developed and implemented by the executive or administrative body (governors, city managers, county administrators, school district superintendents, etc.). The public procurement professional needs to be cognizant of the roles, responsibilities, and balance of power between the legislative and executive bodies that promulgate statutory and administrative laws. The official also needs to be cognizant of the political environment affecting these two groups, as most legislative bodies are elected while most executive bodies are appointed. Public procurement professionals can best influence statutory laws through a consolidated effort of professional associations or collegial groups. In contrast, the public procurement professional can have a greater individual influence on administrative law.
- The authority granted by the legislative governing body to implement administrative law or regulations is often referred to as an "administrative procedures act." This series of statutes determines the manner and extent to which the procurement officer has authority over

procurement rules or regulations. To the extent possible, an administrative procedures act should enable the public procurement officer to promulgate operational policies and procedures that enhance the value of the procurement function.

- Policy issues and procedural details that need to be dynamic to be effective (e.g., bid limits and contract authorization thresholds) should not be included in statutory law to the extent possible.

Within the legal framework, the public procurement professional should continually seek enabling legislation that empowers the public procurement function to add economic, efficient, and effective value to the public entity. As of this writing, new procurement concepts are transitioning from fresh, innovative practices developed by a few public entities to best practices serving as the standard for many entities. Undoubtedly, new concepts and practices will be implemented as the profession grows in stature and credibility.

Public procurement professionals should strive to ensure that their statutory laws and administrative laws enable them to offer the highest strategic value to their entities. Consider the following:

- Laws and regulations should provide ethical guidelines for conduct by public buyers, managers, elected officials, and suppliers;
- Laws and regulations should strive for the greatest efficiency and economy of the public procurement process by providing alternative methods of source selection, such as cooperative ventures and strategic sourcing;
- Laws and regulations should strive for the greatest effectiveness of the public procurement process by establishing realistic bid thresholds based on benchmarks of similar governmental entities;
- Laws and regulations should allow for evaluative methods that consider the total cost of ownership and best-value approaches to public procurements;
- Laws and regulations should promote public-private partnerships that encourage contract incentives and performance-based contracting;
- Laws and regulations should allow for fair negotiations for specified types of procurements; and
- Laws and regulations should provide for the use of technology and electronic processes to create efficiencies and effectiveness.

Conclusion

This chapter added legislative, administrative, and common law topics that are even more central to public procurement than the basic principles and structure of the United States legal system introduced in Chapter 1. A threshold consideration is the government's authority to procure and its agents' authority, defined by the law of agency. Procurement professionals, as the authorized agents of public entities, follow a variety of laws that govern procurement of supplies, services, and public works (construction). The ABA Model Procurement Code was covered in some depth because it is the closest to a common framework in the United States, and it is adopted at least partially in half the states and many municipalities. But relevant laws do not end with procurement codes. Budget and finance laws, digital commerce legislation, laws governing cooperative procurement, and federally funded contract regulations all are examples of other laws with which public procurement professionals must be familiar.

For Further Reading

Pennington, Richard. "Piggybacking on the Law (of Piggybacking)." Government Procurement, December 2011.

———. "State and Local Procurement Liability Allocation: Constitutional and Statutory Limitations: Government Article by Richard Pennington." *Resource Government*, October 16, 2008. www.resourcegovernment.com/articles/view.php?article_id=16513.

Pennington, Richard, and Ed Pabor. "Pros and Cons of Design-Build Construction Procurement Method—Government Procurement Article." *American City & County*. Accessed October 23, 2018. www.americancityandcounty.com/2012/04/01/the-growth-and-growing-pains-of-design-build-construction/.

References

American Bar Association. *The 2000 Model Procurement Code for State and Local Governments*. Chicago: American Bar Association, 2000.

Conway, Danielle M. *State and Local Government Procurement*. Chicago: American Bar Association, Section of State and Local Government Law, 2012.

Federal Transit Administration. "Best Practices Procurement & Lessons Learned Manual (Report 0105)." Federal Transit Administration, October 2016.

NASPO. *State and Local Government Purchasing Principles and Practices*. Lexington, KY: NASPO, 1997.

NIGP, The Institute for Public Procurement. "Global Best Practices." Accessed October 23, 2018. www.nigp.org/home/find-procurement-resources/guidance/global-best-practices.

Pitzer, Jack T., and Khi V. Thai. *Introduction to Public Procurement*. 3rd ed. Herndon, VA: National Institute of Governmental Purchasing, 2009.

State of Oregon. "Reciprocal Preference." Department of Administrative Services. www.oregon.gov/das/Procurement/Pages/Recippref.aspx.

Chapter 3

The Basic Components of a Common Law Contract

This chapter focuses on the basic components of a common law contract. While Article 2 of the Uniform Commercial Code (U.C.C.) (like the Sales Act in Canada) governs contracts for the sale of goods, the common law of contracts governs all other types, most notably of which are service contracts. Under the common law, there are six essential elements needed to form a legal contract: offer and acceptance, definiteness, consideration, mutuality of obligation, capacity of the parties, and legality of purpose. The common law also provides rules for interpreting contracts and remedies for their breach. This chapter ends with a description of key differences between government contracts and those under common law.

What Is a Contract?

Before delving into the legal specifics of the common law of contracts, it may be useful to define the basics of a contract. Unfortunately, there is no simple definition of the term "contract." Non-lawyers generally tend to use the term to mean the written document signifying an agreement between two parties, but in the eyes of the law, the term actually refers to the process by which the agreement is formed. Within the context of this chapter, the term "contract" refers to promises or agreements for which the law establishes enforceable duties and remedies. For the public procurement officer, the law of common law contracts has many applications. For example, not only will public procurement officers deal with contracts for the procurement of goods and services, but also the issuing and writing of grants, intergovernmental and cooperative agreements, facility leases, real property purchases and sales, and a host of other types of contractual agreements.

A contract is nothing more than an agreement between two or more people to do or not to do something. The key to a contract is that there must be an agreement. A promise, proposal, or offer with no agreement is not a contract. In the public procurement context, a contract is an agreement by a seller or supplier to provide goods or services to the public entity in return for receiving payment from the public entity.

The common law of contracts is not designed to make the process of conducting business difficult; rather, the purpose of the law of contracts is to facilitate business by establishing fair and efficient rules of contract law. That being said, the law of contracts wants commerce to flow smoothly, so that everyone involved can make a reasonable profit or secure goods and services without one person or supplier having an unfair advantage toward another person or supplier engaged in the market. This constant tension between making sure business is not unduly hampered, yet making sure business people are legally protected, is the dynamic of modern contract law.

Contracts are primarily governed by state legislation, common law, and the contract itself. Parties to a contract have what is referred to as "the freedom of contract," which principally allows the parties to establish their own law for the performance of a specific contract. This private contract law may override many of the default rules otherwise established by state law.

Statutory law may require that some contracts be detailed in writing and executed with particular formalities, such as contracts for the purchase and sale of real estate, guarantees, and contracts of employment in excess of one year. Otherwise, the parties may enter into a binding agreement without signing a formal written document. Contracts related to particular activities or business sectors may be highly regulated by state and federal law.

When Does a Contract Exist?

Before taking measures to enforce a contract, it must be established whether or not a contract actually exists. To determine existence, the opinion of the involved parties is ignored, and the "reasonable person rule" serves as the basis for determination. By viewing the dynamic as a whole, the court decides if a "reasonable person" would have reason to believe that the parties intend to be bound to a contract. A binding contract requires an offer, acceptance, and consideration. In addition, the parties must have an agreement as to the material elements necessary for the performance of the contract. This understanding and agreement is known as a "meeting of the minds."

In determining whether there is a valid contract, in addition to other factors, the court may consider testimony; written evidence such as notes, emails, or letters; and any actions taken by or on behalf of either party in the performance of the disputed contract.

The court will attempt to determine the intentions of the parties; however, where the parties have not agreed to a key element of the contract, it is unlikely that a court will find an enforceable contract under the common law. It's important to note that the court will not decide terms of a contract for parties—it will rule on whether there was an agreement to terms and what constitutes that agreement.

A letter of intent is not a binding contract. However, if a letter of intent is written in such a way that it contains the consideration and requires performance, a court may find it to be a valid contract, especially if both parties sign off on the letter of intent or one or both parties have fully or partially performed.

Privity of a Contract

Normally, only parties to a contract have the right to enforce its terms. In some instances, third parties who are not in privity with contracting parties may have rights to enforce and sue for breach of contract. These kinds of contracts are third-party beneficiary contracts. For third-party rights to exist, certain contractual criteria must be met. These criteria include the following:

1. A valid contract must exist between two contracting parties;
2. The contracting parties must have intended, either expressly or impliedly, to confer a benefit to a third party;
3. The third party must be named or referred to or be a member of a distinct class referred to in the contract; and
4. The third party must have some knowledge of the contract's existence.

For example, the government once contracted with a data security firm to protect the personal information received from members of the public. Unfortunately, a data breach occurred, disclosing the personal data of a significant number of people who had applied for various kinds of government identification cards and permits. The court determined the members of the public who applied to the government for these cards and permits would be considered third-party beneficiaries of the contract between the government and the data security firm. This is known as the "privity of contract" rule. In some circumstances, third parties who are known beneficiaries to a contract may have rights to enforce and sue for breach of a contract.

Forming a Contract

Contracts are formed through a variety of ways. There are express contracts, which may be written or oral, created when the formal elements for establishing a contract exist. Another kind of contract is an "implied-in-fact" contract, where some of the formal elements occur through conduct rather than express words. This type of contract occurs when someone takes a car to be washed at the local car wash. Although the formalities of an express contract are missing, it is implied that the person taking the car keys will wash the car and that the other person, who has handed over those keys, will pay for that service.

Sometimes, the law affords a person a legal remedy to pursue another person based on that second person's promise, even though critical elements of contract formation do not exist. An example of this type of contract is where a general contractor uses a subcontractor's quote in preparing a bid for a public construction project. Some courts have decided that since the general contractor relied on the subcontractor's quote in preparing its bid, the subcontractor may not withdraw that quote until the general contractor knows whether it has been awarded a contract and has a reasonable opportunity to accept the quote.

In other instances, the law imposes an obligation on a person to achieve justice, even though there is clearly no contract. Those situations are called "implied-in-law" contracts. An example is a circumstance in which a doctor renders necessary medical treatment to someone who is unconscious and obviously cannot enter into a contract for those services. The law implies a reasonable promise to pay the doctor for those services.

The principle of an "implied-in-law" contract does not generally apply to governments. That being said, there are exceptions. In one instance, a court required a city to pay a hospital for services rendered to an arrested person that city police had shot, on the theory that the city had a constitutional duty to provide medical services to that prisoner.

Elements of a Contract

There are six essential elements that must exist for an enforceable contract to be formed:

Offer and Acceptance	Definiteness
Consideration	Mutuality of Obligation
Capacity of the Parties	Legality of Purpose

Because of the formal nature of the public contracting process, disputes about whether the government and its supplier have complied with some of these elements are seldom seen. Nonetheless, issues arise from time to time. This text defines each element in the context of the common law of contracts.

Offer and Acceptance

Formation of a contract requires an agreement—two parties consenting to the same terms. The process by which persons reach an agreement is the offer and acceptance process. An offer generally involves a promise or commitment to do or not to do a specified thing in the future. That promise demonstrates a person's intent to assure that the thing promised will or will not be done.

The words "I will sell you my black horse for $1,000" is an offer because the speaker has made a commitment. However, a mail order catalog that lists items for sale and their prices is not an offer because the supplier has not used any language promising to supply a specific quantity at a specific price.

Acceptance occurs when the person to whom the offer is made exchanges his or her own promise or performance for the promise made in the offer. In the common law, the acceptance may not vary from the terms of the offer. If it does, then that kind of acceptance will not be valid as an acceptance, but constitutes a counteroffer and a rejection of the original offer.

Offer and Acceptance Within the Context of Public Procurement

In public procurement, a solicitation, such as an Invitation for Bids (IFB), is not an offer. Instead, it is a request to suppliers to submit offers. The bids or proposals submitted in response are offers. Acceptance occurs when the public official authorized to award contracts signifies that the jurisdiction has selected the supplier as the winner. That official may be the public procurement officer, a city council, or a board of supervisors.

Nothing needs to be signed for acceptance to occur; it takes place by merely communicating, by words or conduct, assent to the offer. Courts have held that an authorized procurement officer's letter notifying a supplier that it has been selected for award is the point at which a contract is created. Likewise, the vote of a city council may constitute acceptance. That is the case even where the government intends to enter into a signed, formal agreement at some later date but has not made acceptance expressly conditional on the agreement's final execution.

On the other hand, a written notice of award does not form a contract where the public procurement professional sends it so that the supplier receives it after the supplier's offer has expired. Similarly, a government official's statement to a supplier that the supplier has been awarded a contract does not constitute a valid acceptance if that official is not authorized to award contracts.

For small purchases, it is standard practice for the public procurement professional to obtain written or verbal quotes and to issue a purchase order based on the best quote. The procurement professional's issuance of a purchase order in response is generally an acceptance of an offer—the supplier's quote.

In other cases, the procurement professional may simply send a supplier a purchase order for an item from the supplier's catalog without obtaining quotes. Here, the purchase order constitutes an offer, not the catalog listing. The terms of the government's purchase order will likely vary with those on the supplier's order confirmation or in the documents shipped with the goods. Some suppliers' documents state that acceptance is expressly conditional on assent to those varying terms. If the purchase order is for services rather than goods, the common law provides that the supplier has not accepted the government's offer because the supplier proposed terms that differ from those in the offer. It is also important to note that this process of the initial bid and then acceptance of a bid may include a lengthy process of negotiation. As such, the final offer and acceptance may be delayed until such time as the negotiation is completed.

Definiteness

Under common law, an offer must include the important, or material, terms of the proposed agreement so that when a person accepts the offer the resulting agreement is enforceable. Important terms include subject matter, price, payment terms, quantity, quality, duration, and the work to be done. If the parties purport to agree on a material term but do so in a vague manner, as contrasted with omitting the term altogether, there is no agreement because it is too indefinite.

Definiteness Within the Context of Public Procurement

Because of the formal competitive process that most governments follow in purchasing items above a certain dollar limit, indefiniteness of the offer is not a problem. Remember that the bid a supplier submits is the offer. Under the law of public contracts, that bid must be responsive—it must show the supplier's commitment to comply with the solicitation's requirements, which includes supplying a set price. If a supplier submits a bid that says the price will be the one in effect at the time it supplies janitorial services, the bid is not only non-responsive, it is also indefinite.

Many public purchasers today are drafting "floating price" provisions in solicitations for goods subject to volatile price changes, such as personal computers. Those pricing provisions state, for example, that price will be determined monthly based on the manufacturer's commercial price plus the set fee or percentage increase that the supplier-bidder identifies in its bid. That type of pricing provision is not indefinite.

Consideration

The concept of consideration is a tough one for lawyers, and defining it in a meaningful way for non-lawyers is even more troublesome. It concerns the promises made during the offer and acceptance, which common law generally requires to be supported by "consideration." Simply stated, consideration is the "bargained for" exchange of promises. For procurement professionals, this usually means we pay the supplier once they have provided the contracted commodity.

Consideration Within the Context of Public Procurement

A good example of a consideration issue in the government contracts setting arises under what are called term or indefinite quantity contracts. Public purchasers establish these contracts for items commonly used throughout the government. Under this type of contract, a supplier agrees to supply particular goods or services at a set price for a specific period of time, but the quantity of the goods or services that the government will need is unknown, only estimated. If a dispute arises because a supplier claims that the government has ordered too great a quantity of the items under the contract, the estimated quantities in the contract, as well as the size of past orders, will define whether the disputed order is reasonable.

If the contract does not require the government to buy all those specific goods or services that it needs from that supplier, but reserves the discretion to buy them elsewhere, the government has not given any consideration; it has not obligated itself legally to the terms of the contract. That consideration problem is solved by mandating that the government purchase all of the specific goods or services it needs under the contract.

Mutuality of Obligation

This element is really a sub-element of consideration. It applies in situations where the offer requires the person accepting it to make a promise in return rather than by immediately performing. A simple statement of this element is "both parties must be bound or neither one is bound." It really means that both parties must supply consideration to the other. For example, if a contracting party reserves a means by which it may completely avoid performing, the contract may not be enforceable because both parties are not legally obligated to perform.

Competent Parties

There are certain classes of persons whom the law deems incapable of entering into a contract. A person who lacks the authority to contract for someone else under the law of agency is but one example. Others incapable of entering into binding contracts include infants and mentally infirm individuals. Under common law, a person remains an infant until the age of 21. Today, statutes and court decisions set the age at 18.

Some scholars use the concept of "competency" interchangeably with the concept of "consent." Since a contract involves a "meeting of the minds," all parties must be capable of consent. Accordingly, minors and mentally challenged persons may void a contract at the minor's or mentally challenged person's option. A contract with an incompetent person is only voidable on the purview of the incompetence if the other party knew about the mental incompetence or ought to have known under the circumstances.

Legal Purpose

Courts will generally not enforce an agreement, or part of an agreement, that violates statutory law or public policy. The extent to which a court will assist one person to enforce an "illegal" contract against another will depend on the type of violation of law involved and the requirements of applicable statutes or ordinances.

For instance, suppose a supplier does not have the appropriate license to enter into a contract to provide certain services to a government, but does so anyway. Another example is where a supplier submits a proposal to perform a study for a government and receives a contract to do the work. It includes in its proposal a requirement for the government to make payments to it in advance of the work, but the law of that jurisdiction prohibits advance payments. In the first case, the government, on discovering that the supplier does not have the proper license, must terminate the contract. If only part of a contract violates the law, as is the case in the second instance, the government may ignore that portion of the contract because the law will not enforce it.

Assignment and Novation

A person can transfer their contractual rights, benefits, and liabilities to another, unless such assignment rights are limited or eliminated in the contract itself. We refer to this transfer of the benefits, liabilities, and rights of one party to another as "assignment," which must be absolute with no contractual limitations, kickbacks, or additional requirements of the initial party. The law favors assignment, however, and imposes a duty that parties act reasonably when requested to approve an assignment. In addition, assignments can occur by operation of law, such as when a person dies, a firm declares bankruptcy or is purchased by another.

Novation on the other hand, is simply the replacement of one contract between parties with another contract, based on any number of changing circumstances. A novation extinguishes the original contract.

When Can Consent to an Assignment Be Withheld?

A 2010 New York appellate court plainly explained how a novation and assignment are different. In *KIOP Forest Avenue v. Southern Smokehouse of Staten Island* (958 N.Y.S.2d 61 (N.Y. Civ. Ct. 2010)),

Southern had a lease with KIOP for restaurant space in a shopping plaza. When the 2008 recession hit, Southern saw a downturn in sales and requested a rent reduction. KIOP denied the request. Thereafter, Southern sought to sell the business and assign the lease to a new restaurant that offered a Chinese buffet. The lease had an assignment approval provision, and KIOP also declined to accept the assignment. KIOP cited the existence of another Chinese takeout restaurant in the plaza that would interfere with the buffet concept. Southern's business continued to suffer, and Southern stopped paying the lease installments. KIOP sued. Southern's defense was based on improper refusal to consent to the assignment, and Southern sought money damages it claimed were caused by the refusal.

The appellate court found for the landlord. The court noted that under New York law, courts do not favor contractual restraints on assignments. Refusal to consent to an assignment can only be based on consideration of objective factors, such as financial responsibility, the legality of use, or the nature of occupancy. Subjective concerns and personal desires cannot play a role.

Consent to novation is governed by a different rule. A novation operates to discharge (extinguish) the duties under the previous contract. Under New York law, there is no obligation not to withhold consent to novation, unreasonable or otherwise. The court looked at Southern's requests and concluded that a novation, not an assignment, was being requested. The court characterized it as a "disguised novation" seeking a complete release of Southern from the lease. Under its terms, Southern would not be liable for any lease obligations during the remaining lease period. The court entered judgement for KIOP for unpaid rent and ordered a warrant of eviction.

Conditions That May Lead to a Voidable Contract

Mistakes

The process for handling mistakes in bids is discussed in Chapter 5; however, it should be noted here that a contract requires a meeting of the minds. If one or both parties have been mistaken about an element of the contract, then there is no such meeting of the minds. That does not necessarily mean, however, that the contract is void. Such a rule could breed abuse. Therefore, the common law has attempted to develop a fairly sophisticated set of rules for dealing with mistakes. Unfortunately, as is the case with most contract law, the final determination of what those rules are is constantly changing.

In contracts, it is unfortunately common for each party to make similar—or even the same—mistakes. These so-called "mutual mistakes" occur when respective parties know the intention of the other and ultimately accept that intention; however, they are ultimately unclear, mistaken, or under the assumption of an incorrect, key underlying fact. When only one party to a contract is mistaken, this is termed a "unilateral mistake." The common law handles each of these types of mistakes in contracting differently.

When both parties are mistaken on a basic and fundamental element of the contract, the contract is void from the start if the mistake is of such significance that, in the words of the old English common law cases, it is a "false and fundamental assumption." For example, if the identity of a contracting party is a fundamental element of the contract, such as an athlete or artist, a mistake in this regard will void the contract. Another example is a contract involving something that, unbeknownst to the parties, has been destroyed. In contrast, when only one party is mistaken, unless the other party to the contract knows or should have known of the mistake, the contract is still enforceable.

Misrepresentations

Misrepresentation is when one of the parties to a contract lies about or fails to disclose some material element of the contract and, in reliance on this statement, the other party entered into the contract. The common law of contracts treats this kind of fraudulent misrepresentation as grounds for rendering a contract unenforceable. The elements of fraudulent misrepresentation include:

1. That the representations were made by the wrongdoer to the victim before the contract;
2. That these representations were false in fact;
3. That the wrongdoer, when he made them, either knew that they were false or made them recklessly without knowing whether they were false or true; and
4. That the victim is damaged thereby.

Misrepresentation must be distinguished from sales language, or "puffing." A salesperson's sales pitch that hypes a product may constitute a fraudulent misrepresentation. However, merely touting a good or service in generally favorable terms will most likely not constitute a fraudulent misrepresentation. It is also important to note that silence and the failure to disclose material facts can be construed as misrepresentations in certain circumstances, such as when the omission reasonably results in a misunderstanding or the omission is a fact that a reasonable person would want to know before entering into the contract.

Restraint of Trade Contracts

In contemporary, commercial environments, restraint of trade contracts in the form of non-compete and non-circumvent agreements are common. Accordingly, state statutory law and the common law set forth the standards of fairness for such contracts. These standards include that such contracts must be reasonable in relation to the circumstances, time period, and geographical location or, now, Internet marketplace.

Confidentiality agreements, on the other hand, are typically enforced in favor of the restrainer if the information involves trade secrets.

Frustration

Under certain conditions, a person can be relieved of their contractual obligations under the common law doctrine of "frustration." This common law doctrine—sometimes referred to as "impossibility of performance"—will excuse one or both parties from performance of the contract. Impossibility of performance is judged by an objective standard. An act of God or a change in statutory law may render performance of the contract impossible or illegal. For example, Hurricane Katrina rendered performance of many contracts for the delivery of goods to New Orleans impossible to perform. Further, when the law of Florida changed to disallow certain kinds of consumer and other financial loans, such contracts may have become illegal or impossible to perform.

That being said, frustration cannot be invoked just because the contract has suddenly become more difficult or expensive for one of the parties to perform. Likewise, frustration cannot be invoked just because it would be more advantageous for one party to not perform under a contract. For example, if one party to an agreement now believes that the contract price is too cheap and that the value of the goods or services contracted for demands a higher contract price, this kind of reason would not be sufficient to invoke a frustration or impossibility of performance defense to performance of the contract. Finally, parties can, but would be well advised in most instances not to, contract away this defense by specifically barring such a defense in the contract terms.

Rules for Interpreting Contracts

The courts are frequently asked to resolve disputes about the meaning of certain words, sentences, and provisions in contracts. A wide range of general interpretation rules guide the courts in the task of interpreting a contract. However, courts are reluctant to impose their view of what the terms of a contract mean between two parties unless the contract terms, as written, are ambiguous.

If both parties agree on a certain interpretation to be given to a term in a contract, a court has no reason or justification for pursuing the matter further and should accept that interpretation.

A court will always try to discover the intentions of the contracting parties using the plain, ordinary, and popular meanings of the words used. Reference to a common usage dictionary is perfectly in order for a court making this kind of decision. A court will not try to rewrite a contract using interpretation rules, but rather uses these rules to pinpoint the intentions of the parties at the moment of contract. For example:

- Courts presume that no provision of the contract is void of any meaning or superfluous, but rather it must have some purpose. Only in those circumstances where no clear alternate interpretation is available to remove absurdity or ambiguity from a contract provision will the court void any part of a contract.
- Courts can refer to words that have been crossed out or words in headings, margins, recitals, or a preamble for guidance in interpreting ambiguous contract terms.
- Courts may refer to the factual circumstances under which the contract was signed or agreed upon to assist in interpretation of ambiguous contract terms. Such circumstances may include a review of letters exchanged between the parties and prior agreements between the parties. However, the courts will usually refrain from reviewing prior drafts of the existing contract.
- Courts may consider business customs as part of their methodology.
- Where contract terms are ambiguous and open to more than one interpretation, the courts usually interpret the contract term against the author, especially if there is a power imbalance between the parties.
- Courts give greater weight to writing than oral testimony when interpreting ambiguous terms of a contract. In some cases, evidence of oral

amendments or modifications will not be considered where a contract provides that it can only be amended or modified in writing.

- Courts will correct obvious mistakes in spelling, punctuation, and grammar if such corrections do not change the meaning of a contract. For example, if a contract provision uses the word "may," the courts will not change that word to "shall," but it will make sure that the word is spelled correctly and preceded or followed by the appropriate punctuation.
- Courts will interpret contract terms to carry out the general and specific purposes for which the contract was formed.
- Courts will always interpret ambiguous contract terms with a view toward carrying out the intentions of both parties to the contract.
- Courts will interpret contracts in the context of the whole document.
- Courts will view terms not expressly provided for in a contract as not part of the contract.
- Courts may consider prior course of dealing between the parties and custom and trade usage to interpret the meaning of a contract provision.

Parol Evidence Rule

The ability of a court to interpret a contract may be limited by the Parol Evidence Rule. The Parol Evidence Rule prohibits a court from considering evidence outside of the language contained in the contract. This rule is triggered by a finding of the court that the contract is the final and complete agreement of the parties and the final and complete expression of the terms of the contract. If the court finds that a contract is the final and complete agreement between the parties, then no extrinsic or outside evidence can be presented to a court to vary or contradict the terms of a contract. On the other hand, if the court finds that the contract is not the final and complete agreement of the parties, then the court will consider extrinsic or other outside evidence that proves the exact terms and conditions in a contract agreed to by the parties. Therefore, the Parol Evidence Rule does not prevent either party to a contract from presenting evidence to a court that the contract was not the final and complete agreement of the parties.

The customary application of the Parol Evidence Rule, as explained in the previous paragraph, can be altered by the parties to a contract. For example, many contracts will contain specific language that states the contract is the final and complete agreement of the parties. Further, many contracts will contain language that prohibits either party from presenting evidence to a court that the contract is not the final and complete agreement of the parties or evidence of different or additional terms applicable to the contract. Since a court's basic approach to interpreting a contract is to follow the intent of the parties, such contract provisions may limit both parties' ability to try to circumvent the application of the Parol Evidence Rule.

Parameters for Written Contracts

As a general rule, contracts may be written or oral. Under both the common law of contracts and other statutory law, certain types of contracts must be in writing. This requirement does not mean that two persons cannot enter into an oral agreement. It simply means that, for certain types of contracts that must be in writing, neither party may enforce an unperformed contractual obligation unless there is a written contract.

Statute of Frauds

In the early years of common law, the king's courts in England generally did not enforce oral promises. This changed over time, but in 1677, Parliament passed the "Act for the Prevention of Fraud and Perjuries," requiring certain promises and agreements to be evidenced in writing. That law, generally known as the Statute of Frauds, became the common law of this country, though court decisions and state legislatures have enacted their own versions of it.

Agreements That Must Be Supported by Written Documentation

The Statute of Frauds generally mandates that the following types of promises or agreements be evidenced in writing: agreements for the sale of land or of interests in land; agreements in consideration of marriage; a promise by the executor or administrator of a deceased person's estate to pay from his or her own pocket a debt of the deceased; certain promises made by a person to answer for the debt of another; contracts that are not to be performed within one year from the time they are made, including leases; and, under the U.C.C., contracts for the sale of goods valued at more than $500. The most important rules on that list for the procurement professional are the sale of land or an interest in land, contracts not to be performed within a year, and the sale of goods valued at more than $500.

Satisfying the Writing Requirement

The type of writing that will satisfy the Statute of Frauds varies. A memorandum, exchange of correspondence, or receipt, for instance, may suffice if that writing identifies with reasonable certainty the contracting parties, the subject matter of the contract, and the contract's essential terms, especially a description of quantity when dealing with the sale of goods. The writing needs to be signed in some fashion by the party against whom the contract is being enforced. Any mark or sign that is written, printed, stamped, or otherwise placed on the writing may serve as a signature. In certain cases, even electronic signatures can satisfy the requirements.

Differentiating Between Private and Public Contracts

Whatever responsibilities the public procurement professional has in writing contract terms and conditions, they will differ from the responsibilities, and the flexibility, that parties have in the private setting. The following is a list of the general differences between how contracts are formed in public and private settings.

Formation of Private Contracts

In the commercial world, parties create contracts in one of four ways. One party may present the other with a prepared document for signature, and the second party has little bargaining power to change the terms of the agreement. Many consumer sales agreements fall within this category.

The second way a contract is formed is when each party sends the other its prepared document, setting forth differing terms. For example, one party may issue a purchase order for certain goods, and the other sends a confirmation that contains terms that vary from the purchase order. The goods are often shipped despite the differences in the documents, and those differences do not become important unless a problem arises.

The third way a contract may be created is through the process of negotiation, in which the parties bargain for the contract's terms and sign the agreement that results from that negotiation. The contract may be a complex document with pages of tightly drafted clauses, or it may consist of a letter that one party drafts for the other to sign.

The fourth way a contract may be created is through the competitive bid process, which is similar to the process used by governmental entities and provides the same benefits to the party looking to contract for goods or services.

Formation of a Public Contract

Public contracts are, for the most part, created through a different process. Just like in private commerce, however, a public procurement professional may issue a purchase order to a supplier for some small-dollar purchases based on items and prices in that supplier's general catalog. The supplier may ship the goods requested with a confirmation or invoice that contains terms that vary from the purchase order. This scenario generally creates a contract, despite the fact that the parties did not reach an agreement on its precise language. This type of transaction occurs both in private and public contracting.

For larger-dollar purchases, a contract arises as a result of a formal, arms-length process. The public entity issues a solicitation that "invites" suppliers to make an offer that complies with the specific terms of that solicitation. Where the public entity seeks a contractor through the competitive sealed bids process, there is no real bargaining. Under the competitive sealed proposals method, however, the opportunity for discussions and negotiations exists, but is somewhat constrained by considerations of fairness to all proposers.

Once the public procurement professional selects the winning bid or proposal and notifies the supplier submitting that bid or proposal of its selection, a contract comes into existence in most cases. Where the awarding of a contract requires the vote of a town council or board of supervisors, that vote is the event that creates a contract. The solicitation and the bid or proposal becomes the contract voted upon.

In some public entities, procurement professionals prepare a separate contract document for signature once they have selected and notified the winning supplier.

For complex projects, the public procurement professional, their client-agency end user, and the supplier may wish to have one document instead of the solicitation and the proposal that spells out the obligations of the parties. Problems may arise with this practice. The creation of a separate document opens the door for mistakes to occur in the transfer of information from one document to another. An example is the inadvertent change of "125 calendar days" for performance to "125 working days." To the extent that the new document changes the terms of the solicitation, bid, or proposal, it may amend the contractual relationship that was intended by the original solicitation.

Sometimes, public procurement professionals issue a solicitation without many terms in it, particularly when buying goods, and award a contract through a blanket purchase order. Unless the solicitation addresses issues such as termination of a contract, contract remedies, or payment, such terms may not be adequately covered, depending on the language of the blanket purchase order. This practice of issuing an incomplete solicitation may also provide leverage for the supplier to include the supplier's terms and conditions in the contract in any agreement. In addition, some suppliers or contractors innocently, or maybe not so innocently, ask the public procurement professional to sign a separate agreement for "housekeeping" or other similar reasons, but whose legal affect is sometimes unclear. The best approach is for the procurement professional to include all the terms that will become part of the contract in the solicitation. The procurement department should have a set of approved, standard contract terms addressing issues common to all of its contracts, and may wish to draft additional standard terms applicable, for instance, to contracts for the purchase of goods. The public procurement professional must either include those standard terms in every solicitation or simply include language in the solicitation that incorporates them by reference, making copies available to suppliers online, via fax, or at the procurement department.

Scope of the Contract

Private parties can amend contracts any way they want. Governments, on the other hand, may be constrained by competition requirements where added work exceeds the "scope" of the contract. The issue of contract scope arises in two contexts under federal procurement law. A unilateral change directed by the government under a changes clause may be outside of the "general scope" of the contract and may actually be a "cardinal change." That directed change may be considered a government breach of contract and "discharge" (excuse) the obligation of the contractor to proceed with contract performance.

The other context of contract "scope" is whether an amendment to a contract is outside the scope of the contract and should have been treated as a new procurement and competed under applicable procurement laws, a well-known issue in federal government contracting. Chapter 7 discusses this issue in some depth.

Common Law Breaches and Remedies

A breach of contract comes in many forms. There is a "complete breach," or "material breach," of contract, where one party fails to perform the essential and fundamental part of their undertaking or so underperforms the contractual obligation that the purpose of the contract is not satisfied. In other situations, a party to a contract performs most of the obligations under the contract, but omits or refuses to completely perform under the contract. This "minor breach" of contract, because the party to the contract "substantially performed" the contractual obligation, has the effect of binding the other party to the contract to also perform under the contract, at least in an equivalent manner.

The measure of damages for a breach of contract can be set out in the contract itself or can be based on other various common law principles. For example, the parties to a contract can set out the measure of money damages through a valid liquidated damages provision. A valid liquidated damages provision under the common law must be a reasonable measure of the actual damages suffered by either party if the contract is breached. Courts vary, but some courts will not enforce a liquidated damages provision in a contract if the amount of damages recoverable under such a provision does not correspond to the actual damages suffered by a party because of the breach of contract. Predicting at the time of the formation of a contract what the actual damages will be upon the breach of a contract can be difficult. The court, in hindsight, will evaluate a liquidated damages provision to ensure that the application of the provision that may limit or enhance the amount of damages a party may receive is not a penalty.

In addition, the parties to a contract can agree that specific performance of the contract is required because the value of performance of the contract is unique and that money damages would be an inadequate remedy. For example, the remedy of specific performance applies most often in a sale of land contract or in a contract for unique goods or services. In all cases, each party has a responsibility to mitigate their losses. That means that even if the contractual partner is not keeping their end of the bargain, the affected party should use reasonable effort to keep its losses at a minimum.

An injunction is another coercive legal remedy that can be used in some breach of contract cases where a direct order is required to stop a party from continuing an ongoing breach. An injunction will only be granted where monetary damages would not protect the injured party.

The most common form of contract damages are compensatory money damages, the out-of-pocket expenses caused by the breach. Money damages are an attempt by the court to compensate the innocent party to the contract; that is, the party that suffers the breach. The purpose is compensation, not punishment.

Generally, there are two main methods of calculating money damages:

- The diminution of value test—the difference between what was contracted for and what was received; and

- The cost of performance method—whatever it costs to put the plaintiff in the position he would have been in had the defendant fully performed his contractual obligations. The defendant is ordered to pay the cost of fixing the defect necessary to complete the contract.

Conclusion

Contracts are at the core of public procurement. Procurement professionals enter into a variety of agreements and must understand the essential elements for their being enforceable: an offer and acceptance; definiteness; consideration by both parties (mutuality); competency of the parties; and legal purpose. Certain defects in the contract process and rare, unexpected events can permit a party to disavow or void a contract.

Government contracts essentially have the same elements as commercial contracts, although they differ in important ways—not the least of which are legislative competition requirements. Public procurement professionals must understand this core part of their practice in order to effectively satisfy their contractual obligations and protect the rights that contracts legally create.

For Further Reading

Pennington, R. "Lessons to Learn in Options and Competition." Government Procurement, Penton, December 2012/January 2013.

Chapter 4

The Uniform Commercial Code

Historically, commercial business activity in the United States, whether private or public, began at the local level, with small ventures selling goods and services to neighbors and local governments. With the industrial revolution and the ability to travel and communicate on a national level, the mechanics of conducting a simple business transaction either involved a maze of local customs or remained completely unregulated. As the world continued to innovate, it became apparent that a uniform business transactions law would make the business of buying and selling more predictable, more efficient, and less risky.

In response to this need, the American Law Institute and the National Conference of Commissioners on Uniform State Laws published a uniform code of commercial law in 1951. This code, called the Uniform Commercial Code (U.C.C.), essentially incorporated the common law of commercial transactions into a uniform law. The U.C.C. was presented to and adopted by all states, with Louisiana, as the last state to do so, adopting all but three of the U.C.C. Articles in January 1990.

For NIGP's Canadian practitioners, the Uniform Law Conference of Canada's Uniform Sale of Goods Act accomplished similar objectives, and its provisions are analogous to those covered in this chapter. Practitioners engaged in international contracting may encounter references to the United Nations Convention for the International Sale of Goods (CISG). The CISG is a treaty developed by the United Nations Commission on International Trade Law (UNCITRAL) that uses accepted trade terms that apply among ratifying countries where not expressly changed by the terms of the contract. The United States and Canada are among the 91 countries who have ratified the CISG.

The most important part of the U.C.C. for the public procurement professional is Article 2, entitled "Sale of Goods." Absent a specific state or federal statute or administrative regulation, Article 2 will govern the public procurement professional's contract for the sale of goods. It is important to note that Article 2 only covers contracts for the sale of goods, not contracts for the sale of services. Therefore, a contract to purchase 200 boxes of pencils will be covered by Article 2, but a contract for the purchase of a financial auditor to review data would not be.

This chapter focuses on important legal principles in the U.C.C. that play an essential part in the daily tasks of the procurement professional. The U.C.C. plays an especially important role in filling in terms of a written contract and adding essential terms to a contract where the parties have not specifically included such terms. Small dollar purchases in which the purchaser solicits verbal price quotes and issues a purchase order is an example of a public procurement contract that does not use a written contract document signed by both parties. The public purchaser must be familiar with some basic U.C.C. requirements to understand how purchase orders work as contracts and how the U.C.C. supplements what is written. Moreover, some very small purchases may have no purchase order terms and conditions at all; they are completely governed by the U.C.C.

This chapter does not intend to provide a comprehensive review of all U.C.C. provisions. For example, the interplay between U.C.C. *free on board* sections about shipping costs, title, and risk of loss are important for the practitioner, but not among the fundamental legal principles discussed here. The public procurement professional is strongly encouraged to become very familiar with pertinent sections of Article 2 of the U.C.C.

Scope of Article 2 of the U.C.C.

Section 2–102 of the U.C.C. defines the scope of Article 2 to include "transactions in goods." "Goods" that are the subject of sales under Article 2 consist of all things, whether specially manufactured or not, that are movable at the time the contract is executed (U.C.C. Section 2–105[1]).

The use of the term "transaction" rather than "sale" in U.C.C. Section 2–102 is significant in that it makes clear that the reach of Article 2 goes beyond those transactions where there is a transfer of title. Thus, Article 2 sections have been applied in decisions involving transactions that are not bona fide sales, but that are used as substitutes for a sale or have attributes analogous to a sale, such as leases, bailments, or construction contracts.

It is clear that Article 2 of the Code is intended to have broad application; however, it also follows from the Code's continued focus on "goods" that a contract which merely calls for the rendition of services is not subject to the sales provisions of the Code. Therefore, the fact that the party supplying a service does so in conjunction with the delivery of goods does not necessarily mean that the transaction falls within the scope of the Code. Even though the definition of goods includes goods that have been specially manufactured, "[not] all contracts for special manufacture qualify as contracts for the sale of goods under the Uniform Commercial Code" (*Curtis Publishing Company v. Sheridan*, 53 F.R.D. 642, 644 (S.D.N.Y. 1971)). Even in the context of a contract for special manufacture, initial inquiry should focus not on the fact of special manufacture, but on whether the contract is for the sale of goods or for the rendering of services. Most state courts use the "predominant purpose" test to determine if the contract falls within the coverage of Article 2. For example, a pool service contract may also include the purchase of a pool pump or other pool equipment. In this case, the predominant purpose of the contract is to purchase a pool service while the purchase of the pool equipment is an incidental purchase.

The U.C.C. Contract and Its Formation

Formation of a U.C.C. Contract

Section 2–204 of the Code establishes that the formation of an Article 2 contract for the sale of goods is relatively easy. In particular, Section 2–204 states that a contract for the sale of goods may be made in any manner sufficient to evidence an agreement between the parties, including conduct by both parties that recognizes the existence of an agreement. This is true even if one or more terms of the contract are left open, as the contract will not fail for indefiniteness if the parties intended to make a contract and there is a reasonably certain basis for calculating a remedy for a breach of contract. This "easy" definition of a contract contrasts with the more formal strictures and requirements for other types of contracts, such as contracts for services, the purchase of real estate, and construction contracts.

In every Article 2 contract, however, Section 1–304 prescribes that there is an obligation of good faith, defined as honesty in fact, and Section 1–302 requires that parties conduct themselves using diligence, reasonableness, and care. As to other Code provisions, the effect may be varied by agreement of the parties. Consequently, the parties to an Article 2 contract have wide discretion to use and not use the provisions of the Code in making an agreement.

Finally, the Code permits the parties in Section 1–303 to resort to the course of performance of previous contracts, any previous course of dealing between the parties, and usage or custom of the industry to help determine the meaning of any contract terms and the performance of the contract by the parties. Course of performance refers to the conduct of the parties in a particular transaction. Course of dealing refers to the conduct of the parties involving previous transactions between the parties. Custom and usage of trade refers to industry-wide practices or requirements that apply to specific locations, businesses, and vocations.

Armed with these broad directives, the Code's design is to make commercial transactions in goods simple and easy to handle while protecting parties from unreasonable attempts to disadvantage one party over another.

One of the key definitions in the Code is that of a "merchant," defined in Section 2–104 as a person who regularly deals in goods of a kind or holds herself out as having knowledge or skill peculiar to the goods or practices involved in the transaction. The Code believes that a merchant buyer or seller is a more sophisticated commercial actor than an ordinary consumer who purchases or sells goods. As such, the Code treats them differently in certain areas. It is important to note that, based on this Code provision, there is no break for a beginner as the person or entity that sells lumber the first time is just as much a merchant as the person or business that has sold lumber for 30 years. Most of the time, a public procurement officer acting on behalf of a governmental entity looks like a merchant, as will the suppliers.

The Statute of Frauds (Reference Section 2–201)

When dealing with government procurement contracts, by statute, ordinance, rule, or practice, all contracts need to be in writing. In fact, these statutes, ordinances, rules, or other directives will dictate the details and specific provisions in a government procurement contract. Section 2–201 sets out the basic requirements of the Statute of Frauds by requiring that any contract for the sale of goods for a price of $500 or more is not enforceable unless there is some writing or writings taken together sufficient to indicate that a contract has been made between the parties, signed by the party against whom enforcement is sought to be enforced, and such writing or writings taken together states the quantity of goods to be sold. In addition, if in a contract between merchants, a merchant sends a signed, written confirmation acknowledging the contract, this writing is sufficient to satisfy the requirements of the Statute of Frauds. To avoid this consequence, the merchant receiving the written confirmation must object in writing within 10 days. With this provision, the Code is directing merchants to read their mail or suffer the consequence of being bound to a contract. In the public procurement contract circumstance, only a careless public procurement professional should ever fall into this trap.

Missing Terms—The Gap-Filling Provisions of the U.C.C.

Article 2 contains provisions to fill out the terms of a contract for the sale of goods when some contract terms may be missing. These Article 2 provisions are called "gap filler" provisions, as exemplified in the following:

- Section 2–305 makes provisions for supplying a missing price term by reading into a contract a commercially reasonable price in line with the particular circumstances of the contract.
- Section 2–307 states that unless otherwise agreed to by the parties, goods called for by the contract shall be delivered in a single lot with payment due upon delivery.
- Section 2–308 states that unless otherwise agreed to by the parties, the place of delivery of goods is the seller's place of business; or if the seller does not have a place of business, the seller's residence will serve as the place of delivery.
- Section 2–309 provides that time of delivery or shipment or any other reference to time, absent an agreement of the parties, shall be a reasonable time.
- Section 2–310 requires payment for goods at the time and upon delivery of the goods, absent a contrary agreement between the parties.
- Section 2–311 permits option contracts, which permit a designated party to specify in a timely manner the specific terms and performance requirements for a contract.
- Section 2–306 stipulates that output and requirement contracts are sufficiently specific to satisfy the quantity requirement.

The Parol Evidence Rule (Reference Section 2–202)

The basic thrust of the Parol Evidence Rule is to ascertain, in an orderly fashion, the specific terms of an agreement between two parties. This is not always easy, as parties to a written contract often converse over a long period of time about the terms of an agreement. Unfortunately, after a careful review of a written contract, either or both parties to the contract may think the written contract means different things, contains the wrong terms, or is missing essential terms or phrases. The ability of either party to produce evidence of additional terms that have been orally agreed upon to amend a written contract is governed by the Parol Evidence Rule.

Section 2–202 contains the Code's version of the Parol Evidence Rule:

> Terms with respect to which the confirmatory memoranda of the parties agree or which are otherwise set forth in writing intended by the parties as a final expression of their agreement with respect to such terms as are included therein may not be contradicted by evidence of any prior agreement or of a contemporaneous oral agreement but may be explained or supplemented:
>
> a. By course of dealing or usage of trade (Section 1–303) or by course of performance (Section 2–208); and
> b. By evidence of consistent additional terms unless the court finds the writing to have been intended also as a complete and exclusive statement of the terms of the agreement.

The U.C.C. plainly distinguishes between "final" expressions of agreement and "complete and exclusive" statements of agreement between the parties. The completeness of a written contract is entirely a function of the parties' intent.

If a court determines that the parties agreed that the contract was final and complete, the Parol Evidence Rule applies. Under the rule, a court will not admit evidence, either written or oral, of prior understandings or negotiations that vary or contradict the contract's terms.

The Parol Evidence Rule is the reason that public procurement professionals will often see a clause in their jurisdiction's boilerplate contract language that the contract is a "complete and final" expression of the parties' intentions. That type of clause is called a merger clause. Should there be a contract dispute, that boilerplate language is an important factor that a court will consider in determining whether the parties intended for the contract to be complete and final.

The "Battle of the Forms" (Reference Section 2–207)

The goal of Section 2–207 of the U.C.C. is to recognize that a contract may be embodied in more than one written document and may be formed even if the parties to the contract do not use matching forms. In short, just because the "standard" contract form used by one party is different from the "standard" form used by another party does not necessarily mean that the parties do not have an agreement or contract. Section 2–207 clarifies when a contract will and will not exist when the forms do not match.

For example, suppose a school district contracts with Waterworld, Inc. on a one-time basis to supply bottled water for a school picnic. The acceptance form sent by Waterworld states that any dispute arising from the performance of this contract shall be referred to binding arbitration. The school district contract contains no provision regarding the handling of disputes. When Waterworld delivered contaminated bottled water to the school district for the picnic, the school district brought suit against Waterworld. Waterworld argues that, based on its acceptance form, the school district's lawsuit must be dismissed and any claim by the school district must be referred to binding arbitration. Under 2–207 of the U.C.C., if the school district and Waterworld are considered merchants—that is, entities that regularly deal with these kinds of goods—and the arbitration provision in the Waterworld acceptance form "materially alters" the rights and obligations of the parties, then this provision would not be binding on the parties but represent a counter-offer by Waterworld. However, if this arbitration provision would not "materially alter" the rights and obligations of the parties to the contract, then the arbitration provision would become part of the contract between the school district and Waterworld. Courts have consistently viewed a binding arbitration clause as a "material alteration" of the rights and liabilities of contracting parties.

Unconscionability (Reference Section 2–302)

This Article 2 provision is a consumer protection provision designed to deal with "adhesion contracts." Adhesion contracts are those kinds of contracts (typically form contracts) where the consumer who is buying the goods is in no position to bargain effectively with the seller. In this context, the seller presents a "take it or leave it" contract for the purchase of goods with the intent to take advantage of the consumer's lack of knowledge and sophistication in order to get the consumer to sign a patently unfair contract. For example, when a seller of a $25 watch convinces the consumer that the watch is worth $1,000 and gets the consumer to sign a contract to purchase the watch for $1,000, the unconscionability provision of Article 2 of the U.C.C. may apply. If a contract or a term of a contract, such as price, is found to be unconscionable as determined by a court, the contract or contract term is voided.

In the context of public procurement, the concept of unconscionability, a strictly U.C.C.-invented term, may not apply as readily to a public entity or municipal corporation. In many instances, the public entity as a buyer may have superior bargaining power over a supplier. Many times, this stems from the attractiveness to sellers of contracting with public entities. However, in other instances, a public entity acting as a buyer may also be subjected to the superior bargaining power of, for example, a single source and multi-national supplier. Therefore, the U.C.C. doctrine of unconscionability may apply equally to an ordinary consumer buyer and a public entity buyer.

Firm Offers (Reference Section 2–205)

Section 2–205 states that an offer by a merchant to buy or sell goods in a signed writing, which by its terms holds open the offer, is not revocable during the time stated in the offer or, if no time is stated, remains open for a reasonable time not to exceed three months. Therefore, merchants must be cognizant of the legal effect of offering to hold open an offer to buy or sell. This kind of irrevocable offer in a public procurement circumstance can lead to trapping a governmental entity if not careful to monitor such an offer. The best practice may be to avoid these kinds of offers.

Requirement and Output Contracts (Reference Section 2–306)

There may be occasions when whether in a public procurement contract or other kind of commercial transaction that a buyer needs to lock down a supplier to a contract that provides all of the output of a particular supplier because of the short supply of such goods or because there are only limited suppliers. Conversely, a buyer may not know the exact amount of goods needed and wants to lock in a supplier to provide the quantity of goods necessary to the buyer's business. The Code specifically addresses these types of circumstances by validating output and requirement contracts even though a specific quantity is not stated in a signed writing. Section 2–306 specifically states that a term in a written contract that measures quantity by the output of the seller or the requirements of the buyer is valid and covers the actual output or requirements based on good faith. This Code section goes on to caution that no quantity unreasonably disproportionate to any stated estimate or, if no stated estimate, comparable prior output or requirement may be delivered or demanded.

Again, the concept of good faith is embedded in this Code provision and may implicate the course of performance, course of dealing, and custom and usage of trade sections of the Code. A good example of the usefulness of this kind of contract is the Southwest Airlines contract in which the fuel supplier was locked into providing the required fuel to operate Southwest Airlines jets. Southwest Airlines entered into this requirement contract during the period when the price of jet fuel was at its lowest in years. This enabled Southwest Airlines to reap the benefit when fuel prices rose and gave them a competitive advantage over other airlines who failed to utilize a requirements contract.

The U.C.C. and Warranties

Article 2 warranties are important because they create the seller's legal obligations regarding the transfer of title to and the quality and characteristics of the goods sold. A warranty is a seller's promise or representation that the goods will be of a stated quality or character. Warranties may also involve an obligation to repair or replace unsatisfactory goods. The U.C.C. permits sellers to disclaim warranties if done in compliance with the U.C.C. requirements.

The key Article 2 U.C.C. warranties are:

- Warranty of Title (Section 2–312)
- Express Warranties (Section 2–313)
- Implied Warranties of Merchantability (Section 2–314)
- Implied Warranties of Fitness for a Particular Purpose (Section 2–315)

Warranty of Title

The warranty of title, which is implicitly incorporated in contracts by U.C.C. Article 2, is really three different warranties in one. The warranty of title not only warrants good title to the goods sold but also warrants that there are no security interests or other liens on the goods other than those known to the buyer. The warranty of title also warrants against any patent infringement or similar-type claim. The U.C.C. also expressly provides the mechanism for disclaiming or excluding this warranty of title by a seller.

U.C.C. Section 2–312 states:

1. Subject to subsection (2) there is in a contract for sale a warranty by the seller that:
   a. The title conveyed shall be good, and its transfer rightful; and

   b. The goods shall be delivered free from any security interest or other lien or encumbrance of which the buyer at the time of contracting has no knowledge.
2. A warranty under subsection (1) will be excluded or modified only by specific language or by circumstances which give the buyer reason to know that the person selling does not claim title in himself or that he is purporting to sell only such right or title as he or a third person may have.

For example, if a county purchases a tracking system from a supplier used to track inventory of paper products and other goods, and the supplier fails to obtain the various patent clearances before selling the system, the manufacturer/owner of the patented system would have the right to recover the tracking system from the county. The county's legal cause of action would be against the supplier for breach of the U.C.C. Warranty of Title.

Express Warranties

A seller's oral or written statements or promises made to a buyer that relate to the characteristics, qualities, or performance of the goods creates an express warranty. This occurs when a seller either promises or asserts as fact that the goods will provide a certain level of performance or quality and that promise or assertion becomes a reason that the buyer enters into a contract.

The key to whether a seller's statement or promises create an express warranty is that the seller's statements or promises must be of such substance that the promise or statement is capable of measurement or proof. Descriptive literature or a product sample that a bidder submits with its bid describing or showing a certain quality or performance level of the bidder's product may constitute an express warranty.

Section 2–313 defines an express warranty, in pertinent part, as follows:

> Express warranties by the seller are created as follows: (a) Any affirmation of fact or promise made by the seller to the buyer which relates to the goods and becomes part of the basis of the bargain creates an express warranty that the goods shall conform to the affirmation or promise.

For example, suppose a school district purchases erasable wallpaper to cover the walls in various pre-school classrooms. The supplier of the wallpaper not only shows and demonstrates a sample of the wallpaper to the public procurement professional but also demonstrates how easily the wallpaper is applied. The supplier writes and draws on the wallpaper with special marking pens. The supplier then represents and shows that the wallpaper can be wiped clean and reused. The school district purchases the wallpaper and hangs the wallpaper in various classrooms. However, after the first use, the wallpaper does not wipe clean and cannot be reused. The school district, based on the representation, sample and demonstration by the supplier, would have a legal claim against the supplier for breach of a U.C.C. Express Warranty.

Implied Warranties

An implied warranty arises by operation of law without the need for any action by the buyer or the seller. The U.C.C. creates, other than the warranty of title, two very important implied warranties: The Implied Warranty of Merchantability and the Implied Warranty of Fitness for a Particular Purpose.

Implied Warranty of Merchantability and Usage of Trade

If the person selling the goods is considered a merchant of those goods under the U.C.C., there is an implied warranty that the goods will meet certain industry standards. The warranty is that they will "pass in the trade under the contract description" and be "fit for the ordinary purposes" for which those types of goods are used. This concept is commonly referred to as "usage of trade."

The implied warranty of merchantability, as codified under Section 2–314 of the U.C.C., states, in pertinent part:

> Unless excluded or modified . . . a warranty that the goods shall be merchantable is implied in a contract for their sale if the seller is a merchant with respect to goods of that kind. Under this Section the serving for value of food or drink to be consumed either on the premises or elsewhere is a sale.

Section 2–314(1) states that, for goods to be merchantable, they "must be at least such as . . . are fit for the ordinary purposes for which such goods are used." In accordance with Section 2–314(2), to prove a breach of implied warranty of merchantability,

> a plaintiff must prove, first, that the goods bought and sold were subject to an implied warranty of merchantability; second, that

> the goods did not comply with the warranty in that the goods were defective at the time of the sale; third, that his injury was due to the defective nature of the goods; and fourth, that damages were suffered as a result. The burden is upon the purchaser to establish a breach by the seller of the warranty of merchantability by showing that a defect existed at the time of the sale.

There is an interesting note about the application of this warranty in the public procurement arena. Some courts have decided that, if the government regularly sells certain goods as surplus property, it may be a "merchant" under the U.C.C. In those cases, the implied warranty arises unless the government disclaims it as part of the sale.

The Implied Warranty of Fitness for a Particular Purpose

While the implied warranty of merchantability applies to goods used for their ordinary purpose, the implied warranty of fitness for a particular purpose applies to an instance where the seller, at the time of contracting, has reason to know that the buyer wants the goods for a particular purpose and is relying on the seller's skill or judgment to select or furnish suitable goods.

Section 2–315 of the U.C.C. provides:

> Where the seller at the time of contracting has reason to know any particular purpose for which the goods are required and that the buyer is relying on the seller's skill or judgment to select or furnish suitable goods, there is unless excluded or modified under the next section an implied warranty that the goods shall be fit for such purpose.

Disclaimer of Article 2 Warranties

Section 2–316(3) of the U.C.C. provides:

> a. Unless the circumstances indicate otherwise, all implied warranties are excluded by expressions like "as is," "with all faults," or other language which in common understanding calls the buyer's attention to the exclusion of warranties and makes plain that there is no implied warranty.

The key to disclaiming either the Implied Warranty of Merchantability or the Implied Warranty of Fitness for a Particular Purpose is that such disclaimer must be conspicuously written in any document. It should be noted that the clause "unless the circumstances indicate otherwise" provides the buyer an opportunity to prove that the seller did not properly disclaim any implied warranty.

It should be noted that, while Section 2–318 attempts to define the scope in which buyers are entitled to the protections afforded by Article 2 warranty provisions, this is largely a question of state law. Each state is free to extend or restrict the application of the Article 2 warranty provisions as it sees fit.

Performance of an Article 2 U.C.C. Contract

Overview

The performance of a U.C.C. Article 2 contract for the sale of goods is pretty simple—the seller will deliver the goods contracted to the buyer, and the buyer will pay the seller for the goods (U.C.C. Sections 2–301, 2–507, and 2–511). When the Code provisions are read together literally, it appears that neither the buyer nor the seller of goods is obligated to do anything unless the other acts. This is because Article 2 anticipates that the seller's delivery of the goods to the buyer and the buyer's payment for the goods will happen simultaneously. Although many commercial transactions may occur in this manner, some commercial transactions do not happen this way.

Under the common law, a party may require that the other party "tender" his or her performance in a certain way; if that second party does not do so, the first party may reject the performance. For instance, if the contract requires payment in dollars and a party makes payment in pesos instead, the other party may reject the payment without violating the contract. That rule is often called the "perfect tender" rule.

The U.C.C. adopts that rule, but substantially limits it. If none of the U.C.C. exceptions apply, the buyer may say "take these goods away; there is a defect." The rule also applies to installment contracts and permits a buyer to reject goods in a single installment under a contract calling for the goods to be delivered in lots. However, only if the installment substantially impairs the value of the entire contract may a buyer reject the entire contract and cancel any obligation to accept any other installment. Unlike under the common law, the buyer must permit the seller to fix, or "cure," the non-conforming tender of delivery of goods.

If the buyer accepts the goods, he or she no longer has the right to reject them. Acceptance occurs in several ways. On receiving the goods, the buyer must inspect them, identify the defects, and notify the seller in a timely manner. Timeliness depends on the circumstances, such as the difficulty in discovering defects, but the buyer must be diligent about inspection. If the buyer is not diligent or fails to send a timely notice of the defects, he or she has accepted the goods. The buyer also may accept the goods if he or she uses them after knowing about the defects.

The U.C.C. permits the parties to a contract to agree to terms different from those that the U.C.C. specifies. It may be, for instance, that a government wishes to require "perfect tender" in an installment contract; that is, to declare the contract breached if any one delivery is defective. To do so, there must be contract language in the solicitation or purchase order reserving that right to the government.

Article 2 creates room for the parties to fashion not only the terms but also the performance of a contract for the sale of goods to fit their needs. Article 2 attempts to codify existing general commercial practice so that, absent a contrary agreement between the parties, all buyers and sellers know how a contract will be performed. Therefore, the study of the performance obligations of a U.C.C. Article 2 contract for the sale of goods establishes a framework for commercial activity to flourish.

As previously mentioned, it is strongly recommended that the public procurement professional become knowledgeable of all concepts contained in Article 2 of the U.C.C. Within the context of performance issues, the official should focus on the 500 and 600 sections of Article 2. Some key parameters regarding contract performance are highlighted in the following paragraphs.

Tender of Delivery

The "tender of delivery" describes the seller's obligation regarding the provision of goods as specified in a sales contract. Section 2–503(1) provides: "Tender of delivery requires that the seller put and hold conforming goods at the buyer's disposition and give the buyer any notification reasonably necessary to enable him to take delivery."

Buyer's Right to Inspection of the Goods

In accordance with Section 2–513, the buyer of goods has a right to inspect the goods at a reasonable place and time, and in a reasonable manner, before acceptance or rejection of the goods and before making payment for the goods. This "reasonable" time for inspection will vary with the type of goods delivered. For example, the time permitted for a buyer to inspect perishable goods, like food, will be shorter than the time to inspect durable goods, like nails.

Buyer's Rightful Rejection of Goods

Sections 2–601 and 2–602 of Article 2 define the buyer's right to reject goods delivered by the seller if the goods fail to conform to a contract for any reason and also requires the buyer to timely notify the seller of rejection of the non-conforming goods. For example, if a school district purchases athletic equipment and the logo on each piece of athletic equipment identifying the school district is not exactly as contracted for, the school district has the right under the U.C.C. to reject the non-conforming delivery of athletic equipment.

Buyer's Obligations as to Rightful Rejected Goods

Sections 2–602, 2–603, and 2–605 of Article 2 impose an obligation on the merchant buyer and a non-merchant buyer to use reasonable care in holding the rejected goods. The merchant buyer's duties also include following the seller's instructions regarding the goods, including reshipment to the seller at the seller's expense. Both the merchant buyer and the non-merchant buyer may, in the absence of seller instructions, sell perishable goods at the seller's expense. For example, if a county-operated jail facility purchases frozen food from a supplier and rightfully rejects the frozen food as non-conforming to the contract terms, the county must use reasonable care in holding onto the frozen food, including making sure that the frozen food does not spoil. In addition, the county would be able to charge back the cost of storing the frozen food so that it does not spoil.

Buyer's Acceptance of Goods

Section 2–606 specifies what constitutes the acceptance of goods:

a. Acceptance of goods occurs when the buyer:
   (1) after a reasonable opportunity to inspect the goods signifies to the seller that the goods are conforming or that he will take or retain them in spite of their nonconformity; or
   (2) fails to make an effective rejection (Subsection (a) of Section 2.602), but such acceptance does not occur until the buyer has had a reasonable opportunity to inspect them; or

(3) does any act inconsistent with the seller's ownership; but if such act is wrongful as against the seller it is an acceptance only if ratified by him.

b. Acceptance of a part of any commercial unit is acceptance of that entire unit.

In essence, Section 2–606 stipulates that the buyer may accept the seller's delivery of goods, regardless of whether the seller's goods conform or do not conform to the contract. For example, if the county police department purchases and receives radar guns from a supplier to detect speeding cars and uses these radar guns despite the fact that the guns are bigger and bulkier than the contract specifies, by using the radar guns, the county has accepted the delivery of the radar guns under the terms of the U.C.C. However, it is also important to note that by accepting the radar guns, the county has not waived its legal right to sue for breach of contract.

Buyer's Revocation of Acceptance of Goods

Even after a buyer has accepted the seller's delivery of goods, the buyer can revoke acceptance of the goods when the buyer discovers that the seller's non-conforming goods substantially impair the value of the goods. Revocation of acceptance by the buyer requires that notice be given to the seller within a reasonable time after the buyer discovers the goods are non- conforming or that the seller will not correct the non-conforming delivery of goods. The key to revocation of acceptance is that the non-conformity of the goods must substantially impair the value of the goods. The following is a comparison of the U.C.C. sections regarding rejection of goods and revocation of acceptance of goods

Section 2–602 provides the manner and effect of rightful rejection as follows:

a. Rejection of goods must be within a reasonable time after their delivery or tender. It is ineffective unless the buyer reasonably notifies the seller.
b. Subject to the provisions of the two following sections on rejected goods (Sections 2–603 and 2–604).
   (1) after rejection, any exercise of ownership by the buyer with respect to any commercial unit is wrongful as against the seller; and

(2) before rejection, if the buyer has taken physical possession of goods in which he does not have a security interest, he is under a duty after rejection to hold them with reasonable care at the seller's disposition for a time sufficient to permit the seller to remove them; but

(3) the buyer has no further obligations with regard to goods rightfully rejected. Sections 2–601 outline the buyer's rights on improper delivery to (1) reject the whole; or (2) accept the whole; or (3) accept any commercial unit or units and reject the rest.

Section 2–608 Revocation of Acceptance in Whole or in Part

a. The buyer may revoke his acceptance of a lot or commercial unit whose non- conformity substantially impairs its value to him if he has accepted.
   (1) on the reasonable assumption that its non-conformity would be cured and it has not been seasonably cured; or
   (2) without discovery of such non-conformity if his acceptance was reasonably induced either by the difficulty of discovery before acceptance or by the seller's assurances.
b. Revocation of acceptance must occur within a reasonable time after the buyer discovers or should have discovered the ground for it and before any substantial change in condition of the goods, which is not caused by their own defects. It is not effective until the buyer notifies the seller of it.
c. A buyer who so revokes has the same rights and duties with regard to the goods involved as if he had rejected them.

For example, suppose the county accepts the tender of delivery of ink cartridges from a supplier only to discover upon opening the cartridge packages as needed that the cartridges are not full of ink. If this failure to provide full ink cartridges could only be reasonably discovered upon opening the cartridge packages and affects 75% of all of the ink cartridges delivered, the county would have the right under the U.C.C. to revoke its acceptance of the ink cartridges.

Seller's Right to Cure a Non-Conforming Delivery of Goods

The seller's right to cure is perhaps the best example of how far U.C.C. Article 2 will go to give the buyer and seller a chance to complete a deal.

The seller has two different Article 2 rights to cure (i.e., "correct") a seller's delivery of non-conforming goods.

If the time for performance by the seller under the contract has not expired and the seller has received notice of a rightful rejection or revocation of acceptance of the goods by the buyer, then the seller, upon notice to the buyer, can make a delivery of conforming goods before the seller's time for performance expires. Furthermore, the buyer must accept this delivery of conforming goods.

Where the buyer rejects or revokes acceptance of non-conforming goods delivered by the seller, and the seller reasonably believed that the buyer would accept the non-conforming goods, with or without some money adjustment, the seller, upon timely notice to the buyer, may have a reasonable time to deliver conforming goods to the buyer.

In either case, if a seller's notice to a buyer says that the seller intends to cure the non-conforming delivery of goods and the seller does in fact cure this non-conforming delivery, the buyer must accept the "cured" delivery.

Section 2–508 of the U.C.C. regarding the cure by the seller provides:

(1) Where any tender or delivery by the seller is rejected because non-conforming and the time for performance has not yet expired, the seller may seasonably notify the buyer of his intention to cure and may then within the contract time make a conforming delivery.

(2) Where the buyer rejects a non-conforming tender which the seller had reasonable grounds to believe would be acceptable with or without money allowance, the seller may, if he seasonably notifies the buyer, have a further reasonable time to substitute a conforming tender.

The seller's right to cure under the U.C.C. is a major departure from the common law of contracts.

Risk of Loss

The risk of loss provisions of Article 2 addresses the issue of who bears the expense of the loss if the goods are damaged or destroyed in delivery of the goods by the seller to the buyer.

Article 2 attempts to allocate the risk of loss to the goods in transit fairly between the buyer and the seller. The key factor in placing the risk of loss with the seller or the buyer is to first determine if the seller's tender of delivery of the goods was of conforming or non-conforming goods. The allocation of the risk of loss to the buyer will depend in large part on whether the buyer would have had the right to reject or revoke acceptance of the goods delivered by the seller.

Section 2–509 of the U.C.C. regarding the risk of loss in absence of a breach provides:

> (1) Where the contract requires or authorizes the seller to ship the goods by carrier
>
> (a) if it does not require him to deliver them at a particular destination, the risk of loss passes to the buyer when the goods are duly delivered to the carrier even though the shipment is under reservation (Section 2–505); but
>
> (b) if it does require him to deliver them at a particular destination and the goods are there duly tendered while in the possession of the carrier, the risk of loss passes to the buyer when the goods are duly tendered so as to enable the buyer to take delivery.
>
> (2) Where the goods are held by a bailee to be delivered without being moved, the risk of loss passes to the buyer
>
> (a) on his receipt of a negotiable document of title covering the goods; or
>
> (b) on acknowledgment by the bailee of the buyer's right to possession of the goods; or
>
> (c) after his receipt of a non-negotiable document of title or other written direction to deliver, as provided in subsection (4)(b) of Section 2–503.
>
> (3) In any case not within subsection (1) or (2), the risk of loss passes to the buyer on his receipt of the goods if the seller is a merchant; otherwise the risk passes to the buyer on tender of delivery.
>
> (4) The provisions of this section are subject to contrary agreement of the parties and to the provisions of this Article on sale on approval (Section 2–327) and on effect of breach on risk of loss (Section 2–510).

Section 2–510 of the U.C.C. addressing the effect of a breach on the risk of loss provides:

> (1) Where a tender or delivery of goods so fails to conform to the contract as to give a right of rejection the risk of their loss remains on the seller until cure or acceptance.
>
> (2) Where the buyer rightfully revokes acceptance, he may to the extent of any deficiency in his effective insurance coverage treat the risk of loss as having rested on the seller from the beginning.
>
> (3) Where the buyer, as to conforming goods already identified to the contract for sale, repudiates or is otherwise in breach before risk

of their loss has passed to him, the seller may to the extent of any deficiency in his effective insurance coverage treat the risk of loss as resting on the buyer for a commercially reasonable time.

Impossibility of Performance of a Contract for Sale of Goods

Article 2 uses the concept of "commercial impracticability" as the standard by which to judge whether a contract has become "impossible to perform."

Commercial impracticability does include the common law contract notion of "act of God" or "force majeure." Note that Article 2 provides for other situations when performance of a contract may be excused; including Sections 2–613, 2–614, 2–615, and 2–616. A prime example of commercial impracticability can be seen in the aftermath of weather disasters like Hurricane Katrina. For example, contracts let for the delivery of new school busses by a New Orleans bus company to a New Orleans school district would be "commercial impracticable," not only because the roads were impassable but also because many of the school buildings had been destroyed.

Remedies for Breach of an Article 2 Contract

Overview

Before identifying potential remedies, there should be a general acknowledgement and understanding of what constitutes a breach of contract. As stated in Section 2–301, the basic obligation of the seller is to deliver conforming goods, and the basic obligation of the buyer is to accept and pay for conforming goods delivered by the seller. Therefore, by definition, a seller's breach of contract would be the failure to properly deliver conforming goods to a buyer, and a buyer's breach of contract would be the failure to accept and pay for conforming goods delivered by the seller. Regardless, both a seller and a buyer must provide notice to the other that a breach of contract has occurred.

Generally, if a breach occurs by either the seller or the buyer, the party hurt by the breach may pursue all legal remedies that the U.C.C. has devised, including canceling the contract. In general, the purpose of the remedy provisions of the U.C.C. is to hold the party that breached the contract liable for the damages that he or she has caused the other party, namely, the losses caused and the gains prevented. However, the party who has been wronged by a breach of contract may not unreasonably sit by and let damages accumulate. He or she has a duty to take actions that reduce the damages caused.

Under common law, the general remedy for breach of contract is money damages representing the monetary value of gains lost and losses sustained. This is also a remedy available under the U.C.C.

The determination of whether a breach of contract by either party has occurred can be tricky. Section 2–610 stipulates that a buyer or seller may definitely refuse, prior to when the performance of a contract obligation is due, to perform a contract obligation. This refusal to perform a contract obligation not yet due amounts to an anticipatory repudiation of a contract. In this instance, either a buyer or seller may choose to leverage Section 2–609 and seek, in writing, adequate assurance from a party that the party will honor its contractual obligation.

The failure on the part of either a buyer or seller to provide this adequate assurance of performance within a reasonable time not to exceed 30 days will amount to repudiation of a contract. Under Section 2–611, a buyer or seller may retract a repudiation of a contract by providing a clear indication to the other party that the repudiating party intends to perform its contract obligations. Such retraction of a repudiation of a contract will be effective unless the non-repudiating party has already canceled the contract or otherwise changed its position in reliance on the repudiation. An anticipatory repudiation of a contract will also trigger the remedies for breach of contract under the U.C.C.

The provisions of Article 2 cover the basic remedies available for sellers and buyers. The basic remedies are addressed in the following and are detailed within this section of the chapter.

- For the seller's non-delivery or defective delivery of goods, the buyer may recover the difference between the market price of the goods and their contract price, or between the price of substitute goods and the unpaid contract price.
- For the seller's breach of warranty, the buyer may recover the difference between the value that the goods would have had if they had been as warranted and their actual value.
- For the buyer's breach in not accepting the goods, the seller may recover the difference between the contract price and the market price, or the difference in price obtained in reselling the goods and the contract price for the goods.
- The buyer is obligated to pay the price of the goods to the seller if the buyer has accepted the goods or if goods are destroyed after the risk of loss has passed to the buyer.

Essentially, the remedies provided by the U.C.C. are to be liberally administered to make sure that the injured party is put in the same position as if the other party had fully performed the contract.

Seller's Remedies for Buyer's Breach of Contract in General

Section 2–703 establishes the menu of remedies available to a seller for a buyer who breaches a contract. This Section states that the seller's remedies can be triggered when a buyer:

- Has wrongfully rejected the goods; or
- Has wrongfully revoked acceptance of the goods; or
- Fails to pay for conforming goods properly delivered; or
- Repudiates the contract for the sale of goods.

Where appropriate, the seller's first option is to withhold delivery of any undelivered amount of the goods. Where appropriate, the seller can also identify conforming goods to the contract and may even, in some circumstances, complete production of unfinished goods intended for the particular contract that has been breached by the buyer (Section 2–704).

Seller's Remedy—Market Price and Contract Price Differential

Section 2–708 provides the traditional measure of damages when the breach of contract by the buyer amounts to non-acceptance of conforming goods delivered by the seller or the buyer's repudiation of the contract.

Seller's Remedy—Resale Price and Contract Price Deferential

Section 2–706 provides the uniquely U.C.C. measure of damages for a buyer's breach of contract. The U.C.C. permits the seller to resell the goods in a private or public sale and then claim the difference between the resale price of the goods and the contract price of the goods as the amount of damages.

It is important to note that applying either the market price-contract price differential or resale price-contract price differential as the measure of a seller's damages for a breach of a U.C.C. contract may not sustain a legal claim for damages. For example, if the market price or the resale price is more than the contract price, the seller would actually make money because of the buyer's breach of contract. This scenario has occurred when the goods to be sold jump in price, an example of which would be the price of oil.

Seller's Remedy—Specific Performance: The Price of the Goods

Section 2–709 addresses two concepts. First, the seller, upon a buyer's failure to pay, is entitled to recover the actual purchase price of the goods if the goods are accepted, lost, or damaged within a commercially reasonable time after the risk of loss has passed to the buyer. Second, a seller is entitled to the purchase price of goods identified to a contract that the seller, despite a reasonable effort, could not resell because of the unique character of the goods. This remedy provision literally forces the buyer to perform the buyer's contract obligation—pay the purchase price.

Buyer's Remedies for Seller's Breach of Contract in General

Section 2–711 establishes the roster of remedies available for a buyer upon a seller's breach of contract. The section specifically states that the seller's failure to make delivery of goods or the seller's repudiation of the buyer's contract or the buyer's rightful rejection or revocation of the goods permits the buyer to cancel the contract with the seller. In addition to cancellation of the seller's contract, the buyer, where appropriate, will be entitled to the other remedies provided in Sections 2–712, 2–713, 2–714, and 2–716.

Buyer's Remedy—Cover

This clause is the counterpart to U.C.C. Article 2 that creates a resale remedy for sellers in Section 2–706 and is unique to the U.C.C. In this instance, the buyer under Section 2–711 is permitted to seek the purchase of substitute goods based on the seller's breach of contract. It should be noted that the failure of a buyer to choose "cover" under Section 2–712 as a remedy does not preclude the buyer from other remedies listed in Section 2–711.

Buyer's Remedy—Market Price and Contract Price Difference

This provision is similar to the seller's remedy contained in Section 2–708. It should be noted that the market price is determined at the time when the buyer learned of the breach. Section 2–713 also provides the buyer's remedy for a seller's repudiation of contract obligations.

It should also be noted that either applying the market price-contract price differential or the cover price-contract price differential as the measure of damages may not sustain a legal claim for damages under the U.C.C. For example, when the cover price or market price is less than the contract price, the buyer would actually save money because of the seller's breach of contract. This scenario occurs when the price of the contracted goods drops, like the drop in the sales price for automobiles.

Buyer's Remedy—Breach of Warranty

This provision provides the measure of damages for a seller's breach of contract in which the buyer has accepted the goods but the goods are either non-conforming or fail to live up to the Article 2 warranties. Note that in all cases of a breach of contract under Article 2, the injured party to the contract must provide notice of breach to the breaching party. The proper measure of a buyer's damages under this section simply amounts to the difference between the value of the goods at the time and place of acceptance and the value of the goods if the goods had been as warranted.

Buyer's Remedy—Specific Performance: Seller Must Deliver the Contracted for Goods

Section 2–716 is the counterpart to the seller's remedy of specific performance, which requires that the buyer pay for the goods. Under this provision, the buyer's remedy of specific performance requires the seller to deliver conforming goods to the buyer.

Special Remedies for Buyer and Seller Breach of Contract

Liquidated Damages

The parties to an Article 2 contract may agree to set the amount of damages for a seller's or buyer's breach of contract. As a general rule, a liquidated damages clause is upheld unless it is determined to be a penalty.

Liquidated damages constitute a sum that the parties to a contract contemplate should be paid to satisfy any loss or injury following a breach of the contract. Under Subdivision 1 of Section 2–718 of the U.C.C., a liquidated damages clause is valid if the amount is reasonable in light of (1) anticipated or actual harm caused by the breach, (2) difficulties of proof of loss, and (3) inconvenience or non-feasibility of otherwise obtaining an adequate remedy.

With respect to the first requirement,

> a liquidated damages provision will be valid if reasonable with respect to either (1) the harm which the parties anticipate will result from the breach at the time of contracting or (2) the actual damages suffered by the non-defaulting party at the time of the breach.

It should be noted that it is incumbent upon the buyer to demonstrate, through quantifiable means, that damages did exist. According to the U.C.C., "it is not material whether the parties themselves have chosen to call the provision one for 'liquidated damages.'" In short, liquidated damages must meet the U.C.C. test of actual damage or harm in order to be enforceable.

Seller's Incidental and Consequential Damage

Since one of the purposes of the Article 2 remedy provisions is to make a seller "whole" after a buyer's breach of contract, Section 2–708 regarding lost profits and 2–710 concerning incidental damages are important remedy provisions.

Section 2–708 of the U.C.C. regarding the seller's damage for non-acceptance or repudiation provides:

> (1) Subject to subsection (2) and to the provisions of this Article with respect to proof of market price (Section 2–723), the measure of damages for non-acceptance or repudiation by the buyer is the difference between the market price at the time and place for tender and the unpaid contract price together with any incidental damages provided in this Article (Section 2–710), but less expenses saved in consequence of the buyer's breach.
>
> (2) If the measure of damages provided in subsection (1) is inadequate to put the seller in as good a position as performance would have done then the measure of damages is the profit (including reasonable overhead) which the seller would have made from full performance by the buyer, together with any incidental damages provided in this Article (Section 2–710), due allowance for costs reasonably incurred and due credit for payments or proceeds of resale.

Section 2–710 of the U.C.C. regarding the seller's incidental damages provides:

> Incidental damages to an aggrieved seller include any commercially reasonable charges, expenses or commissions incurred in stopping delivery, in the transportation, care and custody of goods after the buyer's breach, in connection with return or resale of the goods or otherwise resulting from the breach.

Buyer's Incidental and Consequential Damages

These two sections contrast with the seller's damages by providing the buyer the right to be made whole. U.C.C. Section 2–715 provides:

> (2) Consequential damages resulting from the seller's breach include any loss resulting from general or particular requirements and needs of which the seller at the time of contracting had reason to know and which could not reasonably be prevented by cover or otherwise.

In order for consequential damages to be recoverable under the Code, they must not only be causally related to the breach but also result from the buyer's requirements, which the seller had reason to know at the time of contracting—in other words, foreseeable damages.

Seller's Stoppage of Delivery

Sections 2–702 and 2–705 permit a seller to withhold or stop delivery of goods to a buyer who is insolvent. Section 2–705 also permits the seller to stop the delivery of goods to a buyer who has repudiated the buyer's contract obligations. Insolvency is defined in Section 1–201(23) as either a person who has ceased paying debts incurred in the ordinary course of business or cannot pay debts as the debts become due. Section 2–702 also permits a seller to reclaim goods delivered to a buyer upon notice and within 10 days of receipt of the goods by the buyer. The 10-day time limit does not apply to the seller's reclamation rights if the buyer fraudulently misrepresented the buyer's solvency to the seller within three months before delivery of the goods.

Conclusion

The common law of contracts made commerce difficult because of its technical rules about how contracts are formed. The Uniform Commercial Code in the United States provides an overall legal structure for sales and other transactions in goods in order to resolve potential issues in commercial contracting. Where not otherwise addressed in contracts, the U.C.C., for example, helps solve common issues with conflicting terms and conditions, although prudent procurement professionals analyze significant inconsistencies, object, and negotiate to resolve them. The U.C.C. furnishes gap-filling rules for missing terms that under common law might have made contracts too indefinite to be enforceable. Among the most important U.C.C. additions to common law are implied warranties that provide a minimum level of quality. Further, the U.C.C. performance and remedy provisions erect a workable system for managing and asserting rights for breach of contract, even though they often are replaced or supplemented in written contracts.

While the U.C.C. applies in the United States, Canadian practitioners have a similar structure in legislation governing sales of goods. Procurement professionals must be intimately familiar with these laws.

Chapter 5

The Legal Context for Formal Solicitations

The most widely used formal solicitation is the invitation for bids (IFB), also known as an invitation to bid (ITB) or an invitation to tender (ITT) in Canada. As a publicly announced request by an entity for bids on its requirements, the entity develops the IFB/ITB's specifications, resulting in suppliers only submitting a price. The entity writes the terms and conditions governing the purchase, requiring use of best practices for contract development.

The solicitation process represents a key difference between public and private contracting. After publication of the IFB, there are legal rules that govern the timeliness of bids, their responsiveness to the IFB requirements, and how mistakes are handled. Laws require contractors with public entities to be responsible—a concept long part of public procurement. Further, states and local governments usually have published procedures for resolving protests, disputes (e.g. claims of contract breach), and barring some suppliers from doing business with the entity.

An Overview of the Formal Solicitation Process

Formal sealed bidding is a method of procurement that involves several steps, including the following:

- The preparation of the IFB;
- The publicizing and issuing of the IFB;

- The submission of sealed bids by qualified prospective contractors;
- A formal bid opening; and
- The contract award to responsible contractors who submitted responsive bids based on price and price-related factors.

To be effective, the IFB must describe the requirements clearly, accurately, and completely. Unnecessarily restrictive specifications or contract terms and conditions should be avoided as they unduly restrict and limit competition. The IFB must also include all documents, attached or incorporated by reference, necessary to enable prospective bidders to prepare and submit bids. In preparing IFBs, procuring entities may be statutorily required to include a statement of all significant price-related factors that the procurement agent reasonably expects to consider in the evaluation of bids. For example, price-related factors might include foreseeable costs of transportation to the entity destination where the delivery is F.O.B. origin.

Invitations are publicized through the distribution of IFBs to prospective bidders, postings in public places, and such other means as may be appropriate. This could include publication in the local newspapers with general circulation, entity websites, electronic distribution lists, and electronic distribution by third parties. Since many entities are eliminating the requirement for publication in a local newspaper due to the cost and the low return, the public procurement professional may want to consider modifying related statutes or regulations if this is still a requirement. The IFB must be publicized sufficiently in advance of the public opening to enable prospective bidders adequate time to prepare and submit their bids.

To be considered for award, a bid must comply in all material respects with the requirements of the IFB. This policy enables all bidders to stand on an equal footing and maintains the integrity of the sealed-bidding method of procurement.

Once bids are received by the procuring entity, they are publicly opened at the specified time and place by the procurement agent or other official and read aloud. Public opening and reading of bid submittals maintains the transparency that is expected in government bidding. All bids received and opened should be recorded in some form of public tabulation, which includes the IFB number, the bid opening time and date, a general description of the procurement, the names of bidders submitting timely bids, the prices bid, and any other pertinent information required for bid evaluation. Once completed, the sharing of the bid opening information should be handled in accordance with local regulations and state statutes.

After bids are opened and recorded, they are evaluated without discussion with bidders, except where necessary to determine if a mistake in bidding has occurred. An award will be made with reasonable promptness to the responsible bidder(s) whose bid, conforming to the requirements of the IFB, is most advantageous to the entity, considering only the price and the price-related factors set forth in the IFB.

Drafting the Contract

What follows is a series of legal issues that should be considered by public procurement professionals as they begin to develop contracts. In those circumstances where the solicitation document becomes a part of the contract, these issues are considered at the time of solicitation development.

More often than not, there are two types of public officials who develop the language of a public contract on behalf of a public entity. The public procurement professional, or the client agency with the procurement professional's review, prepares the specifications for goods, describing the item to be purchased as well as language addressing related issues, such as delivery, packaging, repair, and maintenance. For service contracts, the procurement professional and client-agency prepare the "scope of work," including service elements and delivery; desired contract outcomes; and the level of expertise required from the supplier and its staff. The public entity's attorney drafts those portions of the contract generally directed at the law that affects the formation and operation of the contract, such as indemnification; certifications about independent, non-collusive pricing and gratuities; contract termination; and preservation of remedies. Sometimes, procurement professionals draft those types of terms and the attorney reviews and approves them.

While the actual responsibility for scripting contract language will vary, depending on the size and resources of the government and the level of training of the procurement professional, it is important for the procurement professional to remember two key concepts. First, the specifications that describe the item or service being purchased serve to tell potential suppliers what the public entity wants. Second, the specifications become part of the contract that results from the competition and establishes whether the supplier/contractor is complying with the contract's requirements.

While it may be more appropriate for an attorney to draft, or at least review, certain contract terms, the procurement professional needs to determine whether those terms are reasonable. If suppliers are taking exception to a clause or deciding not to compete because they consider the clause too onerous, the procurement professional should alert the attorney and discuss whether there is other suitable language that will both protect the public entity and be more palatable to suppliers.

Developing a Drafting Strategy

Before drafting any contract language, the procurement professional should understand the objective of the purchase and develop a strategy based on that objective. It is critical that the procurement professional have a good understanding of both the marketplace and the requirements of the internal customer before preparing language that will govern how the purchase and delivery of an essential service or product will operate. Copying language or templates used in the past or from forms is not helpful if the language does not achieve the objective.

Drafting Language to Fit the Type of Contract Used

Another decision that will affect some of the language that the procurement professional must draft is the selection of the type of contract to use. For instance, different contract types necessitate various types of cost or pricing provisions as well as contractor documentation requirements. Two contract types are commonly used: firm-fixed-price contracts and fixed-price contracts with some form of economic price adjustment, such as the Consumer Price Index (CPI) or Producer Price Index (PPI). A contract for a simple commodity that establishes a firm fixed price may not need to state anything further than that the price is fixed for the period of the contract and, perhaps, describe situations—e.g., increases in relevant cost and price indices—in which there may be a price increase or decrease.

On the other hand, a firm-fixed-price contract for a service or construction may state that the contractor is not entitled to anything but the fixed price, unless the government directs additional or changed work that increases the cost. Additionally, the contract may provide that the contractor must, nonetheless, submit monthly reports of work performed or percent completed, particularly if the contract allows progress payments or requires the contractor to meet specific milestones to obtain progress payments.

The procurement professional should ensure that the terms included in the solicitation advise competing suppliers of the type of contract to be awarded and address all other issues that relate to that type of contract. Suppliers need to know the public entity's performance and documentation requirements for payment because those requirements may be key components of the costs that the suppliers need to factor into their prices.

Use of Legal Counsel

Finally, before drafting contract language, the public procurement professional should consider whether any of the issues intended to be addressed in the contract's terms require the assistance of an attorney. The language of a contract may change the outcome that the common law or other statutory law, including the U.C.C., may otherwise dictate on a matter. If the public procurement professional decides, in keeping with the objectives of the purchase, that the contract should address a legal issue in a particular way, that official should consult with the jurisdiction's attorney to make sure that the language drafted achieves the legal objective sought.

Legal counsel can provide helpful advice regarding risks, alternatives, and legal issues about implementing the entity's business decisions. Public procurement professionals and the agencies they support make the decisions about the procurement process, including which risks to accept, but their counsel can help illuminate the legal risks.

Organization of a Basic Contract

Good organization of a contract's terms is as essential as the words used in the contract itself. Basic contracts result from the parties bargaining equally and, through a "give and take" process, writing a document that reflects their bargain. Public contracts generally do not arise in this fashion; but there may be situations in which a procurement professional must negotiate directly with a supplier to create a contract, such as purchases exempt from the procurement law, sole-source procurements, or intergovernmental agreements. It benefits the entity and procurement professional to organize a contract in a way that allows end users to easily identify its relevant parts.

Description of the Document

Contracts have subject matters. If the title of a contract merely says "Agreement" at the top of the page, it does nothing to describe the type of agreement involved for the reader. The better practice is to identify the type of agreement in the title, such as "Contract for Professional Services" or "Agreement for the Lease of Software."

Caption

The caption identifies the parties to the contract and the legal action they are taking. This section of the contract need not be literally identified as the caption, but it should contain the appropriate language. For example,

AGREEMENT FOR THE PURCHASE OF SOFTWARE SERVICES

The City of Timbuktu (City) and Contractor X (Contractor) enter into this agreement on October 11, 20XX, for the purchase of certain software upgrades and services (Agreement). The City and Contractor (Parties) agree as follows:

The procurement professional may put the date of the agreement in the caption or at the end of the contract. Note that the date of the contract may not be its effective date. A contract term may provide a different date for the agreement to become effective; that is, for performance to begin.

Recitals

Drafters sometimes include a "recitals" section in a contract to state the background for it, often for the purpose of clarifying the parties' intentions. It is not necessary to do so. While recitals traditionally begin with "whereas" clauses, the procurement professional should not use the term "whereas" because it does not meet the "plain language" principle of contract drafting.

Recitals should be short and consist of a bare statement of key facts. They should not contain representations, indicate agreements, or contain substantive contract terms and conditions. Those should appear in the body of the agreement. For example,

Background

1. The (public entity) maintains its automated financial system on an XYZ mainframe computer that operates exclusively on BBB operating software. That software requires upgrading and maintenance from time to time.
2. Contractor manufactures BBB software.
3. The (public entity) and Contractor want to enter into an agreement for the purchase of BBB software upgrades and maintenance.

The parties agree as follows:

Definitions

The procurement professional may want to follow the caption or recitals section, if used, with definitions of key terms in the contract. The official should ensure that the words or terms as defined are consistently used throughout the contract. A common convention is to capitalize defined terms throughout the contract.

Operative Language

This section of the contract should consist of the terms that answer the "what, where, when, and how" questions about the purchase. The procurement professional may wish to divide this section into subsections with separate headings. Those subsections might separately address matters such as specifications or scope of work; delivery, warranty, maintenance, and payment for commodities contracts; documentation of work hours, milestones for any progress payments, and format for a final report; or standard and special terms and conditions, such as those addressing indemnification, conflicts of interest, termination of the contract, and liquidated damages.

Mandatory Legal Provisions

Statutes and ordinances often require public contracts to contain certain terms. Examples include rights to audit and inspect contractor records, retention of records, availability of funds, indemnification, and conflict of interest. Procurement professionals should ensure that their solicitations, contracts, and purchase orders contain those required terms. Often the statutes that require these clauses are not the procurement laws of the jurisdiction. Instead, the requirements may be in laws that address, for instance, ethics, finance, or budgetary matters.

Obligations

Statements of obligation concern things that the supplier has promised to do in the future, signified by use of the word "shall." They will appear in the contract's specifications, or scope of work, and in the description of the type or course of performance required.

There are competing preferences about the use of words to express obligation. "Must" has been proposed as a preferred alternative word of obligation over "shall," for example. Coordinate with legal counsel regarding stylistic preferences in contract language.

Representations and Warranties

Representations and warranties should reside in the contract in the same place that the obligations do. The procurement professional should include in the contract language any representations about the supplier and the supplier's product that the public entity has relied on in entering the contract. Unlike obligations, the official must demonstrate in that language that the representations are in the present and are a basis for the public entity contracting with the supplier. For instance, if the contract is for consulting work, the contract language should include something like "the contractor represents that it has ten years' experience in conducting and the specific expertise to conduct a study on the nesting habits of the endangered blue and pink owl." By placing all essential representations in the contract, the procurement professional avoids having parol evidence problems if a dispute arises.

The same is true of warranties. Warranties may either be representations of current facts or may relate to a promise of something in the future. The language in the previous "owl consultant" example could be a warranty as well as a representation. If the procurement professional wishes to ensure that it is, the words "and warrants" should be inserted after the word "represents."

In public procurement, many warranties involve future performance of commodities or items, such as computers, ergonomic chairs, copiers, and carpet. The manufacturer and dealer may offer their own warranties, but the procurement professional may wish to include one in the contract as well. Those types of warranties are promises of something in the future, for example:

> In addition to all other warranties, contractor warrants that its ergonomic chairs will be free of any defects in mechanics or materials for one year after each purchase.

Remember to ask whether the contract terms and conditions ought to include a remedy for the situations in which the promise is not kept or the fact is not as represented. If so, the warranty terms should spell out the consequences.

Declarations

Declarations address the legal principles that govern the parties' agreement. In most cases, those declarations will be the standard terms and conditions along with any special declarations developed for the particular contract, such as liquidated damages. To ensure that the contract contains all necessary declarations, the procurement professional should examine whether those terms and conditions address the possible situations that could arise under the contract.

Closing and Authority

The closing of a contract should show that the parties consent to the agreement. It is the place where their signatures are placed, demonstrating that consent.

A contract must be signed by a person who has the authority to contract for someone else under the law of agency. This is an application of a legal element of contracting: capacity. In the public procurement setting, the capacity issue generally arises because a government employee or a supplier's representative is not authorized to contract.

The wording in the solicitation often states that the person signing for the supplier must be an authorized representative. Contract terms should also state that only an authorized procurement professional can execute a modification of the contract.

The parties who sign the agreement should be the same ones whose names appear in the caption. Since neither a corporation nor a public entity can actually sign an agreement, the closing should designate their "signatures" as follows:

THE CITY OF TIMBUKTU	ABC CORPORATION
By ____________________	By ________________

The closing should include the date that the parties signed it, represented by simply stating "Signed November 11, 20XX" at the end. If the parties are likely to sign the contract at different times, the procurement professional should place a line for the date under each signature line, such as "Date."

Drafting Terms and Conditions

Terms and conditions are the "heart" of any contract. They define and describe the rights and responsibilities of the parties. This discussion emphasizes contract language that establishes the rights and obligations of the parties apart from the specifications and scope of work that define the requirement.

The phrase "terms and conditions" is only one of the phrases that lawyers use to identify the substantive parts of a contract. Other terms used are "clauses," "provisions," "paragraphs," "sections," and the word "terms" by itself. These words describe a whole range of things, such as specifications, delivery and repair response time lines, warranties, pricing for contract option or renewal periods, milestones for performance, termination of the contract, assignment of the contract to another supplier, indemnification, ownership of work products, and notification of debarment or suspension.

For most purchases, the public procurement professional will not draft a complete contract but will rather assemble a solicitation that will result in the formation of a contract and be part of it. The drafting principles and tips in this chapter apply equally to this important exercise. The solicitation is the starting point for a good contract.

The organization of the solicitation is just as important as it is for a basic contract. Each of the parts of the solicitation should be distinct to make the document clear and easy to use. Instructions to bidders, for instance, should not include language defining the circumstances under which the procurement professional may terminate the contract. Instead, those instructions ought to be restricted to advising bidders and proposers about the how, when, where, and what of preparing and submitting their bids or proposals. Likewise, the procurement professional should not mix specifications defining the goods and services to be supplied with other performance requirements that the contract may establish, such as documentation to be submitted with payment requests.

One key to creating good contract documents is the identification, development, and use of some general solicitation provisions (instructions to bidders/proposers, terms and conditions, etc.) that the procurement professional may use consistently for every solicitation. The procurement professional should involve their attorney in the drafting process, and that attorney should approve the end product.

Standard Terms and Conditions

It is easy for the seasoned procurement professional to identify those terms and conditions that are basic for every contract. By asking the question "What if?" the public procurement professional, along with the jurisdiction's attorney, should identify those legal issues that they want to be consistently treated in all contracts. Those legal issues should become terms and conditions that are standard in every contract that the jurisdiction awards.

Laws often require that certain terms appear in every contract of the public entity, and those are clearly candidates for the standard terms and conditions. Here is a useful checklist of contractual topics that the procurement professional may wish to address:

- **Definition of Terms**. A list of terms that frequently appear throughout the contract. Typically, capitalized terms are defined when used repeatedly.
- **Inspection and Acceptance**. Even though the U.C.C. prescribes a statutory process for inspection and acceptance of goods, it is common for all contracts to specify those procedures in more detail.

- **Warranty**. While the U.C.C. has implied warranties, contracts for goods and services may include warranties for a specified period of time, usually running from the date of acceptance or delivery.
- **Applicable Law**. Describes the jurisdiction's law applicable to construction of the contract. Generally, this is the law of the public entity's state, although with the advice of legal counsel, the choice of law may be negotiated. A companion clause, Venue, may be required by contract provisions developed by legal counsel that specify where judicial actions relating to the contract must be filed.
- **Merger Clause**. This clause works with the Parol Evidence Rule and states that the contract is fully integrated, meaning there are no other terms and conditions outside of the four corners of the written agreement.
- **No Waiver Clause**. The no waiver clause states that the public entity's failure to enforce a contract requirement does not waive that entity's right to later enforce the requirement.
- **Applicability of Public Records Laws**. The provision provides that public record/freedom of information laws control the release of information in the contract or arising out of contract performance.
- **Disclosure, Confidentiality, and Public Information**. Where access to sensitive public entity information may be involved, this clause identifies the contractor's obligations with regard to its protection and limits on its disclosure. The clause often includes exceptions and definitions for what is considered public information.
- **Severability**. A clause that states that if a court deems part of the contract as invalid the remainder of the contract is still valid and will be enforced.
- **Independent Contractor Provision**. This clause helps establish the relationship of the parties as independent contractors and not employees of the public entity.
- **Workplace and Safety-Related Provisions**. Contracts commonly include references to statutory requirements for workers' compensation insurance, compliance with occupational safety standards, and other health statutes and regulations.
- **No Assignment Clause**. This provision states that assignments of contract rights (and delegation of duties) are prohibited without the written approval of the authorized procurement professional, although some state laws limit the ability to restrict the assignment of the right to payment only.
- **Subcontract Approval**. Similar to the no assignment clause, this provision requires the authorized procurement professional's approval of subcontracts.

- **General Indemnification**. Public entity contracts typically include a general indemnification provision stating that the contractor will defend, indemnify and hold harmless the public entity against claims by third parties, requiring the contractor to pay defense costs and damages arising out of the contractor's acts.
- **Intellectual Property Indemnification**. This clause is used in contracts where there is a risk of third-party claims of patent, copyright, trade secret, or trademark infringement, requiring the contractor to defend and indemnify the public entity for third-party intellectual property claims that arise out of performance of the contract.
- **Compliance with Applicable Laws**. This common clause states that the contractor must comply with all laws applicable to the performance of the contract.
- **Force Majeure**. Sometimes imbedded in termination clauses, this provision may stand alone and identifies those instances in which the public entity will excuse the contractor's delay or other noncompliance with the contract, such as acts of God and labor strikes, that are not within the control of the contractor.
- **Amendment of the Contract**. This clause typically provides that the sole manner for changing the requirements of the contract is through a written amendment to the contract that the authorized procurement professional signs.
- **Nondiscrimination**. This clause prohibits the contractor from discriminating on racial, gender, religious, or disability grounds, as well as other protected classes under state law. The clause may identify specific laws and executive orders that are pertinent.
- **No Advertising**. Some clauses limit the advertising and promotion of the contract, especially when public entity endorsement is implied, without the procurement professional's approval.
- **Conflicts of Interest, Gratuities, and Kickbacks**. Contract clauses regarding ethical behavior are common, e.g., prohibitions against collusive bidding, conflicts of interest, gratuities, and kickbacks. Some prohibitions are explicitly required in contracts that are federally funded. Individual states and other jurisdictions often have their own statutes and ordinances addressing ethical conduct in contracting that may be cited in the clauses.
- **Availability of Funds**. A common constraint on contract funding states that a contract may not, without explicit legislative authorization, bind future legislatures to the financial commitment. The availability of funds clause conditions future-years' contract performance on funds being duly appropriated.
- **Audit and Inspection of Records**. This clause permits the public entity to inspect and audit the contractor's books and records relating

to contract performance for a specified period of years. In many states, this right is required by statute.

- **Retention of Records**. Often used in connection with (or contained in) the clause reserving a right to audit and inspect records, this clause requires the contractor to maintain records relating to the contract for a specific period of time.
- **Termination for Default**. Prescribes the notice and other procedures required for a public entity to terminate the contract for nonperformance or substantially defective performance.
- **Termination for the Convenience of the Government**. A clause permitting the government to terminate the contract with proper notice and providing recovery of certain contractor costs and profit. This clause is a mandatory clause in most federal government contracts.
- **Nonexclusive Remedies**. This clause reserves all remedies for violation of the contract that the law allows to the public entity, avoiding arguments that listing certain remedies precludes the use of any others available under the law.

There are some additional commonly used terms and conditions that a procurement professional may wish to include in solicitations for the purchase of commodities. The terms address issues that arise under the U.C.C. and include the following:

- **Risk of Loss**. This clause may modify the U.C.C. rules governing the risk of loss: the time when the risk of loss or destruction shifts to the government, e.g., in relation to the tendering of the shipment to the carrier (and before delivery) under certain shipping terms.
- **Inspection and Testing**. While the U.C.C. permits inspection at reasonable times, inspection and testing clauses are common and may allow the public entity to test the commodities and thoroughly inspect them without being deemed to have accepted them. The clauses may also permit access to the contractor's facilities for in-process inspection and testing, and may allocate the costs of testing.
- **Nonconforming Tender**. This clause may permit the public entity greater leeway than the U.C.C. allows to reject an untimely delivery or delivery of defective commodities, e.g., under an installment contract calling for multiple deliveries.

Incorporation by Reference

It is clear from the previous list that the standard terms and conditions may be lengthy. One way to reduce the size of the solicitation is to incorporate those terms and conditions by reference, which can be done by using language in the solicitation such as:

> This solicitation incorporates by reference the Standard Terms and Conditions, Form _____, [Date], as if they were specifically set forth herein. Copies of them are available from _______.

Not only is it good practice, but under some laws, the procurement office must list in the contract where the copies are available.

Special Terms and Conditions

In a solicitation, it is often useful to include a category of terms and conditions designated "special" because they, like the specifications, are unique to that particular purchase or type of purchases, or require adjusting for particular purchases. The public procurement professional should be careful not to react to a one-time problem previously encountered with a bidder, proposer, or contractor by drafting a special term to include in every solicitation. The term drafted in those situations is often too narrow and may simply confuse the meaning of the contract without achieving any commensurate benefit.

Interpretation of Terms and Conditions

A court uses the common law rules of interpretation to determine and implement the intention of the parties to the contract. As a starting place for drafting, the procurement professional should be familiar with those rules to understand how a court will interpret a contract's language if it is ambiguous or not drafted carefully.

Clearly, the best approach is to avoid using language that may require relying on these rules. If a dispute arises, a court will view the language for its objective meaning—the meaning that a reasonable person would give it—and not necessarily the meaning that the drafter intended. One way of determining if language could be interpreted in more than one way is to let someone else read and critique it.

Formalities in Invitations for Bids

Once the elements of the contract are developed for the IFB, the entity is ready to issue it. With respect to the contractual legal element of offer and acceptance, in public procurement, an IFB (and other formal solicitations) is not an offer. Instead, it requests, or invites, suppliers to submit a bid, the term for an "offer" in an IFB. Acceptance occurs when the public official authorized to award contracts signifies that the jurisdiction has selected the supplier as the winner and accepts the offer.

Accordingly, the IFB language should be drafted in a way that defines the point at which acceptance occurs. Letters identifying a supplier as, or implying that the supplier is, the apparent awardee do not constitute acceptance, although solicitation language and practices can be confusing in this regard. If the procurement professional needs to send a letter to an apparent awardee, such as to request certain financial information for determining that supplier's responsibility, the letter should explicitly state that it is not an acceptance of the bid or proposal.

Other legal issues can arise from the unique legal requirements that arise in invitations for bids.

Time Provided to Submit a Bid

In order for the sealed-bidding method of procurement to function effectively, prospective bidders must be given a reasonable period of time in which to prepare and submit bids. Normally, enabling legislation provides a minimum time between the issuance of the solicitation and the opening of the bids, often at least 14 calendar days, unless the public procurement professional determines that a shorter period is both reasonable and necessary to satisfy an urgent requirement. The situation must be urgent to justify compressing bidding time because competition may be restricted. Further, bidders responding to the IFB may be forced to include contingencies in their bids that, with additional time, could have been eliminated.

Amendments to an IFB

An IFB may be amended prior to the time set for bid opening if it becomes necessary to make changes in quantities, specifications, delivery dates, and contract terms or to correct an ambiguous or defective invitation. Prior to issuing the amendment, the public procurement professional is required to consider whether a reasonable extension of time is necessary, and consideration should be given to extend the bid preparation time if only a short time remains between the issuance of an amendment and the time set for bid opening. What is reasonable must be determined on a case-by-case basis. In one case, a federal contracting officer was found to have acted reasonably when bidders were given one day to consider an amendment that was simple in nature and when no bidder objected to the time allowed. However, in another, the award was set aside where the amendment was issued two days before the bid opening date and no additional time for bidding was granted, even though six bidders received and were able to acknowledge receipt of the amendment.

Bidders should be required to acknowledge receipt of amendments. Failure to do so could result in the rejection of their bids as being non-responsive to the requirements of the IFB. For example, a low bidder's failure to acknowledge receipt of an amendment to an IFB for containerized seedlings could not be waived as a minor informality because the amendment significantly reduced the specified quantity of trees and had more than a trivial effect on price. Minor informalities can be treated as such only if the entity can waive the provision.

A bidder's failure to expressly acknowledge receipt can be waived under the constructive acknowledgment theory if the bid clearly indicates that the bidder received the amendment. Such would be the case where the amendment added another item to the solicitation and the bidder submitted a bid on that item. The entity may also waive formal acknowledgment where the amendment involves only a matter of form or has no or negligible impact on price, quantity, quality, or delivery of the item(s) to be bid.

Timeliness of Bid Submission

A bid is timely only if it is received in the office designated in the IFB no later than the precise time set for the opening of bids. A bid received after the time set for bid opening is a late bid and cannot be considered for award unless the public entity expressly permits such consideration in their legislation or regulations. In these cases, a late bid may be considered if received before contract award.

But public entities' rules differ in this regard. For example, in Virginia, the courts have held that late bids/responses cannot be received or considered. In Florida, however, courts have stated that agencies do, in fact, have the discretion to waive the receipt of the late bid after all factors are considered and if the acceptance of the late bid is in the best interest of the entity (*Hewitt Contracting Co., Inc. v. Melbourne Regional Airport Authority*, 528 So.2d 122 (Fla. Dist. Ct. App. 1988)).

The "firm bid rule" is one of the most rigid features of the sealed-bidding method of procurement. Its purpose is to prohibit modification or withdrawal of bids for a reasonable period of time after bid opening. Public policy traditionally prohibits the revocation of a bid after the public opening and during the acceptance period.

Solicitations should include wording, generally in the instructions section, stating that in submitting the bid or proposal, the supplier agrees to hold its bid or proposal open for a stated period of time. That language clarifies that the supplier's "offer" is irrevocable for that specified period of time. If the solicitation does not contain that language, a jurisdiction may have no recourse against a low bidder who wishes to withdraw its bid after hearing the other bidders' prices. Some jurisdictions' procurement laws or judicial decisions limit the instances in which a supplier may withdraw its bid or proposal after submitting it, which may provide the jurisdiction with a remedy. The better practice is to include language in the solicitation making the bid or proposal irrevocable for a period of time.

Responsiveness of Bids

The key element in any public bidding system is the requirement that all bidders must bid on the same effort. This requirement is embodied in both federal statutes—award may only be made to a bidder "whose bid conforms to the invitation"—and also in most public entity rules. The major purpose of this provision is the promotion of objectivity and fairness in the procurement system, assuring that a bidder cannot win the competition by offering to perform the work in a less expensive way that other bidders could also have proposed had they known that the entity was willing to accept such work.

Allowing such bidding on alternate levels of work would inevitably involve the procurement official in further discussions with bidders to ascertain the precise nature of their bids and, ultimately, a discretionary decision on which bid is low, taking into consideration both price and level of performance that was offered. Such a system is tantamount to negotiated procurement with neither the safeguards against unequal treatment of bidders and favoritism, nor the protection from open disclosure of competitors' prices that are necessary parts of fair, competitive procurement. The responsiveness requirement has grown to embody much more than the concept that the successful bidder must bid on the precise level of work called for by the invitation. It has come to stand for the proposition that the procurement official must reject any bid that fails to comply with the invitation in any material manner. Such deviations may occur in many ways.

Required information may be omitted. The bid may contain mistakes or may not be prepared in accordance with bidding instructions. Conditions or provisions not authorized by the IFB may be included. It is immaterial whether these irregularities occur by design or chance, or whether the bidder is willing to correct or modify the bid to conform to the terms of the invitation. The bid must be rejected unless the bidder has unequivocally and unambiguously agreed to perform the work, and its bid was submitted in accordance with the bidding instructions.

These critical requirements have made responsiveness a focal point for award controversies. If a low bidder is disqualified, the next bidder in line stands to receive the award at a higher price. In responsiveness determinations, procurement professionals have much less discretion than in other areas, such as responsibility. Much of the controversy, therefore, focuses on whether a particular issue is one of responsiveness. To be eligible for award, a bid must respond and conform to the requirements of the IFB. Compliance with every aspect of the IFB is essential to assure that all bidders are treated equally and fairly during the evaluation phase. Accordingly, bids submitted under the following circumstances should be considered non-responsive:

- A bid that fails to meet the essential requirements of the IFB;
- A bid that does not conform to the specifications, unless the IFB authorizes an alternate bid and the alternate meets the requirements specified;
- A bid that fails to conform to the delivery schedule or the permissible alternatives set forth in the IFB;
- A bid received from any person or concern that is suspended, debarred, or ineligible for contract award if the period of suspension, debarment, or ineligibility has not expired as of the bid opening date;
- A bid requiring the submission of a bid bond if none was furnished in conformance with the IFB; and
- A bid seeking to qualify the terms and conditions of the IFB, or otherwise seeking to limit contractor liability, or to limit the entity's rights.

The question of responsiveness is extremely critical when dealing with the interrelationship between responsiveness and responsibility. Responsiveness, with no procurement officer discretion, deals with the question of whether the bidder has promised to do exactly what the entity has requested. Responsibility involves the question of whether the contractor can or will perform as promised, and the procurement officer has a great deal of discretion. Questions of responsiveness are determined only on the basis of information submitted with the bid and on the facts available at the time of bid opening. Conversely, responsibility determinations are made on the basis of all information that may be submitted or available up to the time of award.

The rejection of a non-responsive bid has very harsh consequences for the bidder and deprives the entity of the advantage of the rejected bid (often the low price). Thus, where other alternatives are present, there is a reluctance to classify a problem as one involving responsiveness, unless to do so is essential for maintaining the integrity of the bidding process. For these reasons, procuring entities have also adopted a policy of not rejecting bids when the deviation is not material.

Minor Informalities or Irregularities

A minor informality or irregularity is one that is merely a matter of form and not of substance, or pertains to some immaterial or inconsequential defect or variation of a bid from the exact requirement of the IFB, the correction or waiver of which would not be prejudicial to other bidders. The defect or variation in the bid is immaterial and inconsequential when its significance as to price, quantity, quality, or delivery is trivial or negligible when contrasted with the total cost or scope of the supplies or services being procured. Examples of minor informalities or irregularities include:

- Failure of bidder to return the number of copies of signed bids required by the invitation for bids;
- Failure to furnish required information concerning the number of bidders' employees;
- Failure of bidder to sign its bid, but only if (a) the unsigned bid is accompanied by other material indicating the bidder's intention to be bound by the unsigned bid document, such as the submission of a bid guarantee, or a letter signed by the bidder with the bid referring to and clearly identifying the bid itself; or (b) the firm submitting a bid has been formally adopted or authorized, before the date set for opening of bids, the execution of documents by typewritten, printed, or stamped signature and submits evidence of such authorization and the bid carries such a signature;
- Failure of a bidder to acknowledge receipt of an amendment to an IFB, but only if (a) the bid received clearly indicates that the bidder received the amendment, such as where the amendment added another item to the invitation for bids and the bidder submitted a bid thereon; or (b) the amendment involves only a matter of form or is one that has either no effect or merely a trivial or negligible effect on price, quantity, quality, or delivery of the item bid upon; and
- In some cases, failure to execute a required certificate.

Mistakes in Bids

One of the most troublesome areas in sealed bidding is that of mistakes in bids. Whereas a bidder for a commercial contract may be able to withdraw or submit a corrected bid at any time prior to the acceptance of his offer, bidders for public entity contracts are generally not permitted to withdraw or modify their bids after the public bid opening. In sealed bidding, the type of mistake most often made is generally reflected in, or confined to, bid prices. This is attributable to the fact that IFBs are normally quite explicit as to what is required of the bidder, to include specific terms and conditions of the contemplated contract. Other types of mistakes (e.g., failure to sign the bid or failure to acknowledge receipt of amendments) relate to bid responsiveness.

The rules applicable to correction of mistakes in bid prices apply only to bids that are otherwise responsive to the requirements of the IFB. Accordingly, the procurement agent is required, after bid opening but prior to contract award, to examine each bid received to determine if it contains a mistake. If the procurement agent has actual knowledge, or should have known, that a mistake has been made, the procurement agent cannot in good faith bind the bidder to the erroneous bid price by awarding the contract.

Clerical mistakes, apparent on the face of the bid, may be corrected by the procurement agent upon verification of the bid actually intended by the bidder. Examples of apparent clerical mistakes include obvious errors in the placement of a decimal point, obvious figure transposition, obvious discount errors, and mathematical errors in the computation of unit and total prices. Other types of mistakes, typically neither clerical nor correctible, involve failure to include a supplier or subcontractor quotation in the bid price or failure to price out some critical aspect of the work to be performed.

Once a mistake is suspected, the purchasing agent is required to request verification of the bid. This is accomplished by notifying the bidder that a mistake is suspected, calling the bidder's attention to the mistake or to the reason a mistake is suspected, and requesting that the bidder verify the correctness and accuracy of the bid. As to clerical errors, the purchasing agent may permit correction of the mistake by verification of the bid intended. In most jurisdictions, withdrawal of a bid having a material mistake made in good faith is permitted. Correction of mistakes may be made upon a determination by the procurement professional that clear and convincing evidence establishes the existence of a mistake and of the intention of the bidder, unless the correction would result in displacing one or more bids.

There are instances where a bidder's explanation of a mistake may be inadequate to dispel doubts as to its accuracy or the good faith nature of the mistake, requiring the entity to reach a determination as to its acceptability. These corrections may call the integrity of the bidding system into question. For example, if correction would displace a lower acceptable bid, under many rules, the correction may not be made unless the mistake and the bid actually intended are ascertainable on the face of the bid.

Contractor Responsibility

Most procurement laws add one final requirement at the time of the award: responsibility of the contractor. Legal definitions of responsibility vary in the legislation, but the ABA Model Procurement Code definition may be the most widely used. Responsible bidder means "a person who has the capability in all respects to perform fully the contract requirements, and the integrity and reliability which will assure good faith performance."

Typically, the determination of responsibility is made at the time of contract award. The information used to determine a potential contractor's responsibility is not limited to the information in the bid and may consider other information, such as past performance and financial capabilities. Sometimes public entities request information relating to responsibility to be submitted with the bid; others ask for information to be submitted by the bidder who is the apparent awardee. Some laws and invitations for bid explicitly state that failure to provide requested information can result in a finding that the potential contractor is not responsible.

Responsible Contractor?

The concept of contractor responsibility has been around for a long time. A Colorado Court of Appeals wrote the following:

"A broad discretion in the selection among bidders is included within a reasonable construction of the statute as to 'responsible' bidders. The word 'responsible' is not limited to the meaning of pecuniary liability or responsibility, but includes as well skill, experience, and integrity."

This language was penned the year the federal income tax was signed into law, stainless steel was invented, and the British House of Commons rejected a woman's right to vote—1913!

A case from the State of Ohio, *Glidepath, LLC v. Columbus Regional Airport Authority* (2012 Ohio 20 (Ohio Ct. App. 2012)), illustrates the discretion granted to procurement professionals in matters of responsibility. A protest was filed against an award of a contract for the Columbus Airport Authority's baggage handling system. The protestor, Glidepath, LLC, alleged that the evaluation committee had improperly found it not responsible.

The court upheld the determination, finding the responsibility analysis comprehensive. The airport's finance director was a member of the evaluation committee. Financial statements and Dun & Bradstreet reports were analyzed. The committee also considered reports about late payments to subcontractors and evidence that the company had limited project management experience.

The court concluded that it would not substitute its judgment and would "presume that the Airport performed its duties in a lawful manner. . . . [The Airport] made qualitative determinations regarding Glidepath's resources, capacity, and overall ability to perform the project. Based upon our review, the Airport's responsibility determination was supported by logic and reason."

When requested as a part of the bid, the failure to submit information relating to responsibility can become a legal issue of "responsiveness." Some courts may treat omissions of this type of information—that does relate to price or performance—as a minor informality. Public entities sometimes avoid the responsiveness issue by limiting submission of this kind of information to the supplier who is the apparent awardee; they state the requirement in the solicitation. Procurement professionals should work closely with their counsel to develop the best approach to determining responsibility under the procurement laws of their jurisdiction.

Protests Against Solicitation or Award

Protests against solicitation or award and dispute processes for resolving contracting controversies usually are legislatively based remedies available to the prospective contractor or contractor, doing business with the entity. Each remedy has its application during a specific phase of the acquisition process. Contract controversies arising during contract performance are discussed in Chapter 7.

Protests are associated with the award phase and are generally concerned with some irregularity in the selection of a bidder or proposer for contract award, or with allegations of defective specifications or unreasonable terms and conditions of the proposed contract. Suspension and debarment, on the other hand, are remedies available to public entities for dealing with contractors substantially deficient in matters of contractor responsibility.

Unless the right to protest solicitations and awards is legislatively granted, the right to challenge the procurement process is usually based on an implied contract theory. The issuance of a solicitation and the submission of a bid or proposal may be viewed as the creation of an implied contract. This implies that the entity will fairly and honestly consider each bid or proposal received in accordance with the express criteria set forth in the solicitation and in accordance with the entity's rules and regulations and appropriate statutes. Failure on the part of the entity to abide by these criteria may be viewed as a breach of an implied contract.

The administrative protest process is an avenue through which interested bidders or proposers can bring irregularities in the specifications or the terms and conditions of the solicitation to the attention of the procuring entity. As a result, protests may be filed in either the pre-award or post-award phase of the procurement process. Not all jurisdictions extend a right to judicially challenge a contract award, however.

The Availability of Bid Protest Rights

A company competed on an IT procurement conducted by a city and lost. The company's president, Lauren Agile, thought that the company awarded the contract did not have the five years of experience that the RFP required. She made an appointment with an attorney who was experienced in bid protests.

First, they visited the city's procurement office and reviewed the procurement file that included the individual evaluation scores for references and past experience. The awardee's proposal had received good scores with no apparent concern about the length of time the awardee had been in this line of business.

The attorney explained that, in their state, bidders generally do not have "standing" as such to file court actions. Even if she could show standing as a taxpayer to get a court to take jurisdiction, the courts grant relief very narrowly, and then only if there is a departure from bidding practices so substantial that they demonstrate a total disregard for competitive policies in the city's ordinances.

As limited as judicial remedies were, Lauren and her attorney decided to send a protest letter quickly to the purchasing agent who conducted the procurement. The protest was denied, the city finding that they had considered the experience requirement but had interpreted it differently than Lauren. The awardee was considered to have met it.

While Lauren didn't like the result, there was an upside—she appreciated the fact that the city's office considered her protest. She elected not to sue the city.

The public entity's enabling legislation and solicitation practices should encourage protesting suppliers to seek resolution of their complaints with the procurement agent prior to filing a protest with the city/county commission or the courts. In some jurisdictions, when a protest is filed, an award is not to be made until the matter is resolved, unless a designated official determines that: (1) the supplies or services to be contracted for are urgently required; (2) delivery or performance will be unduly delayed by failure to make an award promptly; or (3) a prompt award will otherwise be advantageous to the entity. Some legislation requires that procurements be "stayed" pending resolution of a protest and states the circumstances under which the stay can be lifted. Lifting the stay under this legislation usually requires a determination by a senior procurement officer or other official.

A "protest" is typically defined in the applicable procurement legislation (or implementing rules) as a written objection by an interested party to a solicitation for the procurement of goods or services, or a written objection by an interested party to a proposed award or the award of such a contract. In federal government contracting, an "interested party" means an actual or prospective bidder or proposer whose direct economic interest would be affected by the award of the contract or by the failure to award.

The "interested party" rule is a limit on who can challenge a solicitation or award. A protest by a "concerned citizen" who argues that only one bidder on a challenged procurement provided an appropriate response to the solicitation will often not be considered by an entity because the protestor does not qualify as an interested party. The requirement that a party be "interested" is designed to assure diligent participation in the protest process so that the issues are sharply presented, the record is complete, and frivolous protests are avoided. In making the determination as to what "interest" exists, the courts may consider the nature of the issues raised and the direct or indirect benefits to the protestor.

Procurement professionals must closely follow the established protest and appeals procedures in their statutes, ordinances, and rules. The public entity's enabling legislation should authorize a procurement official to determine whether the solicitation, proposed award, or award complies with statutes and regulations governing the procurement process. If it is determined that the solicitation, proposed award, or award does not comply with appropriate statutes and regulations, typical remedies require that the entity:

- Refrain from exercising any of its options under the contract;
- Re-compete the contract;
- Issue a new solicitation;
- Terminate the contract;
- Award a contract that is consistent with such statutes or regulations;

- Ratify the contract where performance has commenced if authorized by state or other applicable law, a rare remedy that usually requires a determination that the awardee did not act fraudulently or in bad faith and ratification is in the best interests of the state or local government; or
- Perform any combination of the foregoing.

Suspension and Debarment

It is the general policy of government entities to award contracts to, and consent to subcontracts with, responsible contractors only. Debarment and suspension are discretionary actions that are appropriate means to effectuate this policy. The serious nature of these sanctions requires that they be imposed only in the public interest for the entity's protection, not for purposes of punishment.

From the entity's perspective, debarment and suspension are among the most effective administrative remedies available to a procuring entity to protect the entity's interest. From the contractor's perspective, they are the most serious form of sanction that can be imposed because they bar a contractor from doing business with the entity either for a specified period, in the case of debarment, or temporarily, in the case of suspension.

Debarment and suspension may be authorized by legislation as well as by regulation, and the validity of both measures is well established. In the case of both legislative and administrative debarment, it has been held that such are not penalties; rather, if the procedures are reasonable, debarment represents proper regulatory measures for protecting the interests of the entity. Debarment and suspension, although harsh measures from the contractor's perspective, are the essential administrative mechanisms whereby the procuring entities and departments maintain the integrity of the procurement system. Suspension may be imposed as a preliminary step to debarment or as the only action, and immediately precludes the contractor from participating in procurement activities.

The ABA Model Procurement Code recommends that legal advice be sought concerning any proposed suspension or debarment.

Suspension

Suspension is normally for a temporary period, usually not exceeding 12 months. If legal proceedings have commenced during that period, suspension may last until the completion of those proceedings.

Laws vary regarding the grounds for suspension. Generally, the entity may suspend a supplier or individual upon evidence of commission of fraud or a criminal offense in connection with obtaining, attempting to obtain, or performing a public contract or subcontract. Under this criterion, a contractor may be suspended upon indictment for fraud. For an entity to suspend a contractor there must be adequate evidence, which has been defined as information sufficient to support the reasonable belief that a particular act or omission has occurred. Evidence required to sustain a suspension is less than that which must be shown to convict the contractor of fraud but is more than uncorroborated suspicion or accusation.

In *Horne Brothers v. Laird* (463 F.2d 1268 (D.C. Cir. 1972)), the court examined what it described as the serious and fundamental questions regarding the fairness of procedures utilized by the entity in suspending contractors. The oft-cited opinion stated as a general proposition that an action that suspends a contractor and contemplates that the contractor may remain suspended for a period of one year or more is a condition that requires the entity to ensure fundamental fairness to the contractor whose economic life may depend on the ability to submit an offer on entity contracts. Fairness requires that the supplier be given specific notice as to at least some charges alleged against the supplier and be given, in the usual case, an opportunity to rebut those charges. It suggests that, generally, a temporary suspension for a short period, not to exceed 30 days, without notice and opportunity to rebut charges may be acceptable. It also suggests that the kind of evidence the entity may be required to produce to comply with due process and to ensure there is adequate evidence to support the suspension is a question of judgment.

Debarment

Laws vary regarding grounds for debarment. Generally, a contractor may be debarred following conviction of, or civil judgment for:

- Commission of fraud or a criminal offense in connection with obtaining, attempting to obtain, or performing a public contract;
- Violation of federal or state antitrust statutes relating to the submission of offers;
- Commission of embezzlement, theft, bribery, falsification or destruction of records, false statements, or receipt of stolen property; or
- Commission of any other offense indicating a lack of business integrity or business honesty that seriously and directly affects the contractor's present responsibility as an entity contractor or subcontractor.

Under some laws, a contractor may also be debarred for violating the terms of a government contract, but the violation must be of such a serious nature that debarment is fully justified. Such violations include: (1) willful failure to perform in accordance with the terms of one or more contracts or (2) a history of failure to perform, or of unsatisfactory performance of, one or more contracts.

An individual or supplier whose business or livelihood is largely dependent upon government contracts is entitled to procedural due process. This includes the rights to notice of specific charges and an opportunity to present evidence before the contractor can be barred from securing such contracts for actions demonstrating lack of integrity. The entity cannot act arbitrarily, either substantively or procedurally, against a person. That person is entitled to challenge the processes and the evidence before being officially declared ineligible for government contracts. Disqualification from submitting an offer or contracting directs the power and prestige of a public entity toward a particular person and may have a serious economic impact on that person.

The government power must be exercised in accordance with accepted basic legal norms. Considerations of basic fairness require that administrative regulations establish standards for debarment and procedures that may include notice of specific charges and opportunities to present evidence and cross-examine adverse witnesses. These procedures should culminate into administrative findings and conclusions based on the records so made. Conceivably, a temporary suspension for a reasonable period, pending investigation prior to a hearing, might be constitutionally permissible in some circumstances when procedural safeguards are accorded before a final decision is reached; but how long a temporary suspension could be sustained would depend on the need and other circumstances (See *Gonzales v. Freeman*, 334 F.2d 570 (D.C. Cir. 1964)).

Due process includes the right to be notified of the specific charge so as to afford the contractor an opportunity to respond to and attempt to persuade the entity, in whatever time is available, that the allegations are without merit. In so doing, the contractor will at least have the opportunity to explain its actions before adverse action is taken.

Conclusion

An invitation for bids essentially begins with development of a contract. The IFB includes the specifications and states all of the contractual provisions except the price that is supplied by the supplier's bid. The formal solicitation process satisfies the legal requirements not present in commercial contracting. Acknowledgement of IFB amendments, matters of bid timeliness and responsiveness, and rule-based approaches to mistakes in bids all involve legal considerations. Contractor responsibility also is a well-established requirement for the ultimate award decision.

Most jurisdictions have processes for dealing with protests against the solicitation or award, as well as suspension and debarment of contractors found to be seriously deficient in meeting standards of integrity and successful performance. These legal processes are relevant to IFBs as well as other competitive solicitations like requests for proposals, discussed in the next chapter.

Author's Note: This chapter contains text and key elements from Fundamentals of Federal Contract Law *by Eugene W. Massengale (1990). It has been reproduced with permission from Greenwood Publishing Group, Inc., Westport, CT.*

For Further Reading

NASPO. *State and Local Government Procurement: A Practical Guide.* Lexington, KY: NASPO, 2019.

———. *State and Local Government Purchasing Principles and Practices.* Lexington, KY: NASPO, 1997.

NIGP, The Institute for Public Procurement. "Global Best Practices." Accessed October 23, 2018. www.nigp.org/home/find-procurement-resources/guidance/global-best-practices.

Pennington, Richard. "A Legacy Evolves: Responsibility Meets Responsiveness." Government Procurement, May 2013.

References

American Bar Association. *The 2000 Model Procurement Code for State and Local Governments.* Chicago: American Bar Association, 2000.

Burnham, Scott J. *Drafting and Analyzing Contracts: A Guide to the Practical Application of the Principles of Contract Law.* 3rd ed. Newark, NJ: LexisNexis, 2003.

Conway, Danielle. *State and Local Government Procurement.* Chicago: American Bar Association, Section of State and Local Government Law, 2012.

McCue, Clifford P., and Barbara R. Johnson. *Strategic Procurement Planning in the Public Sector.* Herndon, VA: National Institute of Government Purchasing, 2010.

Wright, Elisabeth, and William D. Davison. *Contract Administration.* 2nd revised ed. Herndon, VA: National Institute of Governmental Purchasing, Inc. (NIGP), 2009.

Chapter 6

Legal Issues in Competitive Sealed Proposals

This chapter introduces legal issues involved in the other major type of formal solicitation: competitive sealed proposals—a process that can offer an opportunity for public entities to exchange information with suppliers and negotiate elements of their proposals. Known by various names, including requests for proposals (RFP), invitations to negotiate (ITN), requests for responses (RFR), and competitive negotiation, these procurements are not typically awarded to the lowest-price proposal, but to the "best value." Evaluations require tradeoffs between technical merit and price, considerations of past experience, and award to the proposal determined to provide best value to the public entity overall.

Competitive sealed proposals involve unique legal issues that must be considered during pre-solicitation planning. Market research may highlight special considerations about confidentiality of information, rights in intellectual property, and organizational conflicts of interest involving existing relationships with suppliers. Early in planning, the requirements for cost or price analysis will frame the cost information requested in the solicitation. During the procurement, the process for communication with suppliers about their proposals, and possibly the need to revise them, requires that the process be fair to all the competitors. The evaluation of proposals and post-award activities like debriefing and post-award contract execution also carry their own legal issues.

An Overview of Differences Between RFP and IFB Processes

Competitive sealed proposals and competitive sealed bidding have some things in common. Both publish instructions for submitting responses: bids in the case of invitations for/to bid (IFB or ITB) and proposals in RFPs. The period for submitting responses is typically shorter in IFBs. Both solicitations include the terms and conditions that will make up the contract after award. Depending on the nature of the requirement, RFPs may have more complex terms and conditions.

Bid openings are public and provide an opportunity for the public and competing bidders to inspect the bids and know the prices. Issues of responsiveness are often discovered at bid opening and account for many protests against the solicitation. Missing information in a bid may make the bid ineligible for award, for example.

In RFPs, the policies of responsiveness may be slightly different because the process permits later proposal revisions. Generally, proposals are not opened publicly. Laws may require preparation of a list of proposers on the date and time proposals are due. The 2000 ABA Model Procurement Code Recommended Regulations require two procurement professionals to witness the preparation of the "register of proposals." Under the MPC, that register is made available after award, but practices vary with respect to the identity of proposers. Almost universally, however, proposal prices and contents are not publicly disclosed until after award.

There are other key differences between RFP and IFB processes. In an RFP, there may be an opportunity for communication between the public entity and proposers about weaknesses in proposals and a possibility that proposals can be revised. The revised proposal is incorporated as part of the contract. In IFBs, the only communications with bidders normally involve clarifications of minor informalities and, perhaps, communications prior to award about a potential awardee's responsibility. Another significant difference is the basis for award. In IFBs, the award is based solely on price and cost-related factors—a much narrower basis for award than in RFPs, where evaluation committees also consider technical and management aspects of the proposal.

While approximately half of state governments and many local governments have adopted a version of the ABA Model Procurement Code's process for competitive sealed proposals, states' laws vary. Some competitive sealed proposal processes are more like professional services/architect-engineer selections, where price/cost is not considered until after the most qualified supplier is selected.

The competitive sealed proposal process can be adapted to various service delivery and financial models, including integrated project delivery in construction (e.g., design-build, construction manager at risk) and public-private partnerships. RFPs are especially valuable when communication is necessary to assess whether suppliers fully understand the requirement and whether their proposed approaches are sound.

Pre-Solicitation Planning Issues

Pre-solicitation planning and communications with the industry are critical to the success of a request for proposals. There are four key legal considerations that can shape the ultimate solicitation.

Market Research, Trade Secrets, and Public Records Laws

Information is not protected from public disclosure simply because it is provided in response to a public entity's market research request or a proposal is submitted, even if the information is marked as confidential or proprietary. Some planning is required to properly handle information that may be considered a trade secret and treated as proprietary and confidential by industry.

A trade secret is a type of intellectual property defined by state laws, not the federal laws governing patents, copyright, and trademarks described in Chapter 1. In fact, the information may not qualify as intellectual property under those laws but may still be considered critical to a company—even more important to its commercial success than formal patent or copyright protection, in some cases. A trade secret is broadly defined as information (e.g., a design, formula, pattern, compilation, program, device, method, technique, process, or confidential business or financial information) that gives a supplier an economic advantage over competitors who do not know it. Misappropriation of a trade secret can lead to injunctive relief, award of actual and punitive damages, and award of attorneys' fees for enforcement. Trade secrets are valuable and vigorously protected by suppliers. Under the Uniform Trade Secrets Act, adopted by 47 states, the owner of the secret must have taken measures to prevent the secret from becoming available to persons other than those permitted by the owner to have access to it for limited purposes.

In many states, the trade secret or confidentiality exemption to disclosure in open records statutes extends to confidential business or financial information that is secret and of value. The supplier's obligation to protect trade secrets is why they mark market research information and portions of proposals with confidentiality legends. The extent to which any of this information can be exempt from disclosure is dependent on state law, and in some states the confidential information exemption is much narrower.

Especially during market research, where information is sought from suppliers, broad public disclosure laws may limit the ability to obtain useful information. Requests for information (RFIs) are a common pre-solicitation tool used for market research, but suppliers may be reluctant to provide information that could signal their strategy in any upcoming solicitation. Colorado is one state whose statutes explicitly protect some information from disclosure where submitted by suppliers during market research.

Jurisdictions that have adopted the ABA Model Procurement Code may not permit "disclosure of contents [of proposals] to competing offerors during the process of negotiation," but that prohibition does not address the later release of information like financial data that is submitted with the proposal. Other jurisdictions have taken an expansive view regarding the release of information submitted in a request for proposals. One practice used to better assess documents' qualification as a trade secret exemption under open records statutes is to use solicitation instructions that require proposers to plainly mark and segregate the information considered confidential and proprietary. The process for determining the validity of legends such as confidential and proprietary varies, but usually involves a decision by the public entity about whether the statutory exemption is satisfied and an opportunity for the supplier to challenge an adverse determination, sometimes as part of the solicitation protest process.

Some states' courts refer to federal case law as persuasive precedent in this regard. Federal courts consider whether release may cause substantial harm to the competitive process or impair the government's ability to obtain necessary information in the future. As with other statutory issues, the language in open records statutes differs among states. Nonetheless, the sensitivity of suppliers to disclosure of confidential information is a ripe area for market research discussions. Open records/freedom of information statutes remain relevant throughout the solicitation process.

Rights in Intellectual Property

The industry's approach to protection of intellectual property (IP) rights—patents, copyrights, trademarks, and trade secrets—is an important topic for market research. Requests for proposals for complex services can involve numerous issues of intellectual property ownership and rights. The approaches to IP rights vary among state and local governments.

Ownership of all intellectual property is usually not needed by public entities. Even in the days when agencies funded a good share of information technology (IT) software development, federally funded contracting rules only required license rights permitting use by public entities. Those rights included the right to use the software, prepare derivative works (modify it), and transfer it (to satisfy federal grant requirements, for example). But unless the entity was planning to market the software, which was unlikely, ownership might have been unnecessary. Moreover, retaining only the needed license rights could reduce the prices if suppliers saw opportunities for commercial application.

For over 30 years, the federal government has used a tiered approach to rights in technical data and computer software: unlimited, limited, and restricted rights (in computer software). California uses a similar approach for allocating "government purpose rights" in intellectual property owned by the contractor, as is the case for "preexisting materials" that are developed or otherwise obtained by or for the contractor or its affiliates independently of the contract.

Clauses assigning ownership to the government of intellectual property rights in specially prepared studies by consultants is common. Institutions of higher education have technology transfer offices that develop comprehensive terms and conditions that protect the university's IP rights and ownership of inventions. But in typical state and local government procurements, the licensing approach to intellectual property is often used.

Most public entities have standard (or boilerplate) clauses that address IP rights. Sometimes, however, those standard provisions are not adequate, depending on the requirement and a supplier's proposed approach. One way that entities may provide flexibility is to invite exceptions to RFP terms and conditions within the bounds permitted in its laws. Not all entities, however, permit exceptions.

The market research phase is the time to begin addressing these IP issues. With the assistance of legal counsel, procurement professionals can develop RFP approaches that accommodate industry concerns about intellectual property while preserving the government's interest in having adequate rights to use it.

Organizational Conflicts of Interest

Organizational conflicts of interest (OCI) have received increased attention with the federal Uniform Guidance that covers procurements using federal funds. An organizational conflict of interest exists when, because of activities or relationships with other persons, a company or person is unable or potentially unable to render impartial assistance or advice to the government, or their objectivity in performing the contract work is or might be otherwise impaired, or they have an unfair competitive advantage. Organizational conflicts of interest policies protect the public entity by preventing situations where a consultant or quality assurance contractor would effectively review their own work delivered on a project. OCI policy also prevents a supplier from competing on a solicitation when it has an unfair advantage derived from unequal access to information gained through a prior relationship with the public entity. This type of organizational conflict of interest involves more than the advantages that come from simply being an incumbent contractor, however.

Conflicts can arise, for example, when a company has access to solicitation information (or has assisted in RFP development) and then submits a proposal on the project. The Georgia Procurement Manual cautions procurement professionals to ensure that there are no impermissible conflicts of interest when third-party consultants assist in the development of solicitations. They are required to submit nondisclosure statements and are prohibited from submitting a bid/proposal or otherwise performing work on any contract directly resulting from that solicitation unless the restriction is waived in writing by the state.

As one example, a Florida court upheld an entity's decision to cancel a solicitation and resolicit where the low bidder participated in specification development, even though the governing OCI statute did not technically apply to the entity and the low bidder had been assured that participation as a sub-consultant would not disqualify it from bidding. The court found that the statute stated the public policy of the state: to not permit favoritism or use of insider information to give one bidder an advantage over another (*Sutron Corp. v. Lake County Water Authority*, 870 So.2d 930 (Fla. Dist. Ct. App. 2004)). Policies differ, however, and procurement practitioners must be familiar with OCI rules in their jurisdictions.

Subpart 9.5 of the Federal Acquisition Regulation (FAR) has exhaustive OCI coverage for federal contracting officers. As far back as 1996, some state courts have considered federal precedent when deciding cases involving OCI.

There are steps that an entity can take with the assistance of legal counsel to mitigate the chances an OCI will arise. It's advisable to include OCI language in consultant agreements where they may be assisting in the development of specifications or the scopes of work. Appendix C is an example of an OCI provision in a consultant agreement that could be adapted with the assistance of legal counsel. Negotiated OCI provisions should restrict the ability of the company providing the consulting expertise from participating in proposal development or, in some cases, subsequent contract performance. Provisions should require that the consultant treat procurement-sensitive information as "confidential" and ensure that only authorized employees in the consultant's organization have access to the material. Ideally, the agreement between the entity and consultant would also require the provision to be included in the consultant's subcontracts.

The solicitation itself should include OCI language that clearly explains that suppliers in certain roles will not be permitted to compete. For example, a solicitation provision could state that no person or business entity who was engaged by the public entity to prepare the RFP or has access prior to the solicitation to sensitive information related to the procurement process, requirements, scopes of work, or evaluation criteria, would be eligible to submit or assist another supplier in submitting a proposal. The clauses should state the remedies that may be pursued by the entity if an OCI is later discovered after contract execution. Depending on the nature of disclosures of potential OCIs, legal counsel may be available to assist in analyzing ways to mitigate the effects of potential OCIs.

International Law and Time Permitted for Proposal/Bid Submission

More and more often, clients are asking their attorneys, "Can a foreign company submit an offer?" In an increasingly global economy, foreign companies seek business opportunities in the United States, including government contracts. Of course, sometimes domestic performance may be justified as a contract requirement. Many cloud solutions master agreements, for example, require data storage in the United States, possibly eliminating some foreign companies from participation.

Still, there are international laws that protect the right to compete in the global marketplace. Typically, these only apply at the state level and only when the state has agreed. An example is the World Trade Organization Government Procurement Agreement (GPA, alternatively AGP). The United States Trade Representative manages implementation of the GPA and publishes information describing it and other trade agreements. The nation-parties to the GPA (the United States and Canada both are) achieve some protection for their suppliers. The GPA has an annex of "sub-central" government entities, including some 40 states of the United States (and several large municipalities), although they identify some exclusions regarding GPA obligations.

As NASPO explains in its *Guide to International Trade Agreements*, the GPA and other trade agreements set various minimum requirements for certain government procurements, including explanations to suppliers about why they are not selected for award. Moreover, suppliers must have access to an impartial administrative or judicial authority to seek a review of a covered procurement.

Among the other requirements in the GPA are minimum time periods for submitting "tenders" (i.e., bids) above certain dollar thresholds. The GPA and other trade agreements generally require a 40-day period for large tenders (bids and proposals), with exceptions for some procurements where the time period may be reduced.

Dollar thresholds are periodically set by the United States Trade Representative with respect to obligations under trade agreements. Procurements over those thresholds are required to follow certain procurement requirements, such as the minimum publication periods.

Most covered states have procurement laws and practices that conform to the GPA and other trade agreement requirements, with the possible exception of the time permitted for submission of a bid or proposal. For example, Massachusetts policy states that the 40-day requirement may be satisfied by publishing a Notice of Intent to Procure on their eProcurement system prior to issuing the solicitation. For covered solicitations by states adopting the GPA or other trade agreements, the market research period is the time to plan needed adjustments to procurement practices to conform to international treaty obligations. Especially where international business interest is expected, close coordination with legal counsel is recommended.

Cost and Price Analysis

This section covers common legal compliance requirements for cost and price analysis in public procurement. These issues are distinguished from total cost of ownership (TCO), a measure of all the cost components associated with performance of a product or service. TCO is often used in procurement planning and estimating, as well as evaluation of requests for proposals. Requirements for cost and price analysis are sometimes legally prescribed by law in order to ensure the reasonableness of proposed prices.

Early in solicitation planning, the resource and compliance requirements relating to cost and price analysis need to be identified. They affect the solicitation requirements for offeror submission of contract pricing data. They can also affect the makeup of the team that evaluates cost and pricing aspects of the proposals.

Some states, especially Model Procurement Code states, have comprehensive statutory and regulatory provisions that require submission of cost or pricing data and cost/price analysis under some circumstances. The ultimate objective is to achieve rates and prices that are fair and reasonable. The federal Uniform Guidance has procurement standards applicable to other-than-state public entities that include cost or price analysis as a requirement in some procurements:

> a. The non-Federal entity must perform a cost or price analysis in connection with every procurement action in excess of the Simplified Acquisition Threshold including contract modifications. The method and degree of analysis is dependent on the facts surrounding the particular procurement situation, but as a starting point, the non-Federal entity must make independent estimates before receiving bids or proposals.
>
> b. The non-Federal agency must negotiate profit as a separate element of the price for each contract in which there is no price competition and in all cases where cost analysis is performed.
>
> (42 C.F.R. §200.323)

Price Analysis

Unless there is adequate price competition, some form of price analysis is required for any purchase of goods or services. How the price analysis is conducted depends on the value of the purchase and the circumstances surrounding it. Price analysis is defined as the examination of the proposer's/bidder's price proposal or bid by comparing it with reasonable criteria, without examining and evaluating separate elements of the costs (e.g., overhead and profit) making up the price.

Where there is adequate competition, as in invitations for bids and most requests for proposals, submission of competing priced proposals or bids avoids the requirement for separate price analysis because an open and competitive procurement process is presumed to provide adequate assurance that the government is getting a reasonable price. Under the ABA Model Procurement Code and its recommended regulations, adequate price competition in an RFP is presumed if two responsible proposers who submit responsive proposals independently compete for a contract.

Where there is inadequate price competition, as in a "sole source" contract or when conditions are otherwise not favorable for competition, then other means of price analysis must be found. The nature of price analysis varies among governments, but they can include: comparison of prices and costs in other bids and proposals, established catalog and market prices,

prices of regulated industries (e.g., utilities), historical prices of similar supplies or services, and independent cost estimates.

Cost Analysis

Sometimes, market conditions or contract types are not suitable for price analysis, such as many sole-source situations, pricing of modifications to contracts, and cost-reimbursement-type contracts. In those cases, cost analysis is used to determine whether the price to the entity will be fair and reasonable. Moreover, even when cost analysis is not required in the initial procurement, amendments to contracts do not have price competition, and large-dollar-value amendments may require cost analysis.

Cost analysis is an evaluation of actual or anticipated costs and the individual components of cost, such as profit, overhead, and other indirect costs (including costs for tools, supplies, and materials shared across all of a supplier's contracts and operations). Effective cost analysis requires the application of experience, knowledge, and judgment to raw cost data. The purpose is to forecast expected contract costs and determine an appropriate profit. Cost analysis is used for establishing negotiation objectives for cost/price negotiation. The federal government has a sophisticated structure for cost analysis, including requirements for certified cost and pricing data for cost-reimbursement contracts exceeding $2 million.

States and other public entities whose procurement codes are modeled after the ABA Model Procurement Code often have policies and provisions requiring submission of cost or pricing data, certification of the data, and use of cost analysis techniques. They may have companion cost principles governing allowability of categories of costs in cost-type contracts. States' and other public entities' rules in this regard vary, including the thresholds requiring submission of cost and pricing data.

Reimbursement of costs on cost-reimbursement contracts must be allowable, meaning that they are properly allocated to the contract, reasonable, and not made unallowable by cost principles. In addition, a cost is unallowable if its allocation to a government contract is not reasonable because the allocation methodology is inconsistently applied to government work, essentially subsidizing fixed-price work with government cost-reimbursement contracts. For example, if a company is losing money on a commercial product, it may want to allocate all of its tooling costs to the government product line, distorting the true costs. Allowability rules prevent that distortion when costs of performance are reimbursed (as opposed to when fixed prices are paid).

Cost analysis and allowability rules can affect both modifications to contracts and the original procurement. Apart from contract modifications, even the U.S. Department of Housing and Urban Development (HUD) acknowledges that cost analysis is rare in state and local government procurement, whose procurements tend to be more commercial in nature. Institutions of higher education and departments of transportation and human/social services may have cost-reimbursement contracts and the staffing and expertise to perform cost analysis. Otherwise, price analysis is generally used in procurements by state and local governments.

With respect to RFPs in particular, federal bid protest cases have held that adequate price competition can exist when two or more proposers submit different products to satisfy a government performance specification. When award is made on the basis of price and other factors, there can be adequate price competition so long as price is a substantial evaluation factor in determining which proposal is most advantageous to the government. The MPC recommended regulations also presume adequate price competition to exist where two responsible and responsive proposers independently compete.

Policy and best practices promoted by federal funding entities generally portray a practical approach to price analysis. Both the U.S. Department of Housing and Urban Development and Federal Transit Administration offer practical guidance on price analysis. They also refer to Federal Acquisition Regulation (FAR) policy, such as discouraging unnecessary requests for large amounts of cost and pricing data where the information is otherwise available to the public entity or other reasonable methods of conducting price analysis exist.

The requirement to submit cost or pricing data, whether during the procurement or later for contract modifications, must be included in a solicitation or contract clause. The scope of the requested data can vary from simple budget submissions showing projected expenditures (not really "data," except for the unit prices in categories such as salaries in the budgets) to much more detailed factual descriptions of indirect and overhead rates, proposed hours for the work, salary/benefit breakdowns for all categories of labor, materials costs, subcontractor quotes, etc. In high-value contracts, the entity may also want the offeror to submit subcontractors' quotes concerning subcontracted work as well as their historical employee salary rates, overhead, and material costs. Where a public entity does not prescribe requirements for cost or pricing data in its own regulations or policy, the Federal Acquisition Regulation may provide useful guidance on the types of data to be requested.

Early in solicitation planning, the legal requirements relating to pricing must be considered, along with strategies that may be needed under the open records/FOIA laws that govern disclosure of cost data. The RFP must request the information necessary to comply with the price or cost analysis requirements of the procuring entity and federal funding agencies where applicable. Public entities ideally use memoranda in their files that explain what cost or price analysis was performed in a procurement and the basis for any exemptions.

The Proposal and the Contract

According to the Model Procurement Code, an invitation for bids must include all contractual terms and conditions applicable to the procurement. Using that approach, a bid may need to include nothing more than a price and a signature agreeing to the IFB's terms, with contract formation occurring when the bid is accepted by the publication of an award notice.

In contrast, the MPC recommended regulations require that an RFP include terms and conditions, not necessarily "all" the applicable terms. To the contrary, an RFP typically invites proposals that may be incorporated into the contract. Further, the RFP may permit negotiations and revisions of proposals, both of which are essential to contract formation. Some RFPs start with only a functional description of the requirement that sets forth the essential features of the project, requiring the proposers to propose the specifics of performance.

Despite the availability of such latitude, governments have a long history of structuring their RFPs more like IFBs—including detailed specifications and extensive mandatory contractual terms that suppliers must agree to as a condition of evaluation. This approach has advantages (evaluation time, for example) but can have substantial drawbacks as well, including discouraging innovative proposals.

In an RFP, terms of the contract are included in the solicitation, either as a set of terms and conditions or in a model contract appended to the RFP. The proposer's proposal and revisions to the proposal, when selected for award, become part of the contract. For example, if the RFP requires a mandatory, minimum six-months warranty against defects existing at delivery and requires the proposer to attach its warranty terms, a proposed one-year, failure-free warranty should not only be evaluated, but also incorporated into the contract. A prohibition on an proposer's taking exceptions could forfeit a term that is more favorable to the government. Permitting some exceptions may also promote industry participation when a term is judged to be particularly onerous or impractical by the industry. RFP question-and-answer periods help avoid those situations, but sometimes supplier concerns linger beyond the time set in an RFP for questions.

An order of precedence clause is used to establish a priority for contract interpretation if there is conflicting language. So, if the proposed warranty has a 90-day term, a properly drafted order of precedence clause allows the entity to argue that a six-month warranty requirement in the solicitation takes precedence. Courts prefer to harmonize apparently conflicting language, giving effect to all contract language. Where there is an irreconcilable conflict, though, the order of precedence clause operates to resolve it.

Of course, order of precedence clauses should not be relied on to resolve conflicts. The better practice in an RFP is to evaluate the language as proposed and, if the proposal makes the competitive range or short list, identify the deficiency and discuss it with the proposer. Such a deficiency might be cured in a later, revised proposal if proposal revisions are permitted.

Some thought needs to be given to how the contract is formed. In an IFB, the notice of award sometimes completes the contract execution. In RFPs, on the other hand, the progression of the evaluation process can involve negotiation and revision to proposals and other terms and conditions. Oral presentations during negotiation often involve proposer-provided documents whose contractual effect can be ambiguous. After award, a formal contract execution process that incorporates relevant documents is often the best approach.

There are a variety of approaches to writing the final contract, and caution is advisable. Wholesale incorporation by reference of the RFP may cause confusion about the effect of RFP sections, like protest rights and desirable features, that have little to do with future performance or were not proposed. Incorporation of RFP scopes of work, solicitation addenda having proposer questions and entity answers, and proposals must be carefully constructed so negotiated or revised provisions are properly accounted for and conflicts avoided. Sometimes during the evaluation process, proposers bring documents to oral presentations whose effect as a contractual obligation is unclear. For these reasons, in complex procurements, some professionals write stand-alone contracts with limited incorporation by reference of proposals and RFP provisions.

The RFP should clearly explain when the formal contractual obligation arises. Where the documents explicitly state that later execution of a bilateral contract is required, a court has held that a notice of award does not create a contract (*MacKinnon-Parker, Inc. v. Lucas Metropolitan Housing Authority*, 616 N.E.2d 1204 (Ohio Ct. App. 1992)). Some entities use an "intent to award" notice to avoid the contract formation issue. Massachusetts uses the term "apparent successful bidder" in award notices to avoid contract formation too early.

Responsiveness of Proposals

In traditional competitive bidding, a public entity has a duty to reject bids that are not responsive, e.g., those that fail to comply with the invitation to bid in a material way. The rule promotes objectivity and fairness in the public bidding process, ensuring that suppliers are competing on an equal footing. When a dollar difference in price can determine which bidder receives the award, strict compliance with material requirements is essential to fair competition and the avoidance of corruption. Suppliers have been known to learn during the public bid opening how its bid compared to competitors' bids and then try to revise or withdraw a bid considered improvidently submitted.

In an RFP, the reasons for strict responsiveness rules are not as clear unless the process is conducted like an invitation to bid. Unlike an IFB, the competitive process in an RFP is not essentially over upon proposal receipt and opening. To the contrary, the MPC requires only that award is made to an "offeror whose proposal conforms to the solicitation," a requirement that preserves the fundamental concept that potential proposers must compete on an equal basis, which can only occur if mandatory requirements are not excused when the award is made. Unlike IFBs, though, RFPs often permit discussions and even proposal revisions before award.

Courts in different jurisdictions have taken a variety of approaches to RFP responsiveness, often without discussing the underlying policy. In a design-build procurement, District of Columbia courts have held that the common law definition of "responsiveness" does not apply, and the entity has the discretion to determine responsiveness (*Urban Development Solutions, LLC v. District of Columbia*, 992 A.2d 1255 (D.C. 2010)). State judicial opinions vary in this regard, however. At one end of the spectrum, a New Jersey court proclaimed that a "non-conforming bid is no bid at all" in a request for proposals for a statewide furniture contract.

Non-Responsiveness in a State RFP

In the New Jersey case, *In re Jasper Seating Co., Inc.* (967 A.2d 350 (N.J. Super. Ct. App. Div. 2009)), the state solicited proposals for a state contract for non-modular office furniture. The solicitation required firm pricing for 18 months. The RFP stated that "stickers" showing price increases on previously published price lists were not acceptable.

Jasper submitted a proposal on two furniture lines, but pricing deviated from the RFP instructions. The proposal included Jasper's pre-printed list-price catalogs with stickers on the covers indicating that prices would increase by four percent on a specified date during the performance period. The state rejected Jasper's proposal as non-conforming. Jasper protested, and when it received no administrative relief, Jasper sued.

The court upheld the state's determination that the bid was non-responsive. The court applied sealed bid precedent and a materiality test to the question of whether the proposal was responsive at the time of submission. The *Jasper* court tested materiality of the nonconformity at the time of proposal submission, similar to sealed bid analysis, concluding that, "A non-conforming bid is no bid at all." The court upheld the state's rejection of the proposal, writing, "Generally, courts will not interfere with a Final Agency Determination which pertains to contract awards or rejecting a bid or bidders unless there is a finding of 'bad faith, corruption, fraud or gross abuse of discretion.' "

Pennsylvania courts, on the other hand, have taken a different, more liberal approach. One court even concluded that there are only two mandatory responsiveness requirements in an RFP, "timeliness of receipt and proper signature," a test closer to the federal rule (*Language Line Services., Inc. v. Department of General Services*, 991 A.2d 383 (Pa. Commw. Ct. 2010)). The ABA Model Procurement Code Recommended Regulations use "technical acceptability" as a criterion analogous to responsiveness in sealed bidding. A proposal not following instructions in an RFP and requiring a major rewrite in order to become acceptable (and meaningfully evaluated) might be an example of an unacceptable proposal. Even when a proposal with deficiencies is not rejected as non-responsive, the nature of the deficiencies may be considered in the evaluation and might preclude consideration of the proposal as one in the competitive range or inclusion on the "short list."

RFP language can contribute to confusion about application of responsiveness principles to RFPs. The use of minimum mandatory requirements or pass-fail tests could be lurking protest issues if a proposal that is not technically compliant with all of them is selected for award. While these may be ways to reduce the number of proposals evaluated for award, mandatory language may preclude later discussion of deficiencies or weaknesses in proposals that might have been easily corrected through proposal revision and treated as a matter of evaluation. If the mandatory requirements appear to condition proposal acceptability on strict compliance at the time of proposal submission—a matter of responsiveness—the court could treat deficient proposals as "no bid at all."

After resolving "responsiveness" issues, where award is not made on initial proposals, an RFP evaluation may move into information exchanges and negotiation. There can be issues about whether those exchanges, and opportunities for proposal revisions, are fair.

Competitive Range, Discussions, and Proposal Revisions

This section discusses the period after receipt of proposals and the determination about which proposals are "responsive" or technically acceptable under the rules of the jurisdiction. The ABA MPC process is used here, as its provisions are widely adopted among states and other public entities. The overarching objective of these exchanges is to address notable deficiencies in proposals. Sometimes called discussions and, by other public entities, negotiations, entities communicate with proposers so they do not award a contract with unresolved deficiencies or knowingly "leave money on the table" when negotiating prices.

Competitive Range

The MPC permits discussions to be held with proposers whose proposals are reasonably susceptible of being selected for award. A common term for this step is the competitive range determination, borrowed from years of federal RFP practice. This short-list step (sometimes called a down-select) is especially useful when large numbers of proposals are expected to be submitted, which is more common now with the use of online solicitation publication systems.

The competitive range is typically established after the initial evaluation. Public entities have considerable discretion in establishing the competitive range, i.e., who would be reasonably in line for an award. At this stage, entities usually communicate the deficiencies and weaknesses in the proposals to the proposers in the competitive range to frame the discussions. Practices vary about when excluded proposers are informed.

Meaningful Discussions

Especially in complex RFPs, there is value to conducting substantive discussions. The MPC authorizes discussions. Evaluators gain a better understanding of the proposals, and proposers learn how to sharpen their proposal and make them better if revisions are permitted. That process must be fair, of course.

One of the legal tests for fairness is whether discussions are meaningful, that is, whether proposers are led into areas of their proposal requiring amplification or revision. A 2012 Hawaii case illustrates the importance of fairness in discussions.

Meaningful Discussions with Proposers?

In a 2012 Hawaii case, *Bombardier Transportation (Holdings) USA v. Department of Budget and Fiscal Services* (289 P. 3d 1049 (Haw. Ct. App. 2012)), the city and county of Honolulu issued a request for proposals for a large design-build-operate-maintain contract for the Honolulu transit corridor. The solicitation terms and conditions had a provision limiting contractor liability, but the clause specifically exempted any liability arising out of a contractor-indemnity-of-the-state provision in the contract from the limitation.

In its proposal, Bombardier stated that it assumed that the indemnification exclusion from the limitation of liability cap was an inadvertent oversight because the exclusion would defeat the purpose of the limitation of liability provision, and essentially eliminate any cap on liability of the contractor. During discussions before award, Bombardier argued that the limitation of liability provision should be amended to eliminate the exception for indemnification liability.

The city orally warned Bombardier that a conditional proposal would be considered non-responsive. In its best-and-final offer (BAFO), Bombardier indicated that it was basing its proposal on the assumption that the indemnification exception would be deleted from the limitation of liability provision. The city notified Bombardier that it had submitted an impermissible, conditional proposal and awarded the contract to a competitor.

In its subsequent lawsuit against the city, Bombardier alleged that the city had failed to engage in "meaningful discussions," a term well known in federal procurement law. Hawaii's procurement code is based on the ABA Model Procurement Code (itself modeled on federal procurement law), permitting "discussions" with proposers. Despite differences in language between the Federal Acquisition Regulation (FAR) and the Hawaii procurement code, the court considered federal precedent regarding what constitutes "meaningful discussions."

Federal procurement law requires that once an entity elects to conduct discussions, that the entity ensures that discussions are "meaningful." That is, the entity is required to point out deficiencies or significant weaknesses in a proposal, or adverse past-performance information, with enough specificity that the proposer is led into areas of its proposal which may require amplification or correction.

The court held that the city met its obligations regarding discussions. The court noted that a specific written demand by the city that Bombardier remove the objectionable proposal language might have been preferable. But the court concluded that the progression of RFP amendments, oral warnings about the conditional nature of the proposal, and Bombardier's own proposal language showed that Bombardier had fair notice about the seriousness of the issue with its proposal. The court held also that the city was not required to conduct another round of BAFOs again to permit Bombardier to revise its proposal to remove the conditional language. The court sustained the award.

The *Bombardier* case, federal cases, and other state cases rely heavily on the specific statutory or regulatory language that governs the request for proposals process. The *Bombardier* case is especially relevant to states and other public entities that have adopted the MPC. And while a state's statutory or regulatory language likely is different from that in Hawaii, the *Bombardier* case and the Federal Acquisition Regulation are useful guidelines regarding discussions that help make RFP processes fair to all suppliers.

Technical Leveling, Transfusion, and Auctioning

There are other touchstones for ensuring that discussions are fair. Three of the most well-known in federal practice are the prohibitions against technical leveling, transfusion, and auctioning.

Technical leveling refers to significantly disparate efforts to help one proposer over another. This can arise in the context of disclosure of weaknesses and deficiencies in proposals. Sending a multiple-page letter to one proposer explaining weaknesses in a proposal in detail, and at the same time sending a one-page letter to a competitor that says, "We noted a few weaknesses, but nothing material," could be perceived as helping one proposer disproportionately. Sometimes this principle is incorrectly interpreted to mean the same communication needs to go to all proposers. The requirement is reasonable equivalency in how proposers are treated, but in the context of their own proposals.

Technical transfusion means disclosing to other proposers a competing proposer's technical solutions or innovative approaches. These can include subcontractors' identities, unique uses of commercial items, as well as any information that would compromise a proposer's intellectual property. In federal procurements, this prohibition is embodied in the Procurement Integrity Act that prohibits the release of source selection and contractor bid or proposal information.

Prohibitions on auctioning are related to successive rounds of proposal revisions with the primary objective to simply achieve price reductions. Of course, disclosing another proposer's price is also prohibited. Yet, communications about price with an proposer are permitted where they address affordability, apparently high prices, or inconsistencies between pricing and the technical approach in the proposal.

Proposal Revisions

The ABA Model Procurement Code requires equal opportunity for proposal revisions by proposers whose proposals are reasonably susceptible of being selected for award (e.g., in the competitive range). The MPC's language—like the federal practice it is based on—is flexible enough to permit multiple revisions to proposals. Legal requirements vary here as well, but conceivably, weaknesses and deficiencies could be identified before scheduled oral presentations and proposers asked to submit change-page revisions to their proposals in advance of orals for consideration by the evaluation committee. The oral presentations and negotiation could be followed by another opportunity for proposal revision.

The MPC recommended regulations use the term "best and final offer" (BAFO) as the final opportunity for proposal revisions. The term "best and final offer" is no longer used in the Federal Acquisition Regulation; the FAR expressly permits multiple proposal revisions. Still, the term BAFO remains in widespread use.

A BAFO opportunity need not be a lengthy process; sometimes proposal teams can respond in a matter of days. A common date and time must be established for submission of BAFOs and ground rules for length of the submissions clarified. Remaining weaknesses or deficiencies can be highlighted in the BAFO letter. The letter should clarify the effect of any documents submitted during the oral presentation and confirm that oral representations made during discussions that are not in the proposal will not be considered if not in the proposal revision. Proposers can be told that comprehensive proposal rewrites are not invited, but that they can revise pricing. Proposers should be cautioned not to make changes that are not clearly explained and justified in the proposal revision, and that they assume the risk that proposal revisions are adequately explained so the entity's evaluators understand them. Proposers should be informed that if they choose to not submit a BAFO, their previous proposal will be considered.

While the discussion process leads to a final evaluation, the objective is not to find where points should be added and subtracted in the evaluation. Instead, the goal of discussions is to clarify understandings, identify key deficiencies that can ideally be corrected in proposal revisions, and achieve favorable pricing.

Evaluation

One evaluation present in all procurements relates to contractor responsibility, discussed in Chapter 5. A responsible bidder or proposer is a person or business that at the time of award has the capability to fully perform the contract requirements and the integrity and reliability which will assure good faith performance at the time of the award (MPC §3–101(6)). A public entity's determination of responsibility is an area that enjoys considerable discretion.

Apart from responsibility, RFP evaluations by entities relate to the merits of the competing proposals. Oftentimes, technical, management, and past-performance sections are first evaluated by individual evaluators. Cost/price proposals may be segregated and evaluated separately, often by a procurement professional, with technical information (such as numbers of labor hours) provided to evaluators reviewing technical merits of the proposal. The committee then discusses the evaluations, adjusts scores as desired, and identifies the weaknesses and deficiencies for discussions with proposers found to be in the competitive range. After the process of discussions is complete, and revised proposals (if permitted) received, they are evaluated for purposes of award.

Today, in some entities, the evaluation committee performs all evaluations collaboratively, and numerical scoring is not always used. Even when used, if individual evaluations are scored, the final evaluation is sometimes performed collaboratively without individual reevaluation or even returning to the numerical ratings (i.e., the spreadsheet) at all.

False Precision in Numerical Evaluations?

Serco, Inc. v. United States (United States of Court of Federal Claims, No. 07–691C, March 5, 2008) is a federal case that highlights some considerations when using numerical evaluations in best-value procurements.

Serco involved a procurement by the U.S. General Services Administration (GSA) for master contracts permitting task orders for a wide variety of technology equipment and services available to the entire federal government. The agreement contemplated $50 billion in orders, so there was broad industry interest. The solicitation was announced as a multiple-award procurement, and 62 suppliers submitted technically acceptable proposals. The problem arose when GSA "drew the line" on awards. It ultimately found a "natural break" in the evaluations between the 28th and 29th proposers, and made awards accordingly. Multiple suppliers below the cutoff line protested.

The court eventually sustained the challenge to the awards. With respect to both past performance and the technical evaluation, the GSA's evaluators converted the adjectival ratings (excellent, good, satisfactory, etc.) to whole number (1–5) numerical scores, weighted and averaged them, and used the resulting overall ratings having three digits on the right of the decimal (measuring in thousandths). The court found systemic error caused by "attaching talismanic significance to technical calculations that suffer from false precision." The court reasoned that turning adjectival ratings into whole numbers and then averaging them is akin to rounding errors that limit the precision of the result, a propagation of errors through the evaluation computations. As a result, the natural break points relied on by GSA were essentially statistically insignificant.

The court also was disturbed by the fact that proposers with evaluated prices more than two standard deviations higher than the mean price of the 62 proposers were awarded contracts, without any meaningful analysis about whether the perceived superiority was worth the price premium. The court noted in its factual findings that GSA's cost-technical tradeoff documentation had recurring patterns and repeated language, with bare conclusions that the technical merit justified the increased price. "Simple math, indeed, reveals that the entity apparently was willing to pay a premium of as much as $3.6 million for a technical-ranking advantage of a mere one-tenth of a point—seemingly, a huge premium in a procurement in which the lowest-priced award went for $21,059,803."

Most protests of awards by public entities involve challenges to the award decision. There are few state cases analyzing evaluation practices. Courts considering challenges to evaluations require published evaluation criteria to be followed. Undisclosed evaluation factors may not be used. Statutes, rules, and practices vary regarding whether the numerical weighting has to be disclosed, although many laws require RFPs to at least indicate the relative importance of price and other evaluation factors.

The recurring themes in opinions of the U.S. Government Accountability Office (GAO)—the office that considers the lion's share of federal solicitation and award protests—may help frame the nature of discretion afforded procurement professionals. The GAO's standard of review is deferential to the judgments of evaluators. But in one case, where individual evaluator differences were materially inconsistent with a consensus report, no source selection plan existed to explain the scoring and methodology, and the source selection justification was prepared after the protest was filed, a protest against award was sustained (*Nexant, Inc.*, GAO No. B-407708, January 30, 2013)).

In GAO opinions, the mere difference in evaluation scores is not enough to support an entity's selection of a higher-priced proposal. The GAO repeatedly reminds entities that they should consider and document specific advantages that make a proposal a better value. Even when numerical ratings facially support the cost-technical tradeoff, the GAO has still insisted on written tradeoff analysis when an entity awards to a higher-price proposal. On the other hand, there is deference to source-selection authority determinations that proposals are essentially technically equal, permitting award to the lowest-price proposal even where adjectival or numerical evaluations show some level of technical superiority of the higher-price proposal.

To the GAO, tradeoff analysis need not cover every consideration, nor does the tradeoff have to monetize the technical differences leading to cost or price differences. The record need only show that the source selection official—the term used in federal GAO and court decisions to refer to the official making the award decision—was aware of the relative merits and costs of the proposals. Extensive documentation is not required for every consideration factored into a tradeoff decision.

The kind of analysis performed in these cases necessarily requires the assistance of legal counsel to make a persuasive presentation in protests. But the cases point the way to the kind of procurement file documentation—by far the most important evidence in cases of this kind—that is helpful to explain an award decision.

Debriefing

Most practitioners believe that after completion of a procurement we owe the proposers an explanation about how they can improve their proposals.

The costs to suppliers of assembling proposal teams and developing proposals can be sizable, easily running into six figures in large procurements. Most importantly, debriefings that lead to better proposals can improve competition. Some states (and the federal government) require debriefings by law under certain circumstances.

Courts and administrative agencies that review evaluations and award determinations do not normally substitute their judgment. They defer to the reasonably exercised discretion of evaluators and procurement professionals. Yet, where the record shows that the evaluation was arbitrary or capricious, awards have been overturned.

It's possible for the evaluation process to look arbitrary to a court. A Virginia court considered the fact that different reasons were given during debriefings for the protestor's not winning the contract (*Professional Building Maintenance Corp. v. School Board of County of Spotsylvania*, 725 S.E.2d 543 (Va. 2012)). In that case, the county held two post-award meetings with the supplier. As the court saw the meetings, the first emphasized a weakness in the supplier's environmentally preferable purchasing program. In the second meeting, according to the court's findings, the county raised different reasons for the supplier's not being successful: issues of responsibility, problems with the plan for transitioning from the incumbent contractor, and concerns about the supplier's method of conducting background checks. The justices found that the award decision was arbitrary and capricious.

A well-organized debriefing, however, can help suppliers know how to improve their proposals in the future. But debriefings need to be planned. One needs a clear leader in the debriefing. Even if program or subject matter experts are present, the procurement professional is typically better versed in the issues involved at this stage of the procurement. The procurement professional should stay focused on the evaluation facts, avoiding opinion and speculation. Normally, some informal ground rules are set, even in writing. Among them, as the commentary to section 3–203(8) of the ABA Model Procurement Code states, post-award debriefings should not include point-by-point comparisons of the debriefed proposal with those of other proposers. Procurement professionals should stay focused on strengths and weaknesses in the proposal as shown in the procurement file. They should also set a time limit for the debriefing, request names and titles of planned attendees, and issue an agenda in advance of the debriefing in order to establish expectations and ensure that there is consistency in debriefings for different proposers on the same procurement.

At this point in the procurement process, an apparent awardee has been identified. But how far can the final contract vary from what was in the RFP?

Post-Award Formalization of Contracts

A contract is sometimes prepared based on a model included in the RFP, possibly incorporating some proposal language and exceptions to RFP terms taken by the proposer in its proposal and accepted by the government. It's not uncommon for the resulting contract to have somewhat different terms compared to what was in the RFP.

Laws vary regarding the issue of how much post-award negotiation can occur. When a statute or ordinance permits qualification-based selection followed by contract negotiation leading to a fair and reasonable price—similar to the process used in architect-engineer contracts—there are fewer legal issues with the scope of post-selection negotiation. It is part of the process. In an MPC-type RFP selection, however, an objection may be raised when post-award, substantive contract negotiations with the awardee materially change the RFP and make the initial evaluation appear meaningless.

Is the RFP Evaluation Just a Ranking Tool?

In *State of Florida, Department of Lottery v. GTECH* (816 So.2d 648 (Fla. Dist. Ct. App. 2001)), GTECH filed a court action challenging the award of a gaming contract and claiming that the contract between the Lottery and Automated Wagering International, Inc. (AWI) omitted or altered various material provisions required in the original RFP. The trial court agreed with GTECH and declared the Lottery/AWI contract null and void.

As the appellate court framed the issue, "the pivotal issue before the trial court and in this appeal is whether the [entity] can treat the RFP process as little more than a ranking tool to determine a preferred provider and then negotiate a contract with that provider with little or no concern for the original proposal of that preferred provider." The appellate court sustained the lower court's decision declaring the Lottery-AWI contract null and void, agreeing that "the negotiated contract was financially more favorable to AWI than was the proposal by which it became the winning [proposer]." The appellate court concluded that RFP language did not permit the Lottery to eliminate all but the most favorable proposer and then later privately negotiate the price and terms that bore "little resemblance to the proposal that earned AWI preferred provider status in the first instance."

Some statutes—notably those governing construction—explicitly permit post-award negotiation with the awardee to reduce prices where all bids or proposals exceed the entity's budget. Moreover, laws and regulations may permit voluntary bid price reductions implemented immediately after award.

Bid protest attorneys who specialize in protests against solicitations or awards look closely at post-award communications that may demonstrate that the awardee essentially had an opportunity after award to revise its proposal in a material way. Some entities view this period as the "formalization" of the contract, where negotiated contract language does not materially change what the RFP contemplated, with materiality measured by the possible effect on the award decision had other proposers been given the opportunity. Like many other issues in this chapter, the approach to this one varies among jurisdictions.

Conclusion

The ABA Model Procurement Code approach to competitive sealed proposals has been adopted by many public entities. Yet there are notable differences among jurisdictions in laws and practices. Approaches to proposal "responsiveness" vary. Cost and price analysis requirements differ, although there are often common themes. Likewise, public entities use different terms like "discussions" and "negotiations" to describe the communications permitted between the entity and proposers after proposal receipt and before award; yet the terms apply relatively generically in most situations.

Some entities use very little information exchange in their standard RFPs. However, the exchange of information can help both parties. The proposer can better understand the government's requirements and the entity can better assess the proposer's proposal. But the exchanges with proposers in the competitive range must be fair, with equal opportunities extended for proposal revisions. Evaluation of proposals is a common area of protest, and the touchstone is reasonableness.

Post-award debriefings of unsuccessful proposers are common. The procurement professional ideally leads the preparation and debriefing. Finally, depending on the procurement law's requirements, the post-award formalization of the contract can unwittingly wander into areas that appear unfair to competing proposers when the RFP is materially changed. The issues in this chapter warrant a discussion between procurement professionals and their legal counsel in the context the specific laws and practices in their jurisdiction.

For Further Reading

Federal Transit Administration. "Best Practices Procurement & Lessons Learned Manual (Report 0105)." Text. Federal Transit Administration, October 2016. www.transit.dot.gov/funding/procurement/third-party-procurement/best-practices-procurement-manual.
———. "Pricing Guide for FTA Grantees." Text. Federal Transit Administration, March 14, 2016. www.transit.dot.gov/funding/procurement/third-party-procurement/pricing-guide-fta-grantees.
State of California. "Model Language." Accessed October 23, 2018. www.dgs.ca.gov/pd/Resources/ModelLanguage.aspx.
State of Georgia. "Georgia Procurement Manual." Department of Administrative Services, May 2018. http://pur.doas.ga.gov/gpm/MyWebHelp/GPM_Main_File.htm.
State of Washington Department of Transportation. "Organizational Conflicts of Interest Manual." July 2009, 22.
U.S. Department of Housing and Urban Development. "Quick Guide to Cost and Prince Analysis for HUD Grantees and Funding Recipients." Housing and Urban Development. Accessed October 23, 2018. www.hud.gov/program_offices/cpo/grantees/cstprice.

References

American Bar Association. *The 2000 Model Procurement Code for State and Local Governments.* Chicago: American Bar Association, 2000.
Asner, Michael. *The Request for Proposal Handbook.* 2nd ed. New York: McGraw-Hill, 2000.
Cibinic, John, Ralph C. Nash, and Christopher R. Yukins. *Formation of Government Contracts.* 4th ed. Washington, DC: George Washington University Law School, Government Contracts Program, 2011.
Commonwealth of Massachusetts. "A Guide to Massachusetts Public Records Law." Secretary of the Commonwealth, Division of Public Records, 2017. www.sec.state.ma.us/pre/prepdf/guide.pdf.
Commonwealth of Virginia. "1VAC30–130–10. Agency Procurement and Surplus Property Manual (Filed by Description with the Registrar of Regulations)." 2017. https://law.lis.virginia.gov/admincode/title1/agency30/chapter130/section10/.
Conway, Danielle. *State and Local Government Procurement.* Chicago: American Bar Association, Section of State and Local Government Law, 2012.
Defense Acquisition University. "Contract Pricing Reference Guides (CPRG)." Defense Acquisition University, September 9, 2014. www.dau.mil/tools/t/Contract-Pricing-Reference-Guides-(CPRG).
NASPO. "NASPO Guide to International Trade Agreements." Accessed October 23, 2018. www.naspo.org/ita/index.html.
———. *State and Local Government Purchasing Principles and Practices.* Lexington, KY: NASPO, 1997.
Office of the New York State Comptroller. "Search Comptroller's Bid Protest Decisions." Accessed October 23, 2018. http://wwe1.osc.state.ny.us/Contracts/decisionsearch.cfm.

Chapter 7

The Legal Context of Contract Administration

This chapter changes the focus away from contract formation—including contracts entered through procurement processes—to contract administration. The rights and obligations of the parties depend on the operation of contract terms and conditions, specifications, and the statement of work in service contracts. Most public entities now have mature sets of general provisions for their contracts, often called "boilerplate." Based on their relevancy during contract administration, some of these clauses are more suitable to complex service procurements, while others are more suited to construction. This chapter will look at the operation of the more common clauses.

Contract performance and modifications of contracts involve issues of time, scope, and cost. Contract provisions create rights to relief from delays caused by the contractor or public entity, as well as events that are under no one's control. Inspection, acceptance, and warranty clauses are usually used in contracts to revise the common law and U.C.C. rules. Terminations of contracts need to be orderly, and typical clauses establish the grounds, procedures, and respective rights in termination situations.

Waiver of the contract schedule and other requirements is an important legal concept. When an entity forbears on enforcement of a schedule, especially when it has encouraged the contractor to devote more resources to catch up after a deadline has passed, the entity risks having waived the schedule. The entity cannot then just reverse itself and enforce the original schedule—there are remedial steps that are required.

Finally, some of the most negotiated contract provisions involve indemnification and limitation of liability provisions. Procurement professionals must have a basic familiarity with how those provisions change the common law rules regarding the availability of remedies. Understanding how these clauses operate during contract administration is key to decisions about using them in contracts.

The Order of Precedence Clause

As is well known, there is potential for conflict between various contract terms and conditions covering the issues that arise throughout performance of a contract. Terms and conditions in competitive sealed bidding are established by the public entity. In negotiated contracts, however, terms and conditions can be proposed by either party. Requests for proposals typically have entity terms and conditions and may invite proposals from suppliers that can include their own terms and conditions. In national cooperative master agreements, the terms governing an order by a participating public entity can include provisions from the RFP, the proposal, negotiated terms, and the participating entities' terms and conditions in their ordering document. In short, there can be lots of different—and differently interpreted—language.

The order of precedence clause helps resolve conflict that arises during contract performance when contracting parties disagree about contract interpretation. A typical clause, for example, establishes the RFP specifications as a higher precedence than the contractor's proposal in the event of conflict in language.

Courts prefer to harmonize seemingly conflicting language, attempting to give effect to all contract language instead of throwing out the lower-priority clause. Courts will parse through the language to find an interpretation consistent with both. Where there is an irreconcilable conflict, however, the order of precedence clause operates to resolve it.

Dealing With Changes During Contract Performance

During performance of a contract, an entity's requirements may change. For the contractor, conditions that will increase both the time for and cost of performance may be encountered that were unknown at the time of submission of bids or proposals. A subsequent change to the contract's terms is referred to as a contract modification. Unilateral contract modifications—those that can be directed by the public entity and are commonly called change orders—have both a scope issue and can involve contentious disputes about the measurement of entitlement.

Sometimes, the public entity is not intending to direct any kind of change, believing that its contract interpretation does not entitle the contractor to any additional compensation or time for performance. Directing a contractor to continue without any adjustment in price or schedule may lead to a dispute based on a theory of constructive change, cases that at their heart are matters of contract interpretation.

Unilateral change clauses and constructive change disputes have been present in federal contracting for decades. As an example, consider a city department of corrections contract to build a jail on the north side of town. The contract has a changes clause permitting the city to unilaterally order changes within the general scope of the contract. If the department directed a change to the contract to move the jail to a mountain top on the south side of town where construction conditions were materially different, a contractor could very well argue that the change was a cardinal change, a breach of contract, and refuse to perform. On the other hand, if the city issued a change order substituting a new locking mechanism for the entrance portal, that would likely be within scope, and the contractor would have to perform under the changes clause while being entitled to an equitable adjustment of the contract price and schedule (under typical clause provisions).

If the contractor was losing money on the jail construction because it underbid the work, it could not hold out to renegotiate the entire construction project and "get well" on the locking mechanism change. The usual formula for equitable adjustment is the difference between what it would have cost to perform the work as originally required and what it reasonably would cost to perform the work as changed, with a reasonable profit for the additional effort.

The existence of the changes clause provides considerable flexibility to the public entity. Coupled with a common contract requirement that the contractor continue to perform even in the face of a dispute, the changes clause promotes orderly contract performance and minimizes disruptions that can occur during disputes.

Differing Site Conditions

One special kind of changes provision is the differing site conditions clause in construction contracts. Contractors may encounter subsurface conditions that are unknown, unexpected, and that significantly increase the costs of performance. Without a differing site conditions clause, some courts have held that the contractor assumes the risk that the cost of performance will be higher than expected. This interpretation can lead to large price contingencies in offers; the clause helps avoid them.

So long as appropriate notice is given consistent with the clause, there may be contractor entitlement to recovery for subsurface or latent physical conditions at the site: (1) differing materially from those indicated in the contract (often through furnishing of soil borings), or (2) unknown physical conditions at the site of an unusual nature, differing materially from those ordinarily encountered and generally recognized as inhering in work of the character provided for in the contract.

The federal differing site conditions ("DSC") clause is widely used between prime and subcontractors as well. It is not uncommon for state courts to consider federal precedent in deciding cases involving clauses similar to the federal DSC clause.

Issues in DSC cases include whether the condition is the kind, e.g., subsurface, that the clause covers. Whether the condition is "unusual" is a recurring issue, as well as the contractor's responsibility to be familiar with the site. Even when boring samples are provided, an issue can arise about how representative they are and whether the actual conditions differ materially from what the samples show.

Constructive Change

When the entity has not directed anything it considers a contract change, there still may be theories of recovery that entitle a contractor to more time, money, or both. Constructive change claims generally arise from three circumstances. The first is when a contractor is required to perform work beyond what the contract requires, as when a government inspector is perhaps overzealous and rejects work that complies with contract requirements. Another situation leading to constructive change occurs when a contractor follows the informal directives of an agent, e.g., an architect who is often charged with responsibility for interpreting her own drawings, resulting in the contractor incurring additional costs. A third situation arises from defective specifications themselves, as when construction drawings and specifications, when followed, cannot be acceptably built. In construction law, this is known as the Spearin doctrine—a warranty of specifications based on the 1918 Supreme Court case *United States v. Spearin*.

Constructive change claims also arise from issues of contract interpretation. One issue can be the use of so-called precatory language, e.g., *should* versus *must*, that expresses a desire but not necessarily a requirement. The nature of the contractor's obligation in those cases can be unclear.

Will, Shall, Can, and Should

Early in the 21st century, a state embarked on an ambitious program to develop a computer-assisted management system for benefits and food distributed under the federal supplemental nutrition program for women, infants, and children (WIC). Much of the program was administered by counties, and the WIC program started implementing benefits credit cards to streamline the availability of benefits and more efficient management of the payments.

The state agency responsible for the WIC program applied for a federal grant and described its intended program implementation. Among the dozens of federal requirements was one relating to reporting. The federal grant documents stated that, "The solution should accommodate configurable, customized reports needed for program management." The state was awarded funds to develop a computer system to manage the program. The state used the funds to procure a computer system from a private company.

A year into performance of the fixed-price contract, the contractor encountered problems. The RFP had disclosed a set of 12 reports needed for program management and essentially used the grant language about the requirement for reports. The RFP added an additional requirement, "Contractor shall develop other reports as desired."

The statement of work had essentially incorporated the federal grant requirements that used language like "should" to define desirable aspects of any computer program. The contractor had priced the 12 reports and stated in its proposal that it could and would prepare other reports as requested, adding "contractor and requesting entity will agree on a suitable delivery and testing schedule." But many of the counties were asking for tailored reports, more than quadrupling the number of reports having to be developed.

The state's position was that the contractor was required to deliver "reports as desired" at no adjustment in contract price. Eventually, a formal claim under the contract was submitted. The case settled without going to trial.

One way to minimize the prospect of surprise in this regard is to contractually require written notice by the contractor to the entity, usually within an explicit timeframe specified in the contract. Failure to follow the notice provision is often strictly applied against the contractor by courts, the theory being that the government otherwise loses the ability to investigate and correct its actions. A New York court has strictly applied the notice of change provision even where there was general knowledge by public authority employees that the contractor considered extra work a change (*Ridley Electric Co., Inc. v. Dormitory Authority*, 60 N.Y.S.3d 552 (NY App. Div. 2017)).

Equitable Adjustment of Price and Schedule

For decades, federal government contracts have used equitable adjustment as the measure of entitlement for government-directed changes. The Federal Acquisition Regulation and commercial construction contracts use equitable adjustment in differing site conditions clauses as well. Many other public entities do also. A representative differing site conditions clause states,

> If the conditions do materially so differ [from usual conditions or contract documents] and cause an increase or decrease in the contractor's cost of, or the time required for, performing any part of the work under this contract, an equitable adjustment shall be made.

The measure of equitable adjustment depends on the specific language in the contract provision. The basic measure is the extra cost incurred by the contractor if those costs are reasonable, along with a reasonable profit. Some clauses do not permit recovery of profit when mere suspension of work or pure delay is involved. Further, the equitable adjustment may be reduced to account for the contractor's relative responsibility in contributing to the increased costs.

Sometimes, contractors attempt to submit a total cost claim (also known as a "jury verdict" method) that compares the total project cost to the bid amount without accounting for separate elements of increased costs. That method is not favored and will often not be used by a court if more reliable, alternative methods are available.

Generally, profit is an element of equitable adjustment. In a construction management case involving a three-month extension in a city hall construction project and double the managed contract price, a court used the initial bid fee percentage (applied to the construction price) as evidence to determine the fee for the equitable adjustment (*City of Meridian v. Petra, Inc.*, 299 P. 3d 232 (Idaho 2013)).

One of the most difficult issues in equitable adjustments is the measurement of the indirect cost effects of delay, and federal precedent may be helpful in analyzing those claims. When a contractor is on standby and cannot redeploy a workforce to other projects, for example, there is a cost impact. Likewise, tooling and other equipment whose costs are allocated to indirect cost pools in a company may be underutilized. In construction, the federal courts have an approach known as the Eichleay formula—not a mathematical formula, but named after a seminal case that developed a method of analyzing delay claims. The Ohio Supreme Court has adopted a modified version of Eichleay, with costs adjusted for those considered unallowable under Ohio law (*Complete General Construction Co. v. Ohio Department of Transportation*, 760 N.E.2d 364 (Ohio 2002)). The decision has been cited by other state courts.

Cost or Price Analysis in Contract Modifications

Even if there are exemptions from cost or price analysis in the procurement because of adequate competition, as in construction contracts procured by competitive sealed bidding, modifications to those contracts may require analysis. Cost analysis may be required by applicable law with respect to contract amendments having values above prescribed dollar thresholds.

In federally funded procurements, the Uniform Guidance requires cost or price analysis for amendments above the simplified acquisition threshold ($250,000). Above that threshold, when cost analysis is performed, profit must be separately analyzed.

According to the Uniform Guidance, profit is required to be separately negotiated only when there is "no price competition and in all cases when cost analysis is performed." Unless a public entity is contracting with a nonprofit organization, a large component of total price is the profit. There are no formulas for determining a reasonable profit. In fact, profit is sometimes the cost element that is likely to be negotiated away first by a contractor. Sometimes profit may appear to be negotiated away, when in fact there may be other costs that a contractor expects to reduce during performance.

In general, profit—an element of equitable adjustment—should be a reward for efficiency and the risk assumed by a contractor. Negotiation objectives are sometimes established using profit as a percentage of total estimated cost, e.g., computing the "return of the investment" of time and money. The federal government has guidelines that are used to negotiate profit. They include the nature of professional and management skill, the extent to which contractor facilities and other assets are needed for efficient performance, the complexity, the extent that sources must be developed, cost risk, the initiative shown in support of socioeconomic policies, and the extent to which the contractor has demonstrated effective cost control in the past.

When federal funds are involved, guidance by the federal agency may be useful to understand cost or price analysis expectations. The Federal Transit Administration maintains a useful reference on its website, *Pricing Guide for FTA Grantees*, that covers price and cost analysis of modifications, as does the Department of Housing and Urban Development in its *Quick Guide to Cost and Price Analysis for HUD Grantees and Funding Recipients.*

Matters of Time

Whenever changed circumstances exist entitling the contractor to relief, or if the government unreasonably delays or interferes with contractor performance, requiring the contractor to adhere to the original schedule can result in an additional entitlement from constructive acceleration. The courts look at the impact on the contractor as if it had been explicitly directed to finish earlier than contractually required.

This subsection discusses four other issues related to time. Many contracts have excusable delay provisions, also known as *force majeure* clauses, that excuse certain delays not the fault of the contractor. Some contracts have clauses that exclude damages for delay, the so-called "no damage for delay" clause. Next, suspension of work by the government is treated differently by the federal government and some state and local governments in terms of entitlement. Finally, contract administration illuminates the issues involving enforceability of some liquidated damages provisions, a topic covered in Chapter 4 with respect to transactions in goods governed by the Uniform Commercial Code.

Excusable Delay and Force Majeure

Excusable delay provisions have been in federal government contracting for decades. Notably, they appear in the termination for default clauses in the Federal Acquisition Regulation. In the federal construction clause, delays that are beyond the control and without the fault or negligence of the contractor are excusable. Examples in the clause include acts of God or of the public enemy, acts of another contractor in the performance of a contract with the government, fires, floods, epidemics, strikes, unusually severe weather, or delays of subcontractors or suppliers at any tier arising from unforeseeable causes beyond the control, and without the fault or negligence, of both the contractor and subcontractors or suppliers. These provisions require the contractor to provide notice to the government of the events causing delay.

State and local governments use clauses with different enumerated events, and sometimes separate force majeure clauses. Legal counsel can advise procurement professionals about case law interpreting the various conditions excusing performance or delays.

The District of Columbia borrows heavily from federal terms and conditions. Its courts have struck down terminations for default where the evidence showed that district officials believed that the contractor was entitled to some contract extensions but never fully analyzed the delays. A court rejected the district's contention that the contractor's failure to satisfactorily maintain critical path schedules excused the district from completing the analysis (*District of Columbia v. Kora & Williams Corp.*, 743 A.2d 682 (D.C. 1999)).

These provisions typically require that the event be beyond the control of the party claiming relief and that notice be provided as soon as the event occurs. An Idaho court has concluded that the force majeure clause was not intended to apply to difficulty in securing financial and security obligations under an agreement, such as the posting of a bond, where the events did not affect the contractor's physical ability to perform (*Idaho Power Co. v. Cogeneration, Inc.*, 9 P. 3d 1204 (Idaho 2000)).

No Damages for Delay Provisions

A clause used to mitigate the financial effects of project delay is a "no damages for delay" provision. The clause essentially excludes financial claims solely related to delays on projects.

The effect of the provision was plainly illustrated in a Kentucky case, *Mid States Steel Products Co. v. University of Kentucky* (2003-CA-002509-MR (Ky. Ct. App., May 5, 2006)), involving stadium construction at a university. When the university redesigned the stadium, the university granted extensions of time for performance. The steel construction contractor submitted a claim that included amounts related to underutilization of its shops because of the delay and other claims tied to the delay. The contract included a provision that excluded any compensation because of "impacts, hindrance in the orderly progress of the Work or delay from any cause in the progress of the Work." The clause explicitly stated that the contractor could not make "and hereby waives, any claim from damages on account of any delay," that "the sole right and remedy in the case of any delay shall be an extension of the time fixed for completion of the contract." Because some of the monetary claims were based on delay, the appellate court upheld the trial court's denial of them.

Colorado, Minnesota, and North Carolina are among the states that have statutorily limited the enforceability of no damages for delay clauses in some public works contracts. Other courts give only "restrained approval" of the no damages for delay provisions because of their harshness, and they may not enforce them at all when the public entity has deliberately and wrongfully interfered with the contractor's work.

Suspension of Work

Especially in construction, the "suspension of work" clause is used to permit the government to temporarily suspend performance of the contract. Sometimes, for example, when significant, unknown conditions are encountered, it is advisable to stop work while the conditions are fully investigated.

The federal government does not exclude all damages based on delays. In the federal suspension of work clause, profit is excluded as an element of damage, however. Some federal contract disputes boards and court decisions limit the clause's exclusion of profit to instances involving pure delay, not to cases where work is changed and delay is a natural consequence of the change. In such a case, equitable adjustment law defines the measure of damages, and there may be entitlement to some profit.

Contract provisions govern these cases, of course, and there can be conflicts in the language used. In a case where the Environmental Protection Agency funded a tank and boiler construction, a sanitation district delayed the project eight months using a suspension of work order. The federal suspension of work clause was incorporated in an appendix to the district's contract. In the general terms and conditions, though, elements of permissible damages were limited to extra bonding and direct labor expenses, not overhead that is often part of these claims. The court found no conflict, holding that the district's clause remained an effective limitation on the recovery (*Calumet Construction Corp. v. Metropolitan Sanitation District of Northern Chicago*, 581 N.E.2d 206 (Ill. App. Ct. 1991)).

Liquidated Damages, Penalties, and Effect on Other Remedies

A liquidated damage clause is one that establishes a set amount or rate agreed by the parties payable as damages for certain delays or other contract breaches. The U.C.C. test for enforceability of liquidated damages clauses, e.g., whether the clause is a penalty instead of a reasonable estimation of damages, is generally the test for construction and service contract liquidated damages clauses as well. While liquidated damages commonly apply to delay, they can also be used for other performance deficiencies.

In an application of the "penalty" doctrine, *Boone Coleman Constr., Inc. v. Village of Piketon* (50 N.E.3d 502 (Ohio 2016)), an Ohio trial court found the rate of $700/day a penalty in a road construction case where the claim of 397 days of delay resulted in payment deductions that were one-third the value of the contract. The court noted the absence of testimony linking the daily damage to other than inconvenience; the road was still being used during the traffic signal installation at issue in the case. The Ohio supreme court reversed and remanded the case back to the court of appeals, holding that the lower court's focus on the aggregate amount of the damages was an error. Ohio courts had previously upheld liquidated damages clauses with daily amounts close to $700/day. The court further held that Ohio precedent requires a court to examine a liquidated damages provision in light of what the parties knew at the time the contract was formed.

Another issue with liquidated damages is whether their assessment is an exclusive remedy, or whether other contract remedies like termination for default can still be exercised. This is dependent on state law, but in Indiana, for example, the assessment of liquidated damages does not necessarily preclude later termination for default of a delayed project where parties intended to reserve the additional remedies.

Matters of Scope

There are two major issues involved in the scope of performance when considering post-contract-signing issues. First, the scope of the entity's obligation is discussed in the context of indefinite delivery contracts with an indefinite quantity. Second, there is a scope dimension to contract modifications.

Requirements Contracts

Blanket ordering and cooperative procurement agreements use a contract type known as an indefinite delivery contract, which is a contract in which the time of delivery is unspecified in the original contract but established by the procurement officer during contract performance. Under these agreements, supplies or services are furnished during a specified period with deliveries or performance scheduled by placing orders. The most common subtype is an indefinite delivery/indefinite quantity (IDIQ) contract where there is no fixed quantity in the contract. Typically, a public entity awards the master agreement with participating entities ordering from the agreement and becoming financially committed to the orders they place.

Almost universally, procurements of these master agreements do not commit any minimum quantity, although they often disclose potential volume based on historical usage or estimates. One issue that can arise is a claim by a contractor that they expected either a minimum quantity or that entities would satisfy all their requirements through the master agreement. For example, if one contracts with a lawn maintenance company for a minimum of five lawn mowings at a fixed price, that arrangement is known as a *minimum quantity contract.* If the buyer gets a deeper discount by agreeing to satisfy all mowing needs for the entire summer, an enforceable *requirements contract* has been entered.

Some contracts make it difficult to gauge the nature of the obligation. Courts try to construe agreements so there is consideration, that is, promises are not illusory. But a Rhode Island court rejected claims by a contractor that the contract was expected to be exclusive when the state used its own workforce to self-perform some of the work (*JPL Livery Services, Inc. v. Rhode Island Department of Administration*, 88 A.3d 1134 (R.I. 2014)). The JPL claim was based on a requirements contract theory. The agreement had a five-year term and a termination clause, but no estimates. The court found an enforceable contract existed but held that the department's obligation was only to exercise good faith, not order any specific amount of services.

Procurement professionals should be clear about the extent of the obligation. Specifying minimum quantities or implying that all requirements will be satisfied through a supplier may be legal consideration and lead to an enforceable contract. Unless an entity intends to commit to a requirements contract to achieve reduced pricing, they should avoid language that suggests any exclusivity in terms of satisfying its requirements though the contract.

Modifications and Contract Scope

Private parties can amend contracts any way they want. Governments, on the other hand, may be constrained by competition requirements where added work exceeds the "scope" of the contract.

The issue of contract scope arises in two contexts under federal procurement law. The first scope issue, the cardinal change, was discussed earlier in this chapter in connection with the changes clause. The other context of contract "scope" is whether a bilateral amendment to a contract is outside the scope of the contract and should be treated as a new procurement and competed under applicable procurement laws.

Under the law of federal government contracts, a modification is generally within the scope of the original procurement if potential offerors would have expected it under the contract's changes clause. A broad, original competition may validate a wider range of later modifications without another competition. The original solicitation language is important, including the breadth of stated objectives and any indication that the original work was expected to be expanded.

How Much Can an Option Be Revised?

In *Hanisco v. Township of Warminster* (41 A.3d 116 (Pa. Commw. Ct. 2012)), a Pennsylvania town awarded a waste services contract. The contract had a five-year term with options for two one-year extensions. The options were priced using a unit price based on waste volume.

Four years later, before the expiration of the contract, a public hearing before the supervisors was held and the waste services contract discussed. The supervisors noted that neighboring towns were paying less than the option price for similar trash and recycling services. At the meeting, it was suggested that advertising for a new waste hauling contract should be postponed until a meeting with the incumbent contractor. The supervisors authorized advertising for new bids if the meeting did not result in an acceptable reduction in the option price.

At the meeting, the contractor agreed to freeze the rates near current-year prices. The township and contractor executed an amendment that left the option-year prices the same in the contract but established a "rebate" that would reflect the agreed reduction. The supervisors voted to approve the amendment that exercised both of the option years in exchange for the rebate. The net result? The modified contract options achieved a 10% reduction in price.

Hanisco, the plaintiff, lived in the township and filed a complaint claiming that the township should be enjoined from exercising the options and required to competitively bid a new waste services contract. The trial court denied the request for injunctive relief, and Hanisco appealed.

The township argued that the amendment was a supplement to the existing contract, not a new contract. The township maintained that once a public contract has been lawfully awarded in accordance with

> competitive bidding, a lower price may be negotiated. The appellate court held against the township, however, concluding that "the decision not to advertise its waste services contract for competitive bidding has prevented the parties from knowing whether greater savings could have been achieved had the contract been rebid."

Including a changes clause is an effective way to maintain flexibility in contracts when requirements can be expected to change. But there may be limits on the ability to modify contracts when it looks to the industry and the courts like new work that should have been competed.

Inspection, Acceptance, and Warranties

A fundamental issue in contract administration is whether the work performed is adequate and payment is due. Where contracts do not provide otherwise, the U.C.C. has rules regarding the right to inspection, when acceptance occurs, the right to revoke acceptance, and a suite of implied warranties. Those rules only apply to sales and other transactions in goods, however. Where not addressed in the contract, overzealous or excessive inspection well beyond industry standards can lead to breach or constructive change claims by contractors.

The federal government is not subject to states' commercial codes, and the Federal Acquisition Regulation (FAR) has comprehensive clauses that also define the process and rights surrounding inspection and acceptance. These provisions are useful to procurement professionals because they provide a roadmap to developing clauses for contracts (such as services) not governed by the Uniform Commercial Code.

For example, the FAR Inspection of Construction clause (FAR §52.246–12) requires the contractor to maintain an adequate inspection system and make inspection records available to the government. The clause states that government inspections and tests are for the sole benefit of the government, and do not relieve the contractor of responsibility for providing adequate quality control or constitute acceptance of work, nor does the presence of a government inspector relieve the contractor from any contract requirement or authorize the inspector to change any term or condition (or specification). "Acceptance shall be final and conclusive except for latent defects, fraud, gross mistakes amounting to fraud, or the Government's rights under any warranty or guarantee."

The concept of latent defects—analogous to difficult-to-discover defects under the U.C.C.'s revocation of acceptance—also finds its way into state court opinions. A state court has held that where work was not performed according to the contract, and acceptance of the work and payment of the contract price was made by the public entity without knowledge of latent defects—those unknown and not discoverable by reasonable inspection—an action for breach of contract survives against a performance bond surety (*School Board of Pinellas County v. St. Paul Fire and Marine Insurance Co.*, 449 So.2d 872 (Fla. Dist. Ct. App. 1984)).

The content of warranties (if any) in other than U.C.C. sales of goods is defined exclusively by the contract. A Montana case, *Grass Range High School District No. 27 v. Wallace Diteman, Inc.* (465 P. 2d 814 (Mont. 1970)), illustrates how acceptance and warranty issues interplay. A school district contracted for construction of a gymnasium floor. Two warranty provisions were involved: a one-year warranty (from the date of final payment) by the contractor to remedy defects due to faulty material or workmanship, and a two-year warranty by the surety extending liability for latent defects.

Before acceptance and final payment, several problems with the concrete floor were noted. Notice had not been provided to the architect so she could be present at the pouring. Measurement of the flatness of the slab revealed depressions that later interfered with proper tile installation. Punch lists after final inspection required the contractor to fill and patch some hollows. A certificate of completion was then issued and final payment made.

Sixteen months after final payment, the district demanded correction of defects in the floor. The court held that the warranties did not apply to defects known at the time of final acceptance, and that any rights that existed as to defects known at the time of acceptance had been waived.

The right to inspect, the effect of acceptance, and the operation of warranties are dependent on the specific contract language. These issues may be among the most important to address up-front when writing solicitations and contracts.

Third-Party Beneficiaries and Subcontractors

In general, only a supplier or person having a contract with a public entity can claim breach of that contract. That relationship is known as privity of contract. There are rare exceptions when a person and not a party to a contract has contractual rights, a status known as a third-party beneficiary and described in Chapter 3.

Occasionally, direct subcontractor claims arise from nonpayment of the subcontractor, most commonly in construction contracts. When entities fail to require the prime contractor to obtain subcontractor payment bonds, under some states' statutes, the subcontractor or supplier may have a direct cause of action against the public entity if the prime contractor becomes insolvent.

Care is needed when communicating with subcontractor personnel during performance. Though rarely successful, the course of dealing could later be used to support a claim that a contract was intended between the subcontractor and government. The better practice is to communicate through the prime contractor. And in the case of construction, closely follow the requirements for payment bonds and legal processes for announcing final payment in order to give subcontractors and suppliers the opportunity provided by law to file administrative claims for nonpayment.

Contract Terminations

Enforceable contracts have performance obligations by both parties. Legally, neither can simply change its mind and refuse to perform. Rights and remedies are defined by common law unless the contracts have language to the contrary. Government contracts usually have two provisions that cover early terminations: termination for convenience and termination for default.

Termination for Convenience

The ebb and flow of changes in requirements for goods and services, funding limitations, and continuing advances in science and technology demand that the public entity possess the flexibility to terminate contracts, in whole or in part, when it is in the public interest to do so. The concept of contract termination for the convenience of the entity has evolved over time and is intended to protect the entity from unneeded acceptance of equipment, material, services, or supplies that no longer suit its needs or that have been made obsolete by advances in technology. Such a termination may be ordered when the public procurement professional determines that, usually for reasons other than the default of the contractor, it is in the entity's best interest to discontinue all, or some part, of the remaining work under the contract.

The termination for convenience clause permits the entity to discontinue performance of a contract with only limited liability. The clause states the basis for compensating the contractor—usually payment at contract rates for accepted work or allowable costs of performance and a reasonable profit. The clause has been used in federal contracting for decades (see FAR 52.249-2).

In a private contract, if a party attempts to terminate an agreement without a contractual right to do so, that party would be liable for breach of contract damages. The termination for convenience clause in a public entity contract converts what would otherwise be a breach into an administrative claim cognizable under the contract. Although a small number of contractors have appealed terminations for convenience, alleging bad faith or arbitrariness, they have been uniformly unsuccessful.

Absent bad faith, the public entity alone is the judge of its best interests in terminating a contract for convenience pursuant to the discretionary power reserved to the entity by the clause. In the absence of clear evidence to the contrary, it is presumed that public officials involved in the termination of the contractor's agreement were acting conscientiously in the discharge of their duties when the contract was terminated for the convenience of the entity. While motives are irrelevant to contract administration disputes in general, a bad faith termination for convenience can constitute a breach of contract by the entity. Anticipatory profits can then be recovered. A 2013 Florida case analyzed recent cases and concluded that bad faith could likely only be shown when the government enters into a contract with no intention of fulfilling its promises (*Handi-Van, Inc. v. Broward County*, 116 So. 3d 530 (Fla. Dist. Ct. App. 2013)). The preservation of the right to terminate for convenience is considered such an important public policy in the federal government that, if the mandatory clause is inadvertently omitted from a federal government contract, it is nonetheless construed as if it were included. This action—the clause being added by operation of law—is known as the Christian Doctrine (*G.L. Christian & Associates v. United States*, 312 F.2d 418 (Ct. Cl. 1963)). The doctrine is also applied in the District of Columbia.

Termination for Default

Most government contracts include a termination for default clause that permits the entity to terminate the contract if the contractor fails to perform the services within the time specified in the contract. Default can also be found when the contractor repudiates the contract by clearly expressing an intention not to perform ("anticipatory repudiation").

Typically, the termination of default clause requires the government to issue a cure notice (and the contractor an opportunity to cure) prior to exercising the right to terminate if the deficiencies can be corrected. The contractor is liable to the government for any excess costs incurred if the government must acquire services similar to those terminated. The clauses ideally have an explicit provision stating that if the termination for default is later overturned, then the termination is treated as one for convenience.

Courts have strictly construed the notice provisions in these clauses, meaning that a termination can be overturned for not furnishing the contractual notice. Another commonly litigated issue is the materiality of the default, where substantial performance is the measure of the obligation in services contracts when evaluating whether a breach warrants complete termination. Materiality is the test for the breach.

Procurement professionals should carefully define the role of third-party consultants during contract administration. The relative rights and obligations of parties to a construction contract are sometimes complicated by the role of third parties, e.g., the architect. In a Texas case, *Pelco Construction Co. v. Chambers County* (495 S.W.3d 514 (Tex. App. 2016)), the contractor had submitted applications for three progress payments. The architect certified two of the applications more than 30-days after submission by the contractor and only certified 90% of the amount due. In a lawsuit by Pelco, the court found that the county materially breached the contract's payment provisions because the architect was the county's agent.

Default terminations are very fact-specific. Procurement professionals must closely coordinate with their counsel to ensure that a defensible basis for termination exists. Moreover, they must carefully follow the procedural requirements in the contract. Finally, the termination provisions should be reviewed to ensure that default terminations found to be unsupported by the law are converted into terminations for convenience.

Waiver of Contract Requirements

Waiver is the intentional relinquishment of a known right—conduct that is inconsistent with the intent to assert the right. By accepting late performance or performance known to be deficient, a party may have waived the right to exercise some contract remedies. In a reversal of the usual waiver situation involving governments, a court has held that a contractor could not terminate a contract for default based on the county's failure to satisfy permitting conditions. The contractor had waived the requirement by performing despite the county's delay in approving permits (*Forsyth County v. Waterscape Serv., LLC*, 694 S.E.2d 102 (Ga. Ct. App. 2010)).

A New Jersey appellate court refused to enforce a contractual requirement for a board-approved change order when a contractor (the surety in a protracted construction dispute) performed work directed by the architect, and the board was apparently aware that the work was being performed (*American Motorists Ins. Co. v. N. Plainfield Bd. of Education*, A-4680–14T4 (N.J. Super. Ct. App. Div., Oct. 20, 2016)). This case also illustrates the reluctance of courts to deny contractor claims based on the government's defense that an agent has no authority.

Sometimes contracts include no waiver clauses that are used to reduce the risk of waiver. While the clauses may vary, they usually have language to the effect that the failure of a contracting party to enforce any right does not constitute a waiver of that right. A competing doctrine of estoppel could support a waiver claim, however, where conduct by a party is expected to be relied on by the other to their detriment. No waiver clauses may not entirely insulate a party from having waived a contract requirement, like schedule.

Waivers of schedule and delivery dates pose a special challenge. Once a delivery date is waived, a reasonable one must be established in order to execute remedies based on late performance. This is ideally done through a bilateral agreement, but the schedule can be established unilaterally so long as the new schedule is reasonable given the circumstances at the time it is reestablished. Counsel should be involved if the entity is forced to reestablish a reasonable schedule without the contractor's agreement.

The doctrine of estoppel can operate to waive performance dates (in particular) in termination for default situations. A common practice before terminating for default is to issue a *show cause* letter in order to assess whether the contractor has an excusable delay or other reasons for excusing a default. Where this investigation lasts for a limited time after a performance date has expired, waivers have not been found where the time is reasonable. However, some contracts contemplate *cure notices* before exercising termination for default remedies where defective performance can be corrected. A cure notice issued immediately before a performance due date or otherwise that is impossible to satisfy in the time permitted could be construed as a waiver of a due date where the contractor in reliance performs in order to avoid a termination for default. Procurement professionals should closely coordinate with legal counsel when considering terminations for default near the end of the performance period.

Liability Allocation Provisions

Some of the most contentious contract negotiations involve liability allocation. Broadly, liability allocation falls into three general categories: indemnification (or another party paying for litigation expenses and judgments), exclusion of damages (usually indirect damages like future lost profits), and other limitation of liability caps on damages under the contract. This section looks at the clauses from the perspective of contract administration—what happens to common law liability rules with these provisions.

Indemnification

Indemnification is an agreement of a contracting party to hold the other party harmless, to secure the other party against loss or damage, or to promise that the other party will be reimbursed in case of an anticipated loss. A hold harmless clause is very similar; it requires the contractor to assume liability for damages resulting from an action taken by the contractor and absolves the government or other contracting body from any responsibility for the consequences of the action. In some states' case law, there is a technical legal distinction in analyzing the clauses, but for purposes here, they are treated the same.

In general, governments are not liable to third parties for the acts of independent contractors. Even when a theory is pursued such as agency, attempting to make the government as principal liable for the acts of a contractor, most governments enjoy some governmental immunity for tort liability except as expressly waived by statute. Common waivers include injury from operation of government vehicles and dangerous conditions of public buildings and roads. Even when immunity is waived, there are often monetary limits to the amount of government liability. So many times, when governments are sued, there are various defenses. Still, the litigation costs can be sizable.

One area where governmental immunity does not operate is in constitutional torts: violations of Civil Rights provisions of the U.S. Constitution. Claims of employment discrimination, unlawful detention and excessive force fall into these categories, and are not barred by state and local government immunity. Some outsource contracts—private prison contracts, for example—can involve services that are particularly susceptible to these kinds of claims and can expose the public entity to litigation, even where they involve independent contractors. The litigation costs and potential liability risks account for the use of indemnification clauses.

Absent contractual indemnification, there are few "implied indemnification" situations where the law provides rights among contracting parties to seek reimbursement for liability because another was more responsible for causing the claim. Further, in the United States, the American Rule generally states that a party bears its own costs of litigation and attorney's fees, often the most sizable expense in defending against claims. Indemnification provisions commonly shift responsibility for paying those costs.

Most contracts of states, local governments, and institutions of higher education have a clause requiring the contractor to indemnify the government at minimum for claims based on personal injury (including death) and damage to tangible property arising out of the contractor's acts during performance. Other jurisdictions' indemnification provisions may be broader. Further, where intellectual property is a significant aspect of performance, the clauses require indemnification against third-party claims of infringement of intellectual property, including trade secrets. Common negotiation issues include supplier requests to limit indemnification to their own negligent or willful acts and exclusion of claims to the extent caused by the public entity.

Procurement professionals can expect contractors' counsel to want to negotiate reasonable provisions about control of litigation where the contractor is contractually required to defend the entity. Like the other topics about liability allocation in this chapter, legal counsel should be consulted—and they often lead—on these matters.

There is widespread agreement that there are legal limitations on a government's ability to indemnify or hold harmless contractors. In some states, the limitations are based on the statutory authority of government. In other states, the limitations are constitutional. In general, though, governments may not agree to indemnify or hold harmless a contractor absent specific legislative authority.

One synthesis of the law suggests that a public entity has no authority to agree to indemnify a contractor where it is 1) a contingent liability, 2) not merely incidental to the transaction, and 3) without legislative authorization. A contractual incentive provision authorizing additional payment by the public entity for a contractor's exceeding service level agreement standards, and a construction contract clause granting equitable adjustment for changes, are contingent liabilities, but are typically considered incidental to government contracts. Some states even statutorily authorize them. But an indemnification provision holding a contractor harmless from any third-party personal injury claims would not be incidental to the transaction. The contracting policy in most states prohibits indemnification of contractors by public entities.

Exclusion of Damages

Both the Uniform Commercial Code and common law have rules governing the nature of damages that can be recovered by a party suffering breach. General or direct damages are those that compensate for loss or injuries that actually occur and result from another's breach of contract. The measurement of direct contract damages from breach is defined in the Uniform Commercial Code, other statutes, and the common law. But often the measure of direct damages from breach of contract is euphemistically characterized as the "loss of the benefit of the bargain."

Contract provisions often exclude other categories of damages, notably incidental, consequential, indirect, and special. But definitions vary. For example, suppose that a retail store contracts at $1,000 for snow removal from a parking lot after a large snowstorm, and the snow removal company does not perform. Having to substitute a second company for $1,500 would have a clear measure of direct damage: $500. But the retailer may also lose thousands of dollars in sales. Depending on the state's laws, that damage could be recoverable as consequential, indirect, or special. Precision in language used in excluding damages under that state's laws would be needed for the supplier to avoid being liable for the retailer's lost profits.

Normally, it is not in the best interests of a public entity to exclude or limit damages for breach. When a supplier asks to negotiate exclusion of damages, the issue for practitioners is the absence of any national consistency about what these damage terms mean. For the procurement professional, with the assistance of their attorney, the key is making sure that any contract language excluding damages is clear, and significant potential risk is excluded from the clauses.

Other Limitations of Liability

Essentially, any exclusion of damages in a contract starts the process of limiting liability, usually of the contractor. In fact, the exclusion of damages can be the most significant limitation of liability because the caps placed on liability under a contract only apply to damages otherwise recoverable.

Caps on liability are generally opposed by governments; yet sometimes they are negotiated when industry practice and market conditions require. They are often expressed in one of three ways: a stated monetary limit, as in "contractor shall not be liable under this contract for an amount exceeding $1,000,000"; an amount based on past sales, e.g., the aggregate of sales under the contract over the past year; or an amount based on the total contract value.

The effects of these various types of clauses are too numerous to generalize. Entity counsel should be involved in their negotiation.

One special caution bears emphasis. Procurement professionals should use caution tying limitation of liability clauses to amounts paid under the contract. In the early stages of performance, that amount can be close to zero. That limitation can have the effect of eliminating the ability to recover damages under the contract where there is a breach or third-party claim soon after performance begins.

Contract Controversies

Sometimes disputes arise during contract performance that may require judicial resolution. Ideally, contracts have disputes elevation clauses that encourage resolution of disputes at the project level, with elevation or escalation of unresolved informal disputes to a higher management level before any formal disputes resolution action is initiated.

Contract provisions and legal requirements vary among jurisdictions, however. Many contracts have a formal disputes clause. These clauses (and other administrative dispute resolution processes) are often considered a legal precursor to initiating a lawsuit based on contract breach allegations. In some jurisdictions, the judicial doctrine of exhaustion of remedies—a legal requirement to exhaust available administrative remedies before filing a lawsuit—may be raised as a defense if a party has not availed itself of administrative remedies.

Even among states or local governments who have adopted the ABA Model Procurement Code, though, the statutory or ordinance provisions vary with respect to contract controversies. Generally, the codes require submission of the claim in writing. The procurement professional is given a specific period within which a decision must be made in writing unless the parties agree otherwise.

Then the contractor can usually appeal to a court or to an administrative appeals authority if one is established by the legislation. In some states, the contractor can file an administrative appeal and then file an action in court to challenge the administrative decision. Typically, there is no deference given by courts to public entity administrative decisions unless a formal administrative proceeding has been used for fact-finding (e.g., an Administrative Procedure Act process with an administrative law judge presiding), and the statutes or ordinances limit the judicial scope of review. Where an administrative law judge is used, courts usually defer to the judge's findings of facts.

For a public procurement professional, the entity's attorney will play a predominant role in disputes. Counsel should be consulted early when a likely, unresolvable dispute has surfaced.

Conclusion

Apart from protests against the solicitation or award, most legal issues that pose financial risk to a public entity arise during contract administration and spawn contract clauses to deal with that risk. An understanding of common liability scenarios informs the development and use of clauses in solicitations and contracts. Contract clauses permitting the entity to direct changes or suspend work provide useful flexibility, but raise questions about how to compensate the contractor for delay and other increased costs. The freedom to contract permits parties to frame their relationship, but even agreed-upon contract modifications are constrained in terms of scope by competition policies. Inspection, acceptance, and warranty clauses address legal issues in the finality of acceptance and rights that exist with respect to defective services. Termination provisions define rights surrounding situations where services are no longer needed or they are seriously deficient. Overlying contract administration is the prospect of waiving requirements where a party does not enforce them. Finally, procurement professionals need a basic understanding of various liability allocation principles in order to effectively work with legal counsel about how best to negotiate indemnification, exclusion of damages, and limitation of liability provisions.

For Further Reading

Cibinic, John, Ralph C. Nash, and James F Nagle. *Administration of Government Contracts.* Washington, DC: George Washington University, National Law Center, Government Contracts Program, 2006.

North Dakota Office of Management and Budget. "Contractual Risk." Risk Management Services. Accessed October 23, 2018. www.nd.gov/omb/agency/risk-management-services/contractual-risk.

Pennington, Richard. "State and Local Procurement Liability Allocation: Constitutional and Statutory Limitations: Government Article by Richard Pennington." Resource Government, October 16, 2008. www.resourcegovernment.com/articles/view.php?article_id=16513.

References

Note: The termination for convenience section of this chapter contains text from *Fundamentals of Federal Contract Law* by Eugene W. Massengale (1990) and has been used with permission of Greenwood Publishing Group, Inc. Westport, CT.

Conway, Danielle. *State and Local Government Procurement.* Chicago: American Bar Association, Section of State and Local Government Law, 2012.

Federal Transit Administration. "Pricing Guide for FTA Grantees." Text. Federal Transit Administration, March 14, 2016. www.transit.dot.gov/funding/procurement/third-party-procurement/pricing-guide-fta-grantees.

NASCIO. "Gaining Traction on the Road to Win-Win: Limitations on Liability in State IT Contracting." NASCIO.org, March 2010. www.nascio.org/Publications/ArtMID/485/ArticleID/180/Gaining-Traction-on-the-Road-to-Win-Win-Limitations-on-Liability-in-State-IT-Contracting.

U.S. Department of Housing and Urban Development. "Quick Guide to Cost and Prince Analysis for HUD Grantees and Funding Recipients." Housing and Urban Development. Accessed October 23, 2018. www.hud.gov/program_offices/cpo/grantees/cstprice.

Chapter 8

Legal Considerations in Information Technology Procurement

As the use of technology to perform public sector functions grows exponentially, the models used to acquire information technology (IT) are evolving. Traditional software purchases remain a central part of the procurement office toolkit, but other methods that challenge the traditional processes have emerged. Cloud computing, for example, is a service contract from which public entities may not own anything in the way of technology resources. Agile delivery methods are replacing some historical methods of large-contract IT procurement. Likewise, the federal government's promotion of modular procurement, breaking large system acquisitions into smaller pieces, creates opportunities for more suppliers while adding its own dimension of risk. As these developments evolved, so too have the potential legal issues.

Key Issues When Purchasing Software

Traditional software purchases acquire a license that provides a limited right to copy. Installation of software on a computer involves copying the operating code, a "work" that is protected by copyright law. As the second edition of this book asked, "What are the most important terms of a software contract? Is it the cost of the software? Is it the payment terms? Is it the license rights or the maintenance provisions?" It is critically important to any software procurement that the public procurement professional address all of the key terms necessary to protect the entity's investment and ensure a smooth, ongoing relationship between the public entity and the supplier.

License/Use Rights

Most software contracts do not transfer ownership. Instead, they license the right to use the software, and the software company retains ownership in the underlying intellectual property. Software is protected at least by copyright, although some suppliers obtain patent protection where there is a combination with hardware or processes meeting the patentability requirements for useful inventions or processes under U.S. patent law.

The distinctions between copyright and patent protection are of less importance to the procurement professional than obtaining the rights to use the software in the way needed. Software licenses use various terms like "install," "download," "reproduce," and "use" to describe the licensed rights. Many entities have general terms and conditions that cover most licensing situations.

There should be, as a minimum, a perpetual license right that covers the expected use of the software. The broadest, unrestricted license—virtually never granted in commercial software purchases—grants a nonexclusive, perpetual, irrevocable, worldwide, transferable, fully paid, royalty-free license to reproduce, modify, and distribute the software and use the deliverables without any restrictions, including the right to sublicense any or all such rights to third parties. Generally, commercial licenses offer only a subset of these rights.

Where there has been significant investment in software development, entities may seek ownership rights in the software and unlimited rights in associated data. Where ownership is not sought through assignment of rights, entities should consider whether to obtain the license right to prepare derivative works—the technical term for the right to modify the software (assuming the entity has sufficient documentation and know-how to modify it). Almost universally, commercial off-the-shelf software licenses do not grant the right to modify.

In licensed software, the public entity should ensure that there are no additional or hidden charges for moving the software, changing hardware or operating systems, etc. In a license known as an enterprise license, described and compared to other common license types in Chapter 1, the license can allow for use by anyone in the organization. Licenses may limit use for internal government purposes only, and entities may want to define transferability rights, e.g., to other government entities. Licenses also may limit use in terms of numbers of people, specific names or job titles, or use for specific purposes.

Contract Types

Clearly, the cost of the software is where many procurement professionals focus their attention, as it is initially the highest cost element of the procurement. Commercial software is sold with a firm, fixed-price. With some research, the procurement professional can obtain market cost information (such as amounts others are paying for the same or similar software) in order to determine whether the supplier is offering the software at a fair price. There are various pricing structures, some depending on volume, and commercial advisory services are available to assist public entities in planning their use of enterprise-wide licensing and the most favorable contract types.

For customized software implementations, suppliers may propose "time and materials" pricing. This type of contract places cost risk on the entity. Configuration of software involves less effort, usually setting of product parameters in the software to adapt the software to a customer's use. Some configuration may be included in the software price. Customization (if available at all), on the other hand, involves more effort and uncertainty than configuration; it can involve recoding (reprogramming) some of the software. Customization is discouraged because the software may be difficult to maintain. Where customization is needed, time-and-material contracting poses significant cost risk for the entity.

Payment Issues

Previously, most software suppliers accounted for all the sales revenue at the time of agreement. Because of a number of changes in accounting practices, however, software suppliers have transitioned to recognizing the revenue as it is received, or as certain implementation milestones are reached that give the supplier a firm entitlement to payment. Accounting practices may explain software suppliers' resistance to deferred payments and some warranty terms.

Where there is configuration or customization involved, payments may be based on the supplier's achievement of defined milestones, with final payment due when the software is fully operational. Alternatively, retention of a percentage of price can sometimes be negotiated and released on final acceptance.

Software Warranties

Warranty provisions give rights to the public entity with respect to defects in the software discovered after delivery or acceptance. Warranty provisions can be separate from those defining the supplier's obligation to maintain the software, but supplier practices vary and must be understood. Commercial software purchases will only include the warranties that exist in the product documentation, and they cannot typically be negotiated for off-the-shelf purchases.

Warranties of functionality are often ambiguous and can be improved by promising for a defined period that the software materially conforms to technical specifications or product documentation. Where services are performed in connection with the software installation, the contracts sometimes warrant that the professional services will be performed in a professional and workmanlike manner. The specific content of those warranties would be governed by state law and proven in a dispute using experts (reinforcing the need to have subject matter experts involved during negotiation of warranties). However, implied warranties are commonly expressly disclaimed by suppliers using language consistent with the Uniform Commercial Code even though the contract (if a service) may not be U.C.C.-governed.

Sometimes warranties are defined by service level agreements, discussed later in this chapter, or separately purchased maintenance agreements. Warranties ideally run from the date of system acceptance when services are involved, but some end user agreements begin their term at the date of installation or even earlier. Practitioners must carefully analyze how the various license and warranty terms work together to grant a remedy for defects.

A warranty does not usually promise indefinitely that the software has any specific performance characteristic. They are time-limited and primarily operate to shift some legal risk to the supplier for the correction of certain defects. The remedies granted in a software warranty often provide the supplier with considerable discretion to choose among the remedies of correction, refund, or credits against future payments. They may limit payment to a pro rata amount or possibly a full refund. In most cases, the warranties' language makes them the exclusive remedy and eliminates actions for breach of contract and damage claims for the covered defect.

Maintenance

Over time, maintenance can become the highest overall cost in the total life cycle cost of the software. The initial license is typically perpetual, but without contractual language stating otherwise, the perpetual license only extends to what was delivered. Software maintenance costs are a key revenue and profit producer for software suppliers. Maintenance costs should be a topic in market research.

The contract or supplier's documentation defines what is included as maintenance. Access to updates is usually included, although receipt of new releases may require additional payment. Contracts should address both the entitlement to updates and the timing and method for their delivery. Contracts should define support for prior releases, error/bug corrections, problem priority level definitions (severe, critical, moderate, etc.), and response and resolution times according to priority level. Another important issue is the time when maintenance begins, especially in relation to warranty provisions.

In addition, the agreement should provide the public entity with remedies in the event of less-than-warranted performance by the supplier. These might include a prorated refund of the maintenance fees paid for a given portion of the maintenance period if, for example, the supplier misses a service level over a defined period of time. It is common for suppliers to resist refunds and instead offer credits toward future payments or purchases.

Open Source Software

A license type that has emerged since the last edition of *Legal Aspects* is open source licensing. It is not public domain software that can be freely used and modified without restriction. Open source software has license terms even though the source code is freely distributed and can be modified. Some care is needed when using open source software.

The industry has evolved standard open source license terms that can be accessed online. Some of the least restrictive open source licenses are BSD-type and MIT licenses, developed out of Berkley Software Distribution of Unix and the Massachusetts Institute of Technology. The Mozilla Public License is widely accepted as "friendly" to software developers, although it is slightly more restrictive. The GNU General Public License, sponsored by the Free Software Foundation, provides a bridge to the Linux operating system. GNU's license terms are complex and prohibit incorporation into proprietary programs.

Some licenses, however, may have terms that require entities to use an open source model if they redistribute the open source software. This type of license can operate like a "viral" application and can have adverse implications for any public entities who further distribute the software. Procurement professionals should consult counsel with questions regarding the terms of these licenses.

To avoid unintended licensing problems, consider requiring offerors in solicitations to disclose any third-party license terms, including the use of open source software. Obligations under these licenses should not be ignored just because they are free. Open source software usually comes with warranty disclaimers and is provided "as is." Further, the licenses sometimes require flow-down notices, e.g., warranty disclaimers, if the software is further distributed. Public entities have IT asset management practices, such as inventories, and open source software should be included. IT professionals and legal counsel can assist with these licensing strategies and issues.

Software publishers are moving away from the traditional licensing model. What was born as packaged, shrink-wrapped software with licenses and maintenance has grown to as-a-service models available "in the cloud."

Procurement of Information Technology in the "Cloud"

The new method of software (and associated infrastructure) procurement is "cloud computing," where usual ownership and licensing concerns generally do not apply. Procurement professionals must have a basic technical understanding of cloud computing in order to appreciate the legal issues that are involved.

Cloud is a model for enabling convenient, on-demand network access by a browser to a shared pool of computing resources (e.g., networks, servers, storage, applications, and other services) that can be rapidly provisioned and released. In most commercial cloud applications, costumers get the right to use the services, but they have no access to the software program. Apart from systems specially developed for public entities as cloud deployments, commercial cloud service providers retain all right, title, and interest in the cloud system.

The National Institute of Standards and Technology (NIST) defines cloud computing deployment models: public (accessible to the public and usually shared), private (restricted to a single enterprise), community (shared by government entities having common performance, data, and security needs), and hybrids of those categories. The procurement planning done by public procurement professionals applies equally in cloud computing solicitations. In many instances, though, there is little or no opportunity to negotiate terms and conditions when procuring commercial cloud services because they are standard packages offered to multiple clients.

There are three service models of cloud computing: Software as a Service (SaaS), Platform as a Service (PaaS), and Infrastructure as a Service (IaaS). Common office software suites and email applications are examples of SaaS. End users worldwide can access office applications with a browser and without loading any other software on the client machine. PaaS platforms permit remote access to systems having integrated operating systems and more sophisticated applications—development platforms for programmers, for example. End users and developers can access tools for configuring other applications, creating workflow, and developing reports and databases. IaaS permits access to hardware such as storage, servers, and disaster recovery resources.

Public clouds are largely subscription-based. Their costs can often be charged as operating expenses instead of capital expenditures that may require separate appropriations and oversight. Coupled with the other advantages of cloud—on-demand capability, ease of scalability, and expected cost efficiencies because of the shared use of resources by many end users—the solutions have become very popular.

Public clouds are widely considered not suitable for sensitive information or mission-critical applications. Access using a variety of devices—desktop computer, notebook computer, and smart phone technology—further raises the specter of security breach and privacy compromise. The risk of supplier failure, for example, in critical systems can best be mitigated by the use of competitive sealed proposal practices where financial responsibility is evaluated. Other contract issues like liability allocation are very similar where cloud services contracts can be negotiated, but unfortunately, routine commercial cloud solutions do not provide that opportunity. This section summarizes some key legal risks unique to cloud computing that can possibly be negotiated, or at least should be considered, when subscribing to cloud services.

Internal and External Security Risks

Depending on the expected use of the system, various laws are implicated that affect public procurement. The security risks summarized here are present not just in cloud solutions, but other IT implementations discussed in this chapter. Their relevance has been magnified by cloud deployments.

The Gramm-Leach-Bliley Act is a federal statute governing data security in financial institutions, e.g., credit card transactions. The Health Insurance Portability and Accountability Act of 1996 (HIPAA) governs collection, storage, and release of medical information. The Federal Bureau of Investigation has security policies protecting the storage and transmission of criminal justice information. The 2002 Federal Information Security Act requires federal agencies to develop and implement information security and protection programs. Some elements of those programs may find their way into security requirements imposed on federally funded grantees.

States also have laws covering storage of personally identifiable information (PII). PII is commonly defined as information that can be used to trace an individual's identity—name, Social Security number, and date and place of birth, for example—and other information linked to individuals like credit card numbers and medical, employment, and educational records. The laws establish requirements for operation of the information systems: authentication practices, encryption, password protocols, education and training, and information security programs.

States have various notification requirements when PII is inadvertently disclosed through data breach: hacking or even loss or theft of tangible property like computers, documents, and storage media (CDs and flash drives). State statutes differ in this regard, but typically require the responsible party to notify affected individuals and in some cases even provide credit monitoring. Care should be taken with respect to limitation of liability and indemnification clauses that can expose the public entity to greater risk. One federal court has held that under Georgia law a consequential damages exclusion in a contract precluded recovery of damages relating to a data breach. Counsel should be involved in assessing risk from those provisions and negotiating them (when negotiation is possible).

Procurement professionals would not be the office of primary responsibility for these requirements; IT professionals should be familiar with them. In public cloud services, suppliers will rarely negotiate changes to their systems, but entity personnel—the business process owner, chief information officer, finance, separate security offices if not part of the CIO's office, along with the chief procurement officer—would have to evaluate available information to determine whether the system meets the entity's security requirements. In negotiated cloud solutions, legal counsel could assist in solicitation and contract development to ensure that requirements are adequately specified and flowed down to subcontractors.

Cloud Outages, Loss Risks, and Data Protection

As public entities move more applications into the cloud, disaster recovery is increasingly becoming a critical issue. The risk is avoided by being judicious about moving critical data/infrastructure to the cloud and using first-class suppliers. While there may be little opportunity to negotiate some cloud agreements, assessment of the risk from disaster remains a consideration about whether to use a cloud solution.

Disaster response commitments may be defined by a supplier's disaster response plan that, ideally, can be reviewed. The content of the disaster response obligations includes both prevention and response provisions that can range from a promise to use best efforts to restore the system to supplier commitments to maintenance of duplicate systems in a separate geographical location. Again, IT professionals and the business process owner will be central to reviewing contract or other service-use language or negotiating more robust disaster recovery provisions to ensure they are consistent with the entity's business continuity plan.

Supplier Lock-In and Failure

Reliance on a single supplier throughout a system's lifecycle is a risk for all IT implementations, especially so with business processes deployed on commercial cloud platforms. Supplier lock-in is part of a larger challenge of disengagement and transferability of data.

The first line of defense against supplier failure is robust source selection procedures, such as past-experience evaluation and financial analysis. Subject matter experts like IT professionals should be used in evaluations. Public entity financial and accounting professionals may be available to assist in some aspects of the analysis. Sometimes, the information about cloud solution suppliers is not publicly available, however. As such, competitive sealed proposal processes can be helpful in large, critical infrastructure projects.

Supplier lock-in is also a risk when the data cannot be easily integrated with other cloud applications. This risk can be mitigated by contracting with suppliers who use industry-recognized, service-oriented architecture and accepted interoperability standards.

The right supplier is one who uses third-party-validated best practices in security, is financially stable, has demonstrated experience and a solid portfolio of satisfied clients, and who uses well-recognized standards to avoid integration and portability problems. IT departments must be part of the planning in these kinds of procurements.

Data Management

Disentanglement from single suppliers is an issue related to supplier lock-in. As the *Center for Digital Government's Best Practice Guide* observes, public cloud models are attractive

> because they allow rapid provisioning of applications. . . . This may mean moving data and applications between service providers. As cloud-driven service models proliferate, it will be important for

government agencies to be prepared for smooth disengagement and reengagement between service providers.

Cloud solutions and contracts must provide for these capabilities and the ability to migrate data.

Other data management requirements can be specified that control the location of storage and destruction of data. Moreover, because public entities have certain discovery responsibilities when faced with litigation, the cloud contract provisions should cover litigation-hold scenarios. A litigation-hold letter may be sent by entity legal counsel and direct the entity to suspend routine records and email destruction when litigation is filed, threatened, or reasonably anticipated. The supplier may not expect to incur those expenses, so the standard subscription agreement should be reviewed to make sure there is at least a mechanism for addressing litigation holds and the related expense.

Access to data by the supplier's subcontractors may also be an issue. Subscription or negotiated agreements should define the circumstances under which the cloud supplier can grant access to the public entity's data. Ideally, the contract would require that the supplier include data management clauses, e.g., a requirement to store data in the United States, in its subcontracts. These clauses are "flowed-down" to the subcontractor. The provisions help ensure that subcontractors are aware of and meeting the cloud service provider's obligations and limits on data use.

Service Level Agreements

Service level agreements (SLAs) may be found in both cloud subscriptions and negotiated professional services contracts for large IT system implementations. SLAs may not be a separate agreement. In some cases, they are incorporated in other contracts, online subscription agreements, or even separately negotiated maintenance agreements.

SLAs define the minimum standards for services, such as limits on system downtime. They may also specify the times for downtime during which the cloud system is maintained. They can define the minimum response times for responding to reports of defects, speed of performance, and expectations regarding the correction of technical failures. Typically, suppliers resist refunds of payments for breach of SLAs, but they may agree to credits on future payments.

In most commercial cloud applications, there is little opportunity to negotiate SLA terms. In fact, many cloud services agreements permit the cloud supplier to unilaterally change SLA terms with or without prior notice. The enforceability of unilateral change provisions is unclear and dependent on individual state law. For example, a Texas federal district court invalidated a contract containing a mandatory arbitration provision where the contractor had reserved the right to unilaterally modify the terms of an online video rental agreement. Other courts are more tolerant of changes to online terms-of-use agreements.

Legal counsel, IT professionals, and the business process owner—who may be the chief information officer in enterprise-wide applications—should be consulted in assessing the risks in online SLAs that cannot be negotiated.

Other legal issues can arise that are not discussed here. Online subscription agreements can attempt to limit supplier risk and customer rights in cases of bankruptcy and insolvency, mergers and acquisitions, and a public entity's facing litigation and having e-discovery obligations. Counsel can help explain the operation of those provisions and how they affect the rights and obligations of parties that would otherwise exist.

Procurement "in the cloud" involves different legal issues from traditional software licensing. Likewise, multimillion-dollar software integration and professional IT service contracts have other legal issues that are unique to information technology procurement.

Other Legal Issues in IT Professional Services Contracts

In large IT system implementations—enterprise resource planning (ERP), eProcurement systems, or hybrid cloud solutions, for example—procurement and contract administration issues are similar to those in any large service contract. The term "professional service contract" is used for purposes of this discussion to distinguish them.

In 2013, the California State Controller published a task force report, *Recommendations to Improve Large Information Technology Procurements: A Road Map for Success in California*, that identified best practices in large system IT procurements. Supplier selection is a key element in successful IT implementations, and the report makes recommendations that address other legal issues not highlighted here.

The other topics discussed in this chapter are worthy of consideration in any IT professional services contract. For example, the cloud computing discussion of SLAs is relevant. Discussed later, Agile's use of issue escalation mirrors a recommendation in the California task force report. This section highlights four other significant legal issues encountered when procuring large IT systems.

Ownership Versus License Rights

Where there has been significant investment in software development, public entities often face the question of whether to own or simply license the intellectual property in software.

In federally funded acquisitions, the Federal Uniform Guidance does not require transfer of ownership rights. It requires license rights to be transferable. Called "intangible property" in the rules at 2 C.F.R. Part 200, when copyright (i.e., ownership) is vested in another, the non-federal awarding entity "reserves a royalty-free, nonexclusive and irrevocable right to reproduce, publish, or otherwise use the work for Federal purposes, and to authorize others to do so." Even outside of the grant context, federal policy may offer ideas for allocating rights in computer software in public entity boilerplate. 48 C.F.R. §27.404–2 sets out the rights in computer software under federal government contracts: limited rights and restricted rights. The federal government requires identification during the solicitation process of the rights being claimed by the offeror. Even for rights otherwise characterized as limited or restricted, though, the federal government retains unlimited rights in data describing functional characteristics and performance requirements (but excluding source code and flow charts of the software).

State and local government procurements of commercial software would be analogous to the federal government's retention of only restricted rights in software developed at private expense. The supplier owns the copyright, and the related data is considered a trade secret and proprietary. California uses an approach similar to the federal government—its clauses retain government-purpose rights in preexisting materials that are developed or otherwise obtained by or for a contractor independently of the contract with the public entity.

Procurement professionals encountering these issues must seek the advice of legal counsel to effectively define the respective rights in the software and associated documentation.

Software Escrow

When entities acquire total ownership of software solutions, they also procure the programming code and documentation necessary to maintain them. Where they only license software, however, they do not have the rights or documentation to maintain them—a potential risk to critical IT systems. Sometimes, software escrow is used to ensure adequate protection where a supplier owning the system may become insolvent or otherwise no longer performs.

Software escrow is a contract provision (or separate agreement) that uses a third party as a depository of the supplier's source code for safeguarding. Source code is the human-readable code used to develop software that is not provided with traditional software licenses but is needed to maintain or modify it. The escrow agent is compensated and is often a commercial entity specializing in software escrow. The agreement specifies the events and procedure for permitting entity access to the source code.

Escrow issues are more common in large system implementations involving software licensing for applications supporting critical infrastructure and business processes. Sometimes third-party suppliers have software publisher certifications or other capability to maintain these systems. Software escrow, however, is another contractual tool for mitigating this risk. Attorney advice is especially important when negotiating contracts with suppliers of critical systems where the entity does not own the software.

Contract Changes and Change Control

Change happens in large system implementations. With the time between planning and completion of implementation often measured in years, the vast majority of IT implementations face changing requirements. This brief discussion of changes does not address the larger change management issues—such as internal resistance to change—that often pose as significant a challenge to large IT implementations. This discussion uses the term "change control" to refer to the management of changes in requirements that may be compensable or lead to claims.

The client agency may not know exactly what it wants during initial planning, and its processes may not be perfectly understood or described in contract specifications. Entities may not understand precisely what is being offered in a proposal at the proposed price. Suppliers have often incorporated a "discovery" phase in the early stage of contract performance in their proposals. What is not always clear is whether the outcomes of discovery are intended to result in compensable change, or the public entity expects the contractor to absorb the risk of cost impacts from what it discovers. The other issue with change orders is the speed at which governance bodies approve them.

So, what can be done to mitigate the effects of unanticipated changes? Entities need a clearer understanding and statement of their business requirements in the solicitation. Ambiguous or incorrect statements of business requirements lead to price contingencies in proposals.

To gain a better picture of what the supplier is offering, a best practice that has emerged in RFPs is the use of requirements checklists. RFPs using them ask that key features of the proposed solution be identified with descriptors such as "provided," "provided through configuration," "provided through customization," and "not provided." The proposal explains which are provided at additional cost, and which are included in the proposed price. Further, use of demonstrations can paint a better picture of an existing system's current capabilities and the amount of customization that might be required. Furthermore, the RFP discussion process can sharpen the understanding of requirements and proposals by both the public entity and the supplier. If performance requirements are priced using labor hour assumptions or not-to-exceed amounts, for example, they can be identified and clarified during the discussion process.

Explicit authority limits regarding change must be defined, and where governance bodies are part of the change control process, assumptions should be stated regarding the time within which decisions must be made. Procurement professionals, their legal counsel, IT professionals, and business process owners need to be clear about the expectations and process for change in large IT system implementations.

Notice of Changes

As Chapter 7 advised, provisions requiring written notice of changes by contractors claiming adjustments in price or schedule can protect an entity from unexpected claims. These claims often arise from a lack of transparency. The government client simply does not have visibility into how the contractor is proceeding and what it sees as a change to requirements. Sometimes, project personnel of both the contractor and entity ignore the potential effects of disagreements about requirements.

Processes must be in place to monitor communications between contractors and entity project personnel to avoid later claims of constructive changes. A notice of changes clause in a contract is an additional protection.

Professional services contracts for large system implementations have special challenges, the likelihood of change among the most significant. The uncertainty of requirements and the prospects for change have led to the latest developments in IT procurement: Agile and modular procurements.

Modular Procurement and Agile Project Delivery

It's been widely reported that 80–90 percent of large IT implementations are not achieving expectations, with some third or more outright failures. There is a widely held acknowledgement that a different approach is needed for requirements that are subject to so much uncertainty and change. Agile and modular procurement are evolving approaches to address weaknesses in traditional IT project delivery, increasingly known as "waterfall" delivery. "Waterfall" delivery involves lengthy planning followed by complex, long-term contracts with a single supplier, and implementation often stretching over years and facing contract changes and sometimes contentious government-contractor relationships.

Modular Delivery

The U.S. Office of Management and Budget promotes modular development as

> a more nimble approach to IT contracting. With well-understood system requirements and known system architecture, contracts can be broken down into more manageable chunks. Smaller contracts can be delivered using agile project methods, where orders are placed against contracts as the need arises. Discrete business requirements can be delivered sequentially or in parallel, using single or multiple contractors. Overall system acquisition is simplified through this iterative process. Modular and interoperable business solutions are delivered quickly, with reduced project risk.

Modular procurement breaks down the size of implementations, increasing opportunities for small companies, making contracts shorter, and reducing risk by not relying on single-solution all-or-nothing contracts and implementations.

From a legal perspective, modularity faces some important issues. One is ensuring that interfaces have been adequately defined in the contract that are widely known by industry so the handoffs between suppliers occur seamlessly and systems are interoperable. Another likely contract requirement is transition assistance for other contractors providing integrated modules. And documentation is needed that is adequate to perform later work.

Along with modularity, a project delivery method that is emerging is Agile project delivery. Agile promises to better address the challenges of changing requirements.

Agile Project Delivery

Agile was born as an iterative software development method used in projects having significant uncertainty about requirements and solutions. Iterative project delivery approaches like Agile essentially do away with "waterfall" implementations. Agile includes planning, execution, testing, and closure within rapid, successive iterations, phases, or cycles, each of which delivers useful software.

While traditional project delivery is still used when requirements are reasonably certain, Agile is promoted where there is a likelihood of significant change. Agile requires close involvement of customers during iterations/cycles as requirements are clarified. Agile project delivery reflects the fluidity of requirements development and places schedule at the forefront. The Agile Manifesto frames the philosophy behind Agile development. Among the central guiding principles in Agile are an emphasis on valuing customer collaboration over negotiation, responding to change over following a plan, and working software over documentation.

Development and testing cycles are very short, sometimes as short as a week. When Agile practitioners discuss the triple constraints of project management—schedule, cost, and scope—they conclude that scope is the easiest to change. Deliverable cycles known as "sprints" deliver usable code, although the deliverables are not necessarily "deployable code," especially in complex applications that defer deployment until scheduled releases. Requirements are defined by the customer's end user "stories" that explain needed functionality. Traditional performance-based statements of work are not used, and solicitations and requirements may read more like statements of objectives. Resources and schedules are developed using estimates based on complexity, sometimes known as "story points."

Agile delivery methods require a new perspective on contract management. Decisions about features and other scope tradeoffs happen quickly. So, the government customer must clothe contract administrators with adequate authority and ensure that contractually defined approaches exist for elevating decisions efficiently to approval authorities where needed.

California's Agile Child Welfare Information System Procurement

The State of California used Agile procurement of its child welfare information system. The state first established a prequalified supplier pool. Suppliers on the state's multiple award schedules were eligible to be prequalified.

A supplier profile questionnaire was used to obtain the relevant information to assess qualifications. Much of the experience and technical information was like that requested in more traditional RFPs. However, technical assessments were framed by the functioning prototypes that suppliers were required to provide and a narrative description of their technical approach to creating the prototype.

A prototype repository of documents was available for state review. The documents included source code and associated documentation. The deposited documents described the collaborative approach to development using Agile processes in the U.S. Digital Services Playbook. The instructions defined the various labor categories within the scope of the supplier pool. The process includes periodic refresh of the qualified supplier pool.

After supplier qualification and selection, departments are able to develop and release requests for offers (RFOs) to the prequalified suppliers. The offers are firm for not less than 90 days. The offers are assessed against criteria in the RFO. An updated responsibility determination is performed by the state agency and a contract executed.

California legal counsel were centrally involved with the development of the process and contract terms and conditions. As one can imagine, both technical and legal expertise were needed to adapt the Agile process to the statutes and regulations governing procurement.

While many contracting issues remain the same—liability allocation terms, for example—others are different. The whole premise for Agile development is that requirements in most respects are unknown and are clarified during project delivery. This method of contracting requires an adjustment in historical ways of viewing contracts. While Agile is an overall approach with varying implementation methodologies, the representative issues identified here are based on the Agile contracting model described by Opelt et al. (2013).

- **Supplier Selection**. Scope and final fixed price are not set until well into project execution. Selection processes may use prototyping, where suppliers who are short-listed may participate in a limited number of sprints before the final selection.
- **Trust, Contracts, and the Obligation of Good Faith and Fair Dealing**. Some contractual terms and conditions addressing trust read much like team norms. These contract terms can sound like precatory language, e.g., "we agree to work together and build trust in one

another and each other's expertise." If the relationship breaks down, it is likely that a party's satisfaction of the "trust" obligations would be legally measured only by the obligation of good faith and fair dealing if specific cooperation obligations are not spelled out.

- **Contract Type and Pricing**. Agile contracts use a hybrid contract type, not a firm, fixed-price contract in the classic sense. A provisional or indicative price is set based on available information, such as end user stories, with adjustments made as more is learned about requirements. Workshops can be held during the solicitation process to gain a fuller understanding of requirements before award. After award, some learning occurs during early sprints, and a fixed-price range is agreed to. The model can use a shared savings ratio as an incentive. If costs are less than the lower limit of the agreed fixed-price range, the contractor can receive an agreed incentive share. Likewise, a formula for sharing cost overruns can be used.
- **Changes**. The preferred way to address change is to adjust the scope, either in the current sprint or in later sprints for end user stories in the backlog. A "change for free" clause is used in Agile contracts to permit new features to be added if others of equal scope are removed. Procurement professionals, their counsel, and the suppliers need to clarify operation of these provisions.
- **Software Documentation**. In Agile development, the documentation strategy is "just enough." There are software documentation practices that can be standardized across suppliers, and a contractual means of identifying and prescribing the use of these documentation standards is important, both for product documentation and handoff documentation if different suppliers are involved. Suppliers need to see the code they have to integrate with. IT professionals must steer project documentation requirements.
- **Acceptance and Payment**. The acceptance approach in the Agile methodology known as Scrum is built around a Definition of Done in the contract that includes code quality (i.e., completion of testing) and functionality as components. Some thought needs to be given to ensuring that the project modules are integrated before final acceptance. Contracts may use payment retention until final acceptance.
- **Warranties**. Incremental delivery adds complexity to warranties. When do they begin? Waiting until the end for the warranty to begin may make sense in a fully integrated solution. Where individual components are being used by the public entity after sprint deliveries, however, there may be a need to begin warranty periods at different times.

- **Issue/Dispute Escalation**. Agile contracts may use a scope steering group above the customer and contractor project teams, as well as an executive steering committee as a second level. The steering group is used for escalation of issues that cannot be resolved at the project level. The escalation process advocated by some Agile experts involves eventual use of a third-party "expert," serving not as an arbitrator, but more as a third-party mediator to provide expertise and opinions to the steering groups/committees regarding an issue not resolved at the project level. Some clarity is required about the role of the expert and whether there are other remedies in the event of a dispute.
- **Termination**. Agile contracting uses a series of exit strategies. Agile contracts are not multi-year, committed relationships, and there is usually a "checkpoint" milestone at which a customer (and sometimes the contractor) can elect to terminate. A number of short sprints, however, can be identified as the minimum committed period, before which neither can terminate. Typical termination for convenience clauses may not be adequate to define this exit right.

As can be seen, the Agile method of project delivery has potential to address fundamental shortcomings of the historical waterfall approach to large system implementations. But to adapt the model to public procurement, some innovative and nontraditional contract management practices will have to be used. Perhaps most importantly, government customers must understand and commit to a level of engagement not seen before.

Conclusion

Once one gets beyond purchasing off-the-shelf software, it becomes even more important that procurement professionals collaborate with IT professionals, business process owners, and legal counsel. Cloud computing has moved away from traditional intellectual property concepts toward service-oriented cloud solutions. While online subscription of software-as-a-service in the cloud may not permit negotiation, an understanding of more sophisticated IT concepts and related legal issues is required for assessing the relative merits and risks of those and other cloud solutions. And the recent evolution of modular and Agile project delivery is illuminating different twists on legal issues that also require the advice and involvement of all these professionals, but at speeds never before encountered.

For Further Reading

Asner, Michael. *The Request for Proposal Handbook.* 2nd ed. New York: McGraw-Hill, 2000.

Cibinic, John, Ralph C. Nash, and Christopher R. Yukins. *Formation of Government Contracts.* 4th ed. Washington, DC: George Washington University Law School, Government Contracts Program, 2011.

Conway, Danielle. *State and Local Government Procurement.* Chicago: American Bar Association, Section of State and Local Government Law, 2012.

Defense Acquisition University. "Contract Pricing Reference Guides (CPRG)." Defense Acquisition University, September 9, 2014. www.dau.mil/tools/t/Contract-Pricing-Reference-Guides-(CPRG).

NASPO. "NASPO Guide to International Trade Agreements." Accessed October 23, 2018. www.naspo.org/ita/index.html.

———. *State and Local Government Procurement: A Practical Guide.* Lexington, KY: NASPO, 2019.

Pennington, Richard. "Agile: A New Frontier for Contract Management." Contract Management, July 2018. www.ncmahq.org/stay-informed/cm-magazine/article/august-2018/agile-a-new-frontier-for-contract-management.

———. "Comparative Review of State IT Procurement Practices." NASPO IT Procurement Work Group, September 2010. http://conference.naspo.org/dnn/portals/16/documents/NASPO_IT_Procurement_Whitepaperfinal2.pdf.

References

American Bar Association. *The 2000 Model Procurement Code for State and Local Governments.* Chicago: American Bar Association, 2000.

Commonwealth of Massachusetts. *A Guide to Massachusetts Public Records Law.* Secretary of the Commonwealth, Division of Public Records, 2017. www.sec.state.ma.us/pre/prepdf/guide.pdf.

Commonwealth of Virginia. "1VAC30-130-10. Agency Procurement and Surplus Property Manual (Filed by Description with the Registrar of Regulations)." 2017. https://law.lis.virginia.gov/admincode/title1/agency30/chapter130/section10/.

———. "IT Procurement Manual—VITA." Accessed October 23, 2018. www.vita.virginia.gov/supply-chain/scm-policies-forms/it-procurement-manual/.

Federal Transit Administration. "Best Practices Procurement & Lessons Learned Manual (Report 0105)." Text. Federal Transit Administration, September 28, 2015. www.transit.dot.gov/funding/procurement/third-party-procurement/best-practices-procurement-manual.

———. "Pricing Guide for FTA Grantees." Text. Federal Transit Administration, March 14, 2016. www.transit.dot.gov/funding/procurement/third-party-procurement/pricing-guide-fta-grantees.

Nyden, Jeanette, Kate Vitasek, and David Frydlinger. *Getting to We: Negotiating Agreements for Highly Collaborative Relationships.* 1st ed. New York: Palgrave Macmillan, 2013.

Office of the New York State Comptroller. "Search Comptroller's Bid Protest Decisions." Accessed October 23, 2018. http://wwe1.osc.state.ny.us/Contracts/decisionsearch.cfm.

Opelt, A., B. Gloger, W. Pfari, and R. Mittermayr. *Agile Contracts: Creating and Management Successful Projects with Scrum*. Hoboken: John Wiley & Sons, 2013.

State of California. "Model Language." Accessed October 23, 2018. www.dgs.ca.gov/pd/Resources/ModelLanguage.aspx.

State of Georgia. "Georgia Procurement Manual." Department of Administrative Services, May 2018. http://pur.doas.ga.gov/gpm/MyWebHelp/GPM_Main_File.htm.

State of Washington Department of Transportation. "Organizational Conflicts of Interest Manual." July 2009, 22.

Tollen, David. *The Tech Contracts Handbook Software Licenses and Technology Services Agreements for Lawyers and Businesspeople*. Amer Bar Association, Section of Litigation, 2011.

U.S. Department of Housing and Urban Development. "Quick Guide to Cost and Prince Analysis for HUD Grantees and Funding Recipients." Housing and Urban Development. Accessed October 23, 2018. www.hud.gov/program_offices/cpo/grantees/cstprice.

Chapter 9

Ethics and Professionalism in Public Procurement

The practice of public procurement is a profession, and its practitioners have a special obligation to preserve the attributes that make it so. The concepts of professionalism have evolved through a long history of societies and their groups, developing standards of behavior along the way. To add to the ethical dialogue and discourse of the profession, however, one must highlight the ethical rules of another stakeholder—indeed a teammate—in the procurement process: the attorney. They account for some perspectives on advice, roles, and occasionally operational requirements that flow out of litigation. Regardless of personal perceptions, the interwoven natures of ethics, integrity, and professionalism align together to create true, strategic value for both the public procurement function and the professionals who support it.

Ethics and Professionalism

It is beyond the scope of this book to dive into the historical evolution of behavioral norms that have become known as ethics. There are questions relating to who decides what is ethical, how ethical questions should be decided, and why some standards are more appropriate than others. Some ethical standards are codified in statutes; there may be civil and criminal penalties when they are violated. Other standards are in ethical codes, violation of which can lead to suspension or even termination of the right to practice some professions. Other ethical standards are more informally accepted as norms for the profession.

Professions have long established acceptable standards by which they are governed. Within organizations, ethics concerns itself with the concept of what is right versus what is wrong behavior. It is a reality that what is considered wrong behavior in one organization, country, or region may not be seen as wrong in another. Standards vary from culture to culture and from organization to organization. For instance, in some countries, it may be acceptable for a public administrator to accept a gift as a token of appreciation for expediting a process for an acquaintance. As expressed by Rose-Ackerman (1999), "in many countries, a telephone, a passport, or a driver's license cannot be obtained expeditiously without a payoff. Sometimes the service is available only to the corrupt, but not to the patient but honest citizen." In other countries, this behavior is considered unethical, if not illegal. Compounding this is the fact that what is considered unethical in a government entity may not be seen as wrong behavior in a private sector firm, even in the same country.

For some cultures, if it is not illegal, then it is fair game; anything short of bribes, kickback, blackmail, unauthorized payoff, and other outright lawlessness may be seen as one hand washing the other. To some people in developing countries and the former communist bloc, it is tactical to have someone on the inside of government to look out for your interests; and, as they say, one good favor deserves another. In the United States and other countries, there has been a movement away from this "to insure prompt service" (T.I.P.S.) approach to expediting transactions with governmental organizations. Laws have been enacted to ensure that flagrant disregard for appropriate conduct is not proliferated in government functions. While ordinances have become a guiding light in navigating the treacherous waters of professional behavior, they are not lighthouses. They cannot be solely depended upon, and both written and tacit ethical codes exist and must be heeded. What, then, is the difference between what is unethical and what is illegal?

Laws Versus the Codes of Ethics

Webster's New Collegiate Dictionary defines law as a rule of conduct or action prescribed or formally recognized as binding or enforced by a controlling authority. It is the binding custom or practice of a community that is advisable or obligatory to observe. The concept of law connotes coercion and control, needing an authoritative body to ensure its compliance. An action or activity is considered lawful if it is authorized, established, or in harmony with the relevant law. Issues pertaining to the law are considered legal issues; and, in practice, the term is extended to describe an action that is lawful. Any activity that is sanctioned by law is generally considered good for the society, but sometimes there is room within legal parameters for unethical practices to occur. For example, while freedom of speech provisions under the Constitution may allow workers to have discussion on topics with sensitive sexual content, it is unethical to conduct such a discussion in the presence of others who do not indicate their desire to hear such content. Therefore, while laws are not broken in such a case, ethical standards are violated.

Webster's New Collegiate Dictionary defines ethic as a set of moral principles or values, a theory or system of moral values, and the principles of conduct governing an individual or a group. In non-professional vocations, ethics may not be codified, and are sometimes tacit mores that descended through historical practices. Even when there is no formal approach to educating the individual on the organization's ethics, the person entering the occupation will be acculturated over time. Within professional organizations, conduct is considered ethical if it conforms to accepted professional standards. Quite often, these standards are codified and promulgated and can be learned as part of the professional development of the individual or group. Laws are usually enacted to govern the activities within long-established professions, and additional guidelines are often set by the profession to complement these laws.

To put it simply, differences between legal and ethical issues may be related to the severity of the offenses and the consequences for violating each. Illegal offenses usually have the potential of affecting society at-large in a negative way, or so the laws claim. Violation of laws can carry consequences that are enforceable by the governing authority and require that the offender repay a debt to society. This can also ruin an individual's legal and social status in society. Unethical offenses that are within the law may only affect a limited segment of the society and quite often a small number of people situated close to the incident. The offender in an ethical matter may be castigated within the profession and among interested parties, but may not be required to repay a debt to society at large. As with law, some ethical violations are more serious than others, and the most serious ethical guidelines are sometimes elevated to the status of law. For example, the problem of kickbacks was once an unethical issue; but, when it became a widespread and major problem (graft), laws were enacted against it.

Making a practice a legal issue does not mean that laws will be vigorously enforced, but it shows that it has been identified as a problem that deserves the coercive force of the governing political body. The irony of the situation is that there are legal but unethical issues that could potentially harm society more than other situations that are addressed through law.

The bottom line is that actions can be unethical without being illegal, though everything illegal should be considered unethical. Therefore, the professional should not solely rely on whether or not an action is legal, but should determine what is right or wrong behavior. This requires the constant adherence to professional standards. Callahan (1988) proposes that the law permits many immoralities that could not withstand even the most basic ethical scrutiny, yet we would not want these actions to be made illegal, since that would interfere with individual liberties.

In public service, there is sometimes a tradeoff between efficiency and social obligations, and an increase in one oftentimes results in a decrease in the other. In government procurement, an effective balance must be established in the effort to reduce malfeasance while increasing efficiency. Allowing procurement personnel to operate in a competitive environment without their hands being tied by overly stringent codes or ordinances can pursue this. However, in a time when some commentators advocate for or against a high level of discretion to be granted to public administrators, as demonstrated in the well-known Frederick-Finer public administration debates, it must be noted that "discretion increases corrupt incentives" (Rose-Ackerman 1999). Still, rigid ordinances or codes may not always be the answer, and "reforms [are] needed to encourage discretion and improve incentives for good performance."

Procurement as a Profession

There has been extensive discussion on the concept of professionalism and what constitutes a profession. One simple definition of a profession is that it is any calling or occupation by which a person habitually earns their living. However, some have pointed out that in days of yore the term "profession" was reserved for the privileged occupations, such as doctors, lawyers, professors, and the clergy. To reconcile the difference in definitions, some researchers have long accepted the notion of a professional continuum with different categories like non-professions, marginal professions, would-be-professions, emerging professions, new professions, and old-established professions (Thai 1983). In today's world of advanced information and technology, the concept of professionalism has once again emerged to mean more than just being a member in an occupational group labeled as a profession (Brody 1989). What then do we look for when we seek professionalism in the public sector?

What are the characteristics of a profession? Echoing the views of many experts in the field, Rabin (1983) considers the following elements as integral components of any profession:

- A body of knowledge that supports the practice and study of the profession;
- An established code of ethics that promulgates acceptable standards;
- Autonomy over one's actions as a member of the profession;
- Altruistic service to society and the profession; and
- Regulation of entry into the occupation.

This is not an exhaustive list, and academicians like Thai (1983) believe that the following are also distinct and necessary attributes of a profession:

- Authority over clients;
- Community sanction; and
- An intrinsic culture.

While some scholars believe that the body of knowledge can be specialized and theoretical, others like Glickauf (1971) believe that the professional should be well-educated, with a broad educational background. Having a knowledge base that draws from allied fields complements the specialized training in the administrator's specific area and differentiates the professional from the trained technician. While the technician concentrates on the approach in which he or she is trained, the professional should be broad-based and well-informed about issues related to his or her actions and decisions. Included in this broad body of knowledge should be a clear understanding of laws and ethical standards relevant to the field of work. This is especially true of personnel involved in pivotal governmental activities like public procurement, since the level of interaction with other governmental departments and the private sector is so high.

The attribute of autonomy can be realized when practitioners in their field separate themselves from the laity with the necessary expertise and develop a certain level of immunity from manipulation by others. Some have argued that professionals in fields like procurement cannot function from a position of autonomy, since it is by cooperating with others from management that the greatest effectiveness is realized. However, while some fields like procurement are intertwined with other areas of government, they have to demarcate their territory and exercise control over their responsibilities, activities, and duties. For professionals, the principle of autonomy over their actions in procurement should not be impaired by the actions of other members, from management, or any political entity. Being consistently astute regarding ethical standards is a big plus in the area of professional autonomy. This does not mean that public officials, special interests, and the public at large will not seek to influence the most highly professional public procurement professional, but doing so will not be easily accomplished if the public purchaser truly believes in their professionalism.

The altruistic component will be questioned in these highly individualistic and opportunistic times, but the practitioner's pride of doing what he or she does should culminate in the delivery of service for the sake of civility. Many trained public officials go beyond the call of duty to properly serve their community, without seeking any additional opportunity for self-aggrandizement.

Gaining the public's trust, recognition, and acceptance should be the desire of any true professional, and the push for sanction by the community they serve should be an ongoing effort. For public administration in general, sanction by the community helps legitimize its role in the governance of society. For procurement in particular, it justifies not contracting out the procurement function as is done by some federal departments like the Department of Defense. Besides competency, ethical soundness (incorruptibility) may be the leading criterion in gaining the public's trust. In fact, without the public's acceptance of their integrity, competence, and authority, the public procurement officer will constantly be required to defend actions and decisions.

Another attribute of professionalism that is directly related to ethics is the "authority over clients" factor. Being closely linked with the "community sanction" attribute, authority over clients does not only come through the powers delegated to the bureaucracy by the three branches of government, but also by the professional's image in the organization and the legitimacy ascribed by the public at large. NIGP's Code of Ethics (Appendix A) states that all its members should be "governed by the highest ideals of honor and integrity in all public and personal relationships in order to merit the respect and inspire the confidence of the organization and the public being served." The Code also admonishes members "to believe in the dignity and worth of the service that their organizations provide, and to recognize and respect the responsibilities entrusted upon them as public servants."

Regulation of entry into the field of public procurement will become a necessity as the practice is advanced along the professionalism continuum. Most government entities have established mechanisms to screen entrants into the field, based strongly on concerns for ethical behavior in the future. There has been great progress in developing academic programs that prepare public servants, administrators, and scholars for the practice in and study of public administration. For public procurement to be recognized as a new profession, it will have to prove that its practitioners have acquired a high level of competency through specialized training and education. The common body of knowledge and skills necessary for accomplishing this task is being accumulated and includes studies in professional ethics.

Each profession's intrinsic culture is perpetuated through professional associations, esoteric publications, accepted practices that are passed on through acculturation, and fraternal relationships. Through all of these experiences, the professional learns what actions facilitate effective and desirable results, and is made aware of activities that can be deleterious to one's own career and the profession in general. The profession actively seeks to bolster its image and prestige and gives recognition to people who make this possible. Public procurement as a profession is no different, and its culture permeates its membership through conferences, seminars, publications, workplace interactions, and formal and informal organizations. Professional procurement associations campaign to keep all their members on the same plane as far as the professional culture is concerned. For new members, it only takes a short time to be able to determine what is tolerated and what is unacceptable behavior, and a major component of the procurement culture involves the issue of ethical standards.

Ethics in Public Procurement

The existence of a code of ethics for the professional public purchaser is important because of the level of responsibility that is attached to the duties of the purchaser. There are always opportunities for improper conduct within the occupation, and the professional must be seen as unimpeachable and of an irreproachable character (Glickauf 1971). Many public administration schools offer courses in administrative ethics, and entities have increased ethics awareness in the workplace, which has resulted in improvements over the past decades. The development of a body of knowledge for procurement professionals and the establishment of ethical standards are not left up to academia. Many government organizations, professional associations and societies, and many suppliers have accumulated a set of ethical standards as parts of their operating policies.

Professional bodies such as the NIGP and the Universal Public Procurement Certification Council (UPPCC) have exercised leadership in establishing and fostering professional codes of conduct for public procurement professionals. Special interest groups are also actively seeking conformity to certain standards by those involved in public procurement. A few elected officials are proactive in assuring accountability for the activities of procurement professionals and have made it their personal prerogative to guard against inappropriate procurement practices within their jurisdiction. One area in which special interest groups, politicians, and administrators find common ground is in the area of protecting certain disadvantaged businesses seeking to do business with the government.

In government, the procurement function involves a great deal of power, which stems from the fact that procurement professionals determine how government business is to be awarded among suppliers. There are opportunities for power to be abused and for purchasers to use their positions for personal gains. Since the activities of these officials cannot always be controlled by procedural rules or auditing, there are always opportunities for kickbacks, personal purchases at special prices, entertainment paid by suppliers, gifts in return for favors, and other unethical behaviors. It is, therefore, important for all public procurement professionals to be cognizant of their obligations to their employers, to suppliers, to the public, and to the profession.

Obligations to Your Employer

It should be noted that unethical actions in procurement do not always occur as a reciprocal gesture aimed at benefiting both parties. As a matter of fact, a person could even act unethically without gaining from the action. Sometimes it is even difficult to tell if the person intended to act in a manner deemed unethical. For example, a purchaser could inadvertently divulge information on competitive prices or misrepresent the public entity's requirements.

Public procurement professionals should not underestimate the intent of individuals or groups to extract information on the procurement activities of their entity. This is why it is important for the public purchasers to be consistent in their practices and not allow deviation from guidelines, even when such deviation seems harmless. Most importantly, the professional must always be wary of seemingly harmless offers or gifts from suppliers. This means that receiving benefits, even when it does not place anyone at a disadvantage, should be avoided.

It is the public procurement professional's obligation to protect confidential information belonging to both the entity and real and potential contractors up until the time that such information becomes public information by law. Most information gathered in government contracts becomes public information once the bids and proposals are officially opened, but this does not mean that the procurement professional cannot become aware of information before the opening. For example, suppose, in seeking clarifications regarding a Request for Proposals (RFP), a supplier inadvertently reveals information intended for a separate sealed bid. If such a situation should occur, the procurement professional is expected to respect the privacy of such information until that bid is officially opened. The procurement professional may want to avoid addressing such information in granting the clarification, since any clarification given would be shared with all competing suppliers. This will prevent anyone from suspecting some kind of collusion between the bidder and entity. The procurement professional must remember that procurement information generally belongs to the entity and in some cases is the supplier's trade secret.

The public entity as an employer is entitled to undivided loyalty from its employees, and it can be considered unethical to disagree with the entity's policy in public (Aljian 1974), or when representing the entity in private presentations. Disagreements should be addressed within the organization and among peers and superiors. Public procurement professionals should conduct themselves in such a fashion that they never become more obligated to anyone other than to their employer. In addition, there is no excuse for treating the confidentiality of procurement information lightly or using it for personal reasons. This also involves securing sensitive procurement information from other members of the organization who are not involved in the procurement process. Information gathered on a supplier is information that has been entrusted to the entity, and that trust should not be broken by an employer who uses it for personal gain or for granting an advantage to another supplier.

Procurement professionals have an obligation to reveal any conflict of interest that can affect the fair conduct of procurement activities by their employers. For instance, a procurement professional who has ownership of stock in a company seeking to do business with the entity should make this known to the employer. Such disclosure should also be extended to conflicts of interest involving relatives of the procurement professional or the procurement professional's past employment with a company that is seeking to do business with the public entity. If appropriate, the procurement professional may be asked to excuse him or herself from participation in the transaction in question. This would ensure that the entity is not led into a contractual arrangement that is not fully competitive and that may not be in its best interest. Even in conflict of interest cases where the procurement professional's adherence to strict professional standards can prevent any disadvantage to the entity or any other competing supplier, the perception problem may be too overwhelming to risk such an involvement.

Obligations to Suppliers

Treating the supplier fairly should be the goal of all public procurement professionals. What is fair to all suppliers, the public, and the buyer is usually ethical. The public purchaser has many obligations to the suppliers, and a few are worth noting here. It is important that suppliers be furnished with reliable information at all times. Deliberately misleading a supplier is unethical, even if it is a way to avoid addressing other difficult questions. Under no circumstance should an actual or potential supplier be given erroneous information, since such an incident will result in the kind of negative reaction that could impair future competition. In addition, every reasonable consideration should be given to the suppliers and their products. To invite a supplier to the procurement process with a priori decision to exclude them from consideration is considered unethical (Aljian 1974). Unless serious considerations are being given, a procurement professional should avoid making requests for free samples or demonstrations from suppliers.

Disenfranchising legitimate suppliers, denying them access to the procurement process, and even causing undue waiting are also unethical. Open discrimination and preferential treatment was once a common occurrence, even in government procurement. So severe were these problems that many jurisdictions have enacted laws against those practices and have actively sought to guard against such activities. Equal opportunity rules and affirmative action have helped tremendously in this aspect. Individual jurisdictions have established their own outreach programs for disadvantaged business enterprises, women-owned business enterprises, and minority-owned business enterprises. It is considered unethical for procurement professionals to blatantly circumvent these ordinances and outreach programs aimed at promoting inclusiveness.

Disenfranchisement of legitimate suppliers does not always take on a blatant appearance, and many suppliers have been kept out of the competitive process in subtle ways. For instance, there are times when the merchandise needed may be proprietary, causing the buyer to develop a relationship with the sole supplier. This relationship may be a good one and could last for a long time, with the buying entity being appreciative of the goods or service. Eventually, a time will come when that commodity in question is no longer a sole-supplier item, and there may be many new suppliers in the market offering similar commodities or services. Due to the good relationship between the entity and the supplier, the procurement professional may not want to readily open up the item to competition, especially if the entity is very satisfied with the product. To knowingly maintain a proprietary status on the product could be considered unfair to the other suppliers, non-competitive and, thus, unethical.

Despite these concerns, there are times when, even with other available suppliers, the purchasing entity may have a good reason to maintain the relationship with a specific supplier. Changing suppliers can sometimes lead to hidden costs to the purchasing entity, especially if the new supplier has slightly different specifications that may require modification to the existing arrangement in the entity. For instance, if the commodity in question is technological, it may do the same thing as the original product, but may require time to retrain technicians and end users. Depending on how many people would be affected, the entity may choose to continue buying from the original supplier. Major software changes in some entities could require the loss of valuable resources, which means lost manpower while end users are trained, the delay of activities in the interim, and cost to do the actual training. The entity must, therefore, balance the need for equity and fairness for suppliers and efficiency and effectiveness within the organization.

The actions of a procurement professional should not diminish a supplier's advantage or competitive "edge" in the procurement process. One of the instruments used by procurement professional in the procurement process is the RFP. In responding to such a document, the supplier will sometimes divulge unique and novel ideas. This happens quite often in presentations by the competing suppliers, where they offer innovative approaches to the problem facing the entity. It is the obligation of the procurement professional to protect and guard such ideas from that supplier's competitors until such time that the information is deemed public by law. Even then, the practice of actively directing other suppliers to the existence of such ideas may constitute a violation of the relationship with the affected supplier.

Additionally, even when the law prescribes public disclosure, there are times when statutory exemptions protect some information from public disclosure. Competing suppliers should find competitive information on their own, even when the purchaser's organization can benefit immensely. It is not only ethical to protect such information, when possible, but it makes good business sense because suppliers who know that their ideas are protected will be more willing to participate in competitive bidding with the purchasing entity.

The obligation of treating all suppliers equitably means that information, explanations or clarifications, allowances for deviation in specifications, time allowances, and other conditions be afforded equally to all potential suppliers. In all business transactions, it is possible for either the supplier or purchaser to make honest mistakes that could be of great cost to the party committing the error. It is considered unethical to capitalize on an apparently honest mistake by the supplier. It is certainly not fair to the supplier for the purchaser to try to hold him or her to an erroneously quoted price, especially if the quoted price is obviously a small fraction of the fair market price. This does not mean, however, that the buyer should accept a correction that will make a purchase non-competitive and would exclude another supplier who is offering a better value. The purchaser's obligation to the supplier goes beyond the discussion here, and the main focus is on fairness. There must be the awareness that fairness should be both real and perceived, and it is important to convey the image of the purchaser doing what is ethical and, thus, right.

Obligations to the Profession

There are laws that govern the function of procurement, and the ones that will be mentioned here are the Uniform Commercial Code and the antitrust laws. The Uniform Commercial Code (U.C.C.) has been effective in all the states and consists of provisions that govern commercial transactions conducted by government entities. Each state has enacted its own version of the Code and may provide its own interpretation and discussion based on varying case law. Because of the voluminous nature of the U.C.C., procurement professionals need only acquaint themselves with the relevant concepts and provisions that affect the government as buyer. Antitrust laws include several laws aimed at curbing anticompetitive practices by both suppliers and public procurement professionals. They include The Sherman Act, The Clayton Act, The Federal Trade Commission Act, and other miscellaneous and related acts.

In addition to national laws that relate to procurement, there are international rules that have been established to regulate government procurement. The World Trade Organization (WTO), in noting that government procurement represents approximately 10% to 15% of gross domestic product (GDP), addresses the issue of discriminatory procurement practices:

> A growing awareness of the trade-restrictive effects of discriminatory procurement policies and of the desirability of fulfilling these gaps in the trading system resulted in a first effort to bring government procurement under internationally agreed trade rules in the Tokyo Round of Trade Negotiations. As a result, the first Agreement on Government Procurement was signed in 1979 and entered into force in 1981. It was amended in 1987, with this amended version entering into force in 1988. In parallel with the Uruguay Round, Parties to the Agreement held negotiations to extend the scope and coverage of the Agreement. The Agreement on Government Procurement (1994) (GPA) was signed in Marrakesh on 15 April 1994—at the same time as the Agreement Establishing the WTO. The new Agreement entered into force on 1 January 1996. The GPA is one of the "plurilateral" Agreements included in Annex 4 to the Agreement Establishing the WTO, signifying that not all its members are bound by it.

It behooves professional procurement professionals to familiarize themselves with the relevant sections of these laws. In most instances, government procurement professionals are exempt from legal actions brought against them for procurement violations involving their actions on behalf of a government entity. In cases where the question of the liability of government officials in actions violating antitrust laws have surfaced, the courts have indicated that state officials cannot be held personally liable if their actions were within the authorized parameters granted by their entities. However, they may not be protected if they acted beyond their scope of authority. This means that if a violation should occur and it is proven that the procurement professional acted without authority, then the procurement professional may be held personally liable for the violation. This is sufficient reason for public procurement professionals to walk a straight line and try their utmost to operate within the laws and ethical standards that are established.

As mentioned earlier, professional procurement associations, like NIGP and the UPPCC, have established codes of ethics to guide purchasers in their capacity as procurement officers (See NIGP and UPPCC Codes of Ethics, Appendices A and B, respectively). These codes of ethics warn against public procurement professionals being engaged in the direct or indirect acceptance of gifts, gratuities, and other things of value from suppliers. Things of value can include excessive entertainment or private trips, promise of future employment, and personal favors to the procurement professionals or their families and friends. The American Bar Association (ABA) publishes a Model Procurement Code that addresses the issue of ethics in public contracting. Article 12 of The 2000 Model Procurement Code for State and Local Governments covers standards of conduct, remedies for breach of these ethical standards, and a discussion of ethics commissions. Provisions from the Code have been adopted by some states and local governments.

Perhaps one of the most overlooked aspects of ethical conduct in the profession involves the individual's behavior off the job. If a person is seen as lacking integrity in activities that are not job related, such a reputation may be extended to their position as a procurement representative for the public entity. If individuals cannot be trusted in their private lives, why should they be trusted in their public roles? In the same way that the private behavior of an elected official can ruin his or her reputation in the public realm, the same is true for procurement professionals. Public procurement professionals have an obligation to project a favorable image of themselves to the general public and anyone who comes into contact with them. The public purchasing agent should be seen as someone truthful and honest in personal transactions. An individual who is seen as discriminatory in their personal life will have a hard time convincing others that such a reputation does not affect their work. Above all, procurement professionals should not portray the image of being opportunistic, avaricious, or corrupt in their personal endeavors.

The public procurement professional also has an obligation to the end user department. The end user department must be assured that the procurement professional handling its purchases is someone who will provide the department with the best quality at the best price. Some authors in the field of procurement (Leenders and Flynn 1995) have summed up the basic elements of the procurement function as the "six rights." That is "ensuring that the right goods and services, of the right quality, arrive at the right time, in the right place, in the right quantities, at the right price" (p. 6). In public procurement, the term "quality" can be taken to mean "suitability." The goods or services do not necessarily have to be the highest overall quality, but must be the right quality for the purpose intended. Going above the required quality may result in unnecessarily elevated prices that would not equate to the "right price." Although it may not ostensibly seem to be a matter of ethics, it is good business practice to try and meet the end user department's needs as best as possible. All of this must be accomplished within the confines of the legal limits and under the ethical standards of the organization and profession.

Obligations to the Field of Public Administration

In addition to their obligations to the employer, the supplier, and the profession, the public procurement professional has an obligation to the field of public administration in general. There are ethical standards that are general to the field of public administration, and the public procurement professional must abide by these standards. This means that the public procurement professional must oppose any discrimination based on race, color, religion, sex, sexual orientation, national origin, political affiliation, physical handicaps, age, or marital status in any and all aspects of public policy. Likewise, a person's private personal lifestyle should not give cause or excuse for discrimination if it is legal and does not impair or impede the ability to perform required tasks, and appropriate channels should be provided for harassed persons to seek redress. In the event of a proven offense, support should be given for appropriate action to take place.

Supervisors should be alert that no illegal action originates from or is sponsored by their immediate office; and they should inform their subordinates, when necessary, that no illegalities will be tolerated within their offices. Public employees who reasonably suspect illegal action in any public entity should channel information regarding the matter to appropriate authorities. It is the ethical duty of all to help eliminate all forms of illegal discrimination, fraud, and mismanagement of public funds; and to give support to colleagues who experience any difficulty because of responsible efforts to correct such illegal discrimination, fraud, mismanagement, or abuse. All public servants should support authorized investigative agencies and should support, when appropriate, independent auditors reporting to committees independent of their management or entity.

Effective fiscal and management controls and inspections should be viewed as important protections for supervisors, staff, and the public interest. If a bid is advertised as being a formal sealed bid, then the bidding process should be treated in that manner. This means that if the rules for formal bidding stipulate that sealed bids must be opened in the presence of two or more procurement employees at a prearranged time, two or more procurement employees should always be present for such bid openings at the stated time, even if no one outside the division would know. Procurement professionals should not deviate from these principles, even under those conditions where no supplier was present and there was no need to ensure that the process was ostensibly conforming. Supervisors should assure their staff that constructive criticism can be aired without reprisal and that such criticism may be carried to an ombudsman or other designated official if the organization's structure and protocol provides for such an arrangement.

One area of ethics that should not be overlooked is that which deals with information technology. In government, inadequate equipment, software, procedures, supervision, and poor security controls give rise to both intentional and inadvertent misconduct. The procurement division has an ethical obligation to seek adequate equipment and software, outline procedures, and establish controls to reduce the organization's vulnerability to inappropriate computer activities. Special care must be taken to secure access to confidential information stored on computers. Care must also be taken to ensure that information gathered electronically is protected and guarded from intrusion. Procurement professionals must remember that in some entities, email correspondence is not confidential. One should be wary in asking for sensitive supplier information to be sent via email. This becomes even more important as entities seek to expand their e-government, since it is unethical to render sensitive government information vulnerable to unauthorized access.

While there are disclosure laws, some information in public offices is privileged because of laws or ordinances. However, when other governmental entities have a legitimate public service need for information possessed by the procurement division or department, procurement professionals should do all they can to facilitate them within the limits of statute law, administrative regulations, and promises made to those from whom the procurement professional acquired the information. Still, when procurement professionals undertake discussions with colleagues about privileged information, they should be sure those colleagues need the information discussed; and the procurement professional should seek assurances of confidentiality from them.

Obligations to the General Public

The procurement department's relationship with the public should not be overlooked, even though it sometimes seems that the public has no significant role to play in the procurement function. As a public servant, the procurement professional must remember that part of servicing the public responsively is to encourage citizen cooperation when appropriate and to involve civic groups when possible. As pointed out by the American Society for Public Administration (ASPA), administrators have an ethical responsibility to bring citizens into contact with the government as far as practical, both to secure citizen support of government and for the economies or increased effectiveness that will result from such interaction. ASPA urges public servants to respect the right of the public to know what is going on in their entities, even though certain interest groups may raise queries for partisan or other nonpublic purposes.

ASPA also notes that Americans expect government to be compassionate, well-organized, and operating within the law. Citizens within a given jurisdiction should be assured that public servants are adhering to local ordinances and procedures. For instance, local jurisdictions have local ordinances and procedural rules that govern procurement. Conducting purchasing outside the purview of these rules constitutes unauthorized procurement. Some offenses may be as simple as conducting unauthorized procurement of goods or services from suppliers when the same goods or services are available within the entity. Others may involve obtaining items under contract from suppliers other than those who hold entity contracts, adding unauthorized purchases to previously approved purchase orders without obtaining permission, or giving false information that informal quotes were obtained without actually contacting the suppliers. Disregarding the rules that are established by the duly elected representatives of the citizenry is clearly unethical.

Public employees should understand the overall mission of their entity and the role they play in achieving that mission. As such, answers to questions on public policy should be complete, understandable, and true. The procurement staff must exhibit courteous conduct when dealing with citizens and should devise a system to ensure helpful and pleasant service to the public. Wherever possible, public procurement professionals should show citizens how to avoid mistakes and be effective in their relations with their government. It will do no harm to share information on the accomplishments of procurement activities with the citizenry, and avenues for public feedback should be opened. On the other hand, not every procurement blunder must be aired in public, but procurement professionals must be willing to give accurate accounts of incidences if the public or media should launch an inquiry. In the final analysis, the tax-paying public is best served when the individuals conducting the procurement processes are capable of effectively, efficiently, and ethically executing their duties.

Nuances of Ethical Integrity

The discussion on ethics was quite general in its approach, and no attempt was made to compile a list of ethical or unethical practices. This was intentional, since different entities in different states have slightly different rules of operations. The obligations discussed, and the examples used, were generic and typical of the kind of issues that procurement professionals face in their daily activities. Still, they may not apply in every public organization. The goal was to convey the idea that even when clear rules are absent, it is incumbent upon the procurement professional to decipher what is right or wrong and what is acceptable and unacceptable behavior. Treating others the way you would want to be treated if you were in a similar situation may not always be good enough, and sometimes rules or laws require much more from the government employee conducting procurement for a government entity.

The discussion was not intended to discourage friendly relations with suppliers, and it does not mean that procurement professionals cannot go the extra mile to be helpful to suppliers who seek their help. It also does not mean that the procurement professional cannot be firm in dealing with contractors who lapse in important stages of the procurement process. No one expects the public procurement professional to operate in a vacuum, and no one says individuals cannot err. However, it must be remembered that procurement professionals may be asked to account for their actions, and when that time comes, they would want to be on the right side. Remember that the actions of procurement professionals are their own, and they should be vigilant of what favors are asked of them by suppliers or by their fellow purchasing coworkers.

While they ensure that their actions are honorable, public procurement professionals should also encourage and help fellow workers to also be upright in their undertakings. This is good, not only for the organization, but for the profession and public administration in general. Procurement professionals should strive to know the ordinances that are established for procurement within their jurisdiction and familiarize themselves with the relevant laws. NIGP's Code of Ethics (Appendix A) is a good place to start in understanding the environment of public procurement. Procurement supervisors and their staff should strive for personal professional excellence and should encourage the professional development of new recruits and those seeking to enter the field of public procurement.

Staff members, throughout their careers, should be encouraged to participate in professional activities and associations for procurement professionals at both the national and regional levels. These associations help to disseminate information and new direction important to the field, thus, perpetuating the "intrinsic culture" needed to fortify the profession. They should also be reminded of the importance of doing a good job and of their responsibility to improve the public service. When possible, procurement administrators should make time to meet with students and to help bridge the gap between classroom studies and the realities of public jobs. Administrators should also encourage and lend their support to internship programs that can help attract public administration students who have acquired a "body of knowledge" desirable for the profession. This would be helpful in the "regulation of entry" into the field, which is another important attribute of professionalism.

Attorney Ethics and Professionalism

A book about legal aspects of public procurement is a good avenue to explore the perspectives of ethics and professionalism of another procurement partner: lawyers who serve as agency counsel. Some of their ethical obligations in particular can affect operations and must be understood.

In recent years, state bar associations and governing bodies have focused on the professionalism aspects of the legal profession, civility in particular. The altruistic canons of the legal profession strive for equal access to justice and providing needed legal services to the less fortunate through pro bono practice programs. They also elevate the relationship between attorney and client to the predominant role and emphasize model professionalism principles. Still, a small part of the profession remains that may not always adhere to the highest standards of professional conduct.

Attorneys have a well-developed ethical code; the first canons of professional ethics were adopted in 1908. Now, the various states' codes often are patterned after American Bar Association Model Rules of Professional Conduct. Notably, California has its own code that is not based on the Model Rules, but it is similar in many respects. The model code serves as a useful reference to highlighting aspects of attorney ethics and professionalism that impact the practice of procurement.

Conflicts of Interest

Attorneys may not represent a client if the representation involves a conflict of interest with another client. That is why, in some government matters, attorneys general may have to obtain separate counsel for another government client where interests are adverse. Some conflicts can be waived. For the procurement professional, these rules can sometimes result in delays and even requests to waive conflicts of interest. Attorneys are obligated to fully explain the issue and options.

Attorney-Client Privilege

The attorney-client privilege is a rule of evidence and an ethical rule, requiring that an attorney not disclose communications with a client within the scope of the privilege. Privileged communications are generally not admissible as evidence in an administrative or judicial proceeding.

Merely having an attorney in the room or on a phone call is normally not adequate to gain the protection of privilege. Moreover, in internal investigations, an attorney conducting the investigation is typically representing the organization, not individuals. In those cases, some communications may not be privileged. It's important to talk with counsel and have a complete understanding about the scope of privilege.

In procurement and contracting, there often are multiple parties, and the scope of attorney-client privilege can be confusing. The Colorado Supreme Court clarified the scope of attorney-client privilege in *Alliance Construction Solutions, Inc. v. American Insurance Co.* (54 P. 3d 861 (Colo. 2002)). The court held that a state attorney's communications with an independent contractor serving as the construction manager for the state were protected by the attorney-client privilege. That ruling has been followed by other states.

Communications With Third Parties and Represented Persons

Under the ABA Model Rules, a lawyer may not knowingly make a false statement of material fact or law to a third person. They do not have a duty, however, to inform an opposing party of relevant facts. The comments to the Model Rules state that under generally accepted conventions in negotiation, certain types of statements are ordinarily not taken as statements of material fact. Estimates of price or value of a transaction and a party's intentions as to an acceptable settlement of a claim are ordinarily in this category.

Generally, a lawyer may not communicate about a matter with a person the attorney knows to be represented by another lawyer unless the consent of the other lawyer is obtained.

The Duty to Preserve Evidence

Procurement practitioners may receive "spoliation" letters from counsel. Today, in most jurisdictions, attorneys have a duty to inform clients about the duty to preserve evidence when litigation is filed, threatened, or reasonably anticipated. The timing, nature of the duty of preservation, and who is subject to the duty must be discussed with counsel. There are judicial sanctions that can be imposed, including sanctions that can compromise the case if evidence is excluded by the judge for failure to preserve. Especially with respect to electronic records and records destruction schedules, close coordination with counsel is required.

The procurement professional is not expected to sort out these issues. Attorneys are ethically required to clarify the nature of the representation and attorney-client privilege issues with the client. But procurement professionals should be aware that issues can arise about confidentiality, and they are encouraged to discuss them with their counsel.

Conclusion

Among the most celebrated and taught principles in public procurement is the duty to act ethically and professionally. The public, government, profession, and suppliers expect it. Some ethical obligations are found in legislation, others in the codes that procurement professionals abide by. Professional behavior is not always defined by strict compliance with ethical standards, however. Professionalism means more.

Lawyers have codified ethical rules, and their observance can occasionally affect procurement operations. Lawyers are obligated to zealously protect and pursue a client's legitimate interests, within the bounds of the law. But lawyers are cautioned that zealousness does not justify conduct that is unprofessional, discourteous or uncivil toward any person involved in the legal system. Though rare, in the heat of battle, procurement professionals may occasionally see an opportunity to have a discussion about tactics and professionalism with their lawyer. More likely, attorney obligations with respect to confidentiality, conflicts of interest, and their obligation to the courts may occasionally affect the operations in procurement departments.

Authors' Note: Part one of this chapter is based on a dissertation by Mr. Leroy Harvey, Ph.D. candidate at Florida Atlantic University, and is used with his permission.

References

Aljian, G. W. *Purchasing Handbook.* 3rd ed. New York: McGraw-Hill Book Co., 1974.

American Bar Association. *The 2000 Model Procurement Code for State and Local Governments.* Chicago: American Bar Association, 2000.

Barry, Donald D., and Howard R. Whitcomb. *The Legal Foundations of Public Administration.* Lanham, MD: Rowman & Littlefield Publishers, 2005.

Brody, E. W. *Professional Practice Development: Meeting the Competitive Challenge.* New York: Praeger, 1989.

Callahan, Joan C., ed. *Ethical Issues in Professional Life.* New York: Oxford University Press, 1988.

Glickauf, J. S. *Footsteps Toward Professionalism.* Chicago: Arthur Anderson and Co., 1971.

Leenders, Michiel R., and Anna E. Flynn. *Value-Driven Purchasing: Managing the Key Steps in the Acquisition Process.* The NAPM Professional Development Series, vol. 1. Burr Ridge, IL: Irwin Professional Pub, 1995.

Lysons, C. K. *Purchasing.* The M and E Handbook Series. Plymouth: MacDonald, Evans, 1981.

Maister, David H. *True Professionalism: The Courage to Care About Your People, Your Clients, and Your Career.* Place of publication not identified: Free Press, 2014. www.myilibrary.com?id=899292.

Pitzer, Jack T., and Khi V. Thai. *Introduction to Public Procurement.* 3rd ed. Herndon, VA: National Institute of Governmental Purchasing, 2009.

Rabin, J. (Ed.). "Professionalism in public administration: Towards conceptual Clarity-A symposium." *Review of Public Personnel Administration*, vol. 4. Place of publication not identified: Fall 1983.

Rose-Ackerman, Susan. *Corruption and Government: Causes, Consequences, and Reform.* New York: Cambridge University Press, 1999.

SCCE. "Develop and Implement an Effective Code of Conduct." *The Compliance and Ethics Blog* (blog), December 21, 2016. http://complianceandethics.org/develop-implement-effective-code-conduct/.

Thai, K. V. "Public administration: A professional education." Review of *Public Personnel Administration*, vol 3. Place of publication not identified: Spring 1983.

Chapter 10

Relevant Procurement Case Law

This chapter presents selected court decisions that may affect decisions made by a procurement professional. These decisions and hypothetical situations are intended to be used for discussion and as examples of how the principles in the book apply to real-world situations. As always, advice of the public entity's legal counsel should be sought when applying law to any set of facts. Further, decisions and rulings discussed in this chapter are only binding on the jurisdiction in which they were decided (assuming they have not been overruled in subsequent cases). Yet, they offer examples of legal analysis of procurement and contract disputes. In some cases, there are significant differences in how the law is applied in different states.

Cases Involving Acceptance and Rejection of Goods

When purchased items arrive at the plant damaged, the procurement professional must act quickly because a number of issues may be at stake. These issues include rejection, withholding payment, making the decision on repairs, and determining how much time is allowable to respond. The following cases illustrate practical points that will guide procurement managers in handling these difficult breach-of-contract situations.

Where There Is an Installment Contract and One of the Delivered Installments Contains Defective Goods, What Are the Buyer's Rights?

The court dealt with this question in *Midwest Mobile Diagnostic Imaging v. Dynamics Corp of America* (965 F. Supp. 1003 (W.D. Mich. 1997)). The contract involved the purchase of four trailers designed to hold magnetic resonance imaging (MRI) equipment. The trailers had to be specially designed and built because of the technical nature of MRI equipment. The purchaser received the first of the trailers but found it to be defective. As a result, the buyer was forced to cancel appointments that had been made with prospective patients.

Eight days later, the seller presented to the buyer a redesigned trailer that purportedly solved the problem. However, the buyer still claimed that defects existed, rented a substitute trailer from another supplier, and notified the seller of its intent to cancel the contract. In deciding the lawsuit, the first question for the court was whether to treat the contract as an installment contract.

As is frequently the case, the parties did not specifically use the words "installment contract." However, since the contract authorized separate deliveries of the four trailers and the payment schedule called for payment of the balance due for each trailer upon shipment, the court concluded that this was an installment contract. The court then explained that the buyer's right to reject goods under an installment contract differed from the right to reject goods under other types of contracts. In the non-installment type of case, U.C.C. Section 2–601 allows the buyer to reject the goods by reason of any defect, whether it is in the quality of the goods, the timing of performance, or the manner of delivery. In other words, Michigan, like many other states, follows the "perfect tender" rule. However, under U.C.C. Section 2–612, which covers installment contracts, the buyer may not reject a non-conforming tender unless the defect substantially impairs the value of the installment.

Moreover, if the non-conformity is curable and the seller gives adequate assurances of cure, the buyer must accept the installment. Furthermore, even if the buyer properly rejects the goods, it may not cancel the contract unless the defect substantially impairs the value of the whole contract. Here, the buyer had no choice but to permit the seller the opportunity to fix a defect that both parties thought could be cured. Since the amount of time the seller was allowed for cure was not fixed in the contract, the seller had a "reasonable" time to cure under U.C.C. Section 2–508. Thus, when the seller provided a purportedly conforming trailer eight days later, it was considered timely.

However, the court found that the second trailer was, nevertheless, also non-conforming and not suited to accommodate the effective use of the MRI machine. The court stated that even under an installment contract, the seller's right to cure is limited. When the seller's redesign attempts failed on the second try, and the buyer faced the loss of patients unless it obtained suitable equipment elsewhere, the buyer had a valid basis for canceling the contract. The seller's breach had now substantially impaired the entire contract, the court said. The court then held that the buyer could recover the amount it had paid for the first installment plus the cost of rental of a substitute trailer. Although the rental of a trailer, as opposed to purchase, technically did not constitute "cover" within the meaning of the U.C.C., the rental costs were recoverable as incidental damages.

Where the Equipment Purchased Proves To Be Defective, Can the Buyer Recover as Incidental Damages the Cost to Have the Equipment Repaired by a Third Party?

The purchaser should proceed with caution before having the equipment repaired. In *Magnum Press Automation, Inc. v. Thomas & Betts Corp.* (758 N.E.2d 507 (Ill. App. Ct. 2001)), the buyer of industrial presses brought a claim against the seller for the costs of unsuccessful attempts to repair the machinery prior to the buyer's revocation of acceptance. The equipment was valued at approximately $46,000, and the repairs cost approximately $11,000. Although the trial court awarded the buyer the cost of repairs as incidental damages, the appellate court reversed and remanded the question for retrial.

The appellate court questioned whether it was proper for the buyer to go through with such a major repair without previously warning the seller of its intention to do so if the seller did not promptly fix the problem. The message for buyers is that, at the very least, they should issue a written warning to the seller before undertaking a major repair.

What Is the Risk of Reselling Goods When the Buyer Has Not Had Sufficient Time to Determine Whether the Goods Conform to the Contract?

The court dealt with the question of resale in *Ricky Riddle v. Heartland Nursery* (No. M.2000–02190, 2001 WL 1346261 (Tenn. Ct. App., Nov. 2, 2001)). In the seller's action to collect the purchase price for the sale of nursery stock, the buyer alleged that the goods did not conform to the contract. In deciding the case, the court analyzed the effect of U.C.C. Section 2–606. This section of the Code states that the buyer has accepted the goods if he has done any of the following after a reasonable opportunity to inspect the goods: (1) signifies to the seller that the goods are conforming, (2) indicates that he will take or retain them in spite of their non-conformity, (3) fails to make an effective rejection (even though such acceptance does not occur until after the buyer has had a reasonable opportunity to inspect them), or (4) does any act inconsistent with the seller's ownership.

Some U.C.C. experts, such as White and Summers, say that U.C.C. Section 2–606 should be applied only where the buyer does something, such as sells the non-conforming goods, which is inconsistent with the seller's rights. This court, however, held that even though the non-conformity became apparent later (when the buyer's own customers complained that trees had died), the buyer had already accepted the goods and it was too late to reject them. This did not leave the buyer without remedies, but the buyer now had the burden of proving that the trees were non-conforming. Since the buyer was unable to prove why the trees died, the seller prevailed.

When the Buyer Has Paid for the Goods on a C.O.D. Basis, Is There Still Time to Reject Goods if They Turn Out To Be Non-Conforming?

In *Gragg Farms & Nursery v. Kelly Green Landscaping* (674 N.E.2d 785, 32 UCC.Rep.Serv.2d 1119 (Ohio Mun. Ct. 1996)), the Gragg Farms nursery shipped "cash on delivery" (C.O.D.) willow oak trees to Kelly Green, who planted them properly. However, they all eventually died, and the evidence showed that Kelly Green took reasonable steps to water the trees, but they were too dry at delivery. The court held that even though the buyer had already paid the freight charges for delivery of the goods, it still had a reasonable time to inspect them. Payment on delivery did not constitute acceptance. When the buyer notified the seller the following day that the goods were "junk" and were being rejected, notice had been provided within a reasonable time. The buyer was entitled to refund and damages.

What Must a Buyer Do to Revoke Acceptance Under the U.C.C.?

U.C.C. Section 2–608 does not specify the manner in which revocation is done. The Official Comment says that the content of the notice is to be determined by considerations of good faith, prevention of surprise, and reasonable adjustment. In *Cissell Manufacturing Co. v. Park* (36 P. 3d 85 (Colo. Ct. App. 2001)), the court said that for the notice of revocation to be sufficient, it should fairly apprise the seller that the buyer wants to give back the goods and receive a substitute or money in return. The court found that Park's letter that described in detail the alleged non-conformity in the good (a dryer) was sufficient to constitute revocation of acceptance because it attempted to "reject acceptance," demanded that Cissell remove the machine from the premises, and requested that damages be paid.

Do Industry Standards Have Any Effect Upon the Time in Which the Buyer Must Reject Non-Conforming Goods?

Said simply, yes. In *B/R Sales Co., Inc. v. Krantor Corp.* (640 N.Y.S.2d 204 (NY App. Div. 1996)), the seller's representative testified, without contradiction by the buyer, that the custom and practice in the industry is that all claims had to be made upon delivery or within a "reasonable" timeframe, normally 48 hours after acceptance of the first shipment or any additional shipments. Since the buyer did not reject the goods until four weeks after delivery, the court held that the rejection was untimely.

Cases About Contract Formation and Award

How Are Formation and Terms of an Online Contract Analyzed?

Re Zappos.com. Inc. Customer Data Security Breach Litigation (893 F.Supp.2d 1058 (2012)) addresses the issue of identifying terms and conditions in online orders. Zappos is an online retailer of consumer products. Several customers ordered products online from Zappos. Zappos posted on its website, accessible through a hyperlink, the Terms of Use for ordering items from Zappos. The written Terms of Use included a statement that all disputes regarding any service or product ordered from Zappos shall be exclusively resolved through arbitration, namely, the Federal Arbitration Act. Dissatisfied customers sued, challenging the Terms of Use stated by Zappos on their website.

The court referred to the Zappos scheme of contracting as a "browser wrap" agreement. The court went on to contrast this "browser wrap" agreement with a "click wrap" agreement. The difference between a "click wrap" and "browser wrap" agreement is that in a "click wrap" agreement, the customer is required to click the icon signifying acceptance of the terms and conditions of the contract while in a "browser wrap" agreement, the customer is not required or offered the opportunity to click or otherwise indicate acceptance of the terms and conditions of the contract.

The plaintiff customers contended that a valid contract with Zappos was not formed, specifically because the agreement to submit all disputes to arbitration was not agreed to. In addition, the plaintiff customers alleged that even though the hyperlink to the Terms of Use is presented on each page of the Zappos website, either in the middle or bottom of the page, if the customer scrolls down the pages of the website, there is nothing in the website that directs the customer to the Terms of Use when setting up an account, logging into an existing account, or if the customer just makes a purchase. Further, the Terms of Use hyperlink is not distinguishable from a multitude of other hyperlinks included in the website. Finally, the plaintiff customers contended that since the hyperlink to the Terms of Use is not conspicuous and that customers are not directed to this hyperlink as a prerequisite to purchasing, the customer is not only not aware of the Terms of Use and the exclusivity of the arbitration provision but also never agreed or consented to such a contract term.

The court ruled that this kind of "browser wrap" agreement, absent some showing that the customer actually viewed and read the arbitration provision, does not form a valid and enforceable contract that includes an exclusive arbitration provision to handle disputes. The court also noted that "click wrap" agreements that condition any purchase of goods online to the customer consenting to the terms of use, including any exclusive arbitration provision for handling disputes, would satisfy the requirements for producing a binding contract.

Does a Bidder Have Standing to Sue When It Is the Apparent Low Bidder But Is Not Awarded a Contract?

In *Ardmare Construction Company, Inc., v. Freedman* (467 A. 2d. 674 (Conn. 1983)), Ardmare was the lowest bidder on a project but was not awarded the bid due to its failure to meet the signature requirements on the bid form. A suit was filed as an action for mandamus (command) to require the named defendant (Freedman, Commissioner of Administrative Services) to award the plaintiff (Ardmare) a contract for labor and materials on a certain state project.

The case involves whether Ardmare had standing to sue.

Standing to sue is the legal right to set judicial machinery in motion. One cannot rightfully invoke the jurisdiction of the court unless he has, in an individual or representative capacity, some real interest in the cause of action, or a legal or equitable right, title, or interest in the subject matter of the controversy.

Originally, the district court ruled that the plaintiff had standing to sue. However, the Supreme Court disagreed with the basis of the court's decision and remanded the case back to the district court, with instructions to dismiss the lawsuit. The Supreme Court found that the plaintiff did not have standing to sue because he had no enforceable legal or equitable right in contract; therefore, not unlike any other person whose offer has been rejected, a disappointed bidder has no right to judicial intervention. This court declared, "[a] bid, even the lowest responsible one, submitted in response to an invitation for bids is only an offer which, until accepted by the municipality, does not give rise to a contract between the parties." The announcement that the plaintiff had submitted the lowest bid did not amount to acceptance. Acceptance occurs only after it is determined that the bid conforms to the statutory requirements and the bidder is "competent to perform the work."

The Supreme Court further ruled that the competitive bidding statute does not provide the disappointed bidder with standing to sue. The court stated: "municipal competitive bidding laws are enacted to guard against such evils as favoritism, fraud, or corruption in the award of contracts, to secure the best product at the lowest price, and to benefit the taxpayers, not the bidders."

It should be noted that there is no uniformity of decisions among the states on this issue of standing to sue. The competitive bidding statute in each state will control the outcome of this question. For example, some state courts have held that an unsuccessful bidder has absolute standing to sue under the competitive bidding statute. Other state courts have found that unsuccessful bidders have limited standing pursuant to a particular state statute. Still other state courts have found standing to sue only if the unsuccessful bidder was a taxpayer.

Can a Public Entity Award a Contract to the Apparent Low Bidder if This Bidder Fails to Acknowledge an Addendum as Required in the Bid Specifications?

In *Martel Construction, Inc., v. Montana State Board of Examiners* (668 P. 2d, 222 (Mont. 1983)), a case on bid responsiveness, Martel Construction, Inc. and Volk Construction, Inc. were both licensed Montana contractors. In late 1982, the Montana State Board of Examiners issued a solicitation for competitive bids for the construction of the Montana Children's Treatment Unit to be built in Billings, Montana. The bid opening was to be held on February 9, 1983. Prior to the bid opening date, the state officers amended the solicitation for bids by addendum 1, dated January 18, 1983; addendum 2, dated February 2, 1983; and addendum 3, dated February 4, 1983. Because of the late issuance of the last two addenda, the architect contacted all bidders on February 8 to confirm they received them.

The solicitation for bids contained a section entitled "Instructions to Bidders," which provided, "[bidders] shall acknowledge receipt of all addenda issued." The bid form had on it a place for the acknowledgment of each addendum, with the date of each addendum. The bid submitted by Volk failed to acknowledge, on the envelope or on the bid form, receipt of addenda 2 and 3.

When bids were opened on February 9, 1983, Volk had a low general contractor's bid of $1,698,000. The next bid submitted by Martel for the same options was $174,600 higher. The architect again contacted Volk to inquire whether the company received addenda 2 and 3. He was assured that Volk received and considered all addenda.

The Montana Board of Examiners received a memorandum from its legal counsel advising them not to accept Volk's bid and to re-bid the project. Nevertheless, the Board concluded that Volk was aware of addenda 2 and 3 and could be bound to a contract, including all the addenda. The Board then awarded the contract to Volk as the lowest bidder.

Martel sued. The trial court held for Martel, emphasizing the importance of protecting the competitive bidding process for the construction of public works and the importance of acknowledging solicitation addenda. The State Board of Examiners eventually appealed to the Montana Supreme Court.

The Supreme Court reversed the ruling of the trial court. The court held that the evidence that Volk was contacted by telephone regarding the last two addenda, and that Volk had begun preparation for fulfilling the obligations of addenda 2 and 3, were adequate to show that Volk had actual knowledge of the addenda, and that Volk was obligated to perform the contract. The solicitation had stated that "All written addenda issued by the Architect/Engineer will become part of the Contract Documents and all Bidders shall be bound by such addenda, whether received or not by the Bidder."

The court found that the defect in permitting oral acknowledgement of the addenda was a minor informality. Volk was obligated to perform at the bid price, and the amount of bid price attributable to addenda 2 and 3 accounted for only one-third of the difference in bid prices.

Can a Public Entity Decide to Reject a Bid if the Bidder Was Encouraged to Submit a Bid by the Project Architect but Failed to Attend a Mandatory Pre-Bid Conference?

In the case of *Gibbs Construction Co., Inc. v. Board of Supervisors of Louisiana State University* (447 So.2d 90 (La. Ct. App. 1984)), the University of New Orleans advertised for public bids to construct certain alterations to the university's graduate school building. The contract documents included a date, time, and location for a pre-bid conference and provided that "no bid shall be accepted from any contractor who does not have a responsible representative attend this meeting." Only one contractor attended the pre-bid conference. Gibbs Construction Co., Inc. did not have a representative at the pre-bid conference.

Subsequent to the pre-bid conference—and without the knowledge or consent of the university—the project architect contacted Gibbs Construction Co. and requested that the company submit a bid. The architect told the company that it could submit a bid although it did not have a representative at the pre-bid conference. The architect even drew a line through that portion of the documents requiring attendance at the conference.

In reliance upon the architect's representations, but without communicating with anyone at the university, Gibbs Construction Company, Inc. submitted a bid. The university did not accept Gibbs' bid, although it would have been the lowest, because Gibbs had not had a representative at the pre-bid conference. The contract was awarded to the only bidder with a representative in attendance at the pre-bid conference, although this bid was higher than Gibbs' bid would have been.

Gibbs filed suit on the theory that Gibbs was the lowest responsible bidder and should have been awarded the contract.

The court ruled that Gibbs Construction Co., Inc. did not qualify as a bidder because it failed to comply with the pre-bid procedures mandated by the bid advertisement.

Gibbs argued that its bid was acceptable and should have been considered by the university because the architect had requested the bid and had represented that the bid would be acceptable. The plaintiffs also argued that the architect was the agent of the university and that the university should be bound by his representations. Further, the plaintiffs argued that the university had the power to waive the requirement of attendance at the pre-bid conference.

According to the court, the facts as alleged by plaintiffs did not indicate the existence of any type of agency relationship between the university and the project architect concerning the advertising and letting of the contract.

Further, even assuming the university had the power to waive attendance at the pre-bid conference, the university was not obligated to and did not waive the requirement as indicated by the non-acceptance of Gibbs' bid. The court found that this action by the university was not arbitrary but was in accord with the advertisement. Gibbs' lawsuit was dismissed.

Does a City Have the Legal Authority to Accept a Bid, Which, at the Time of Bid Opening, Was Nonconforming as to Acceptable Materials and Components but Was Subsequently Amended, Prior to Acceptance, to Conform to the Specifications as Stated in the Original Proposal?

In *Harry Pepper & Associates, Inc. v. City Cape Coral*, 352 So.2d 1190 (Fla. Dist. Ct. App. 1977), the City of Cape Coral desired to build a water treatment plant. The advertisement for bids contained the following provision:

> Prior submittal by manufacturers whose equipment has not been specified is required. The City Engineer's written approval of that equipment must be obtained for that equipment to be authorized for inclusion in the Bid Documents' Equipment Schedule or project work.

Since a major component of the water plant required the use of expensive and powerful pumps, the specifications for the bids said the following about the various types of pumps to be used: "As a point of information, this project has been designed based on the use of [pumps] . . . as manufactured by Johnson Pump Company; FMC Corporation, Peerless Pump Division; or equal." Each bid required the bidder to specify the manufacturer of the pumps that it proposed to supply under its bid.

At the time of bid opening, Gulf Corporation submitted the name of a pump manufacturer that was not acceptable to the city or the project engineers; however, Gulf was the low bidder. Subsequently, the city engineer contacted Gulf and asked them to indicate whether they would use an acceptable pump manufacturer. Gulf agreed to use an acceptable pump manufacturer and made no other changes. At the next City Council meeting, a contract was awarded to Gulf, as the low, responsible, responsive bidder.

The Pepper Company, the number two bidder, filed for injunction, contending that the award was unlawful because of the change allowed to the bid. The city contended that this was a minor change and was in the best interests of the city. The trial court held that the city had such authority. Pepper appealed the case.

The appellate court reversed, ruling in favor of Pepper, following court precedent holding that the purpose of the bidding process is:

> To protect the public against collusive contracts; to secure fair competition upon equal terms to all bidders; to remove not only collusion but temptation for collusion and opportunity for gain at public expense; to close all avenues to favoritism and fraud in its various forms; to secure the best values for the county at the lowest possible expense; and to afford an equal advantage to all desiring to do business with the [government], by affording an opportunity for an exact comparison of bids . . . [a] bidder cannot be permitted to change his bid after the bids have been opened, except to cure minor irregularities.

The appellate court stated that

> the test for measuring whether a deviation in a bid is sufficiently material to destroy its competitive character is whether the variation affects the amount of the bid by giving the bidder an advantage or benefit not enjoyed by the other bidders.

To the appellate court, the difference between the conforming and nonconforming pumps was material, yet Gulf was permitted to modify its bid. Further, the inclusion of the non-conforming pumps was an advantage not enjoyed by other bidders, who were required to only specify approved equipment.

The court concluded,

> Faced with Gulf's substantially nonconforming bid, the City had but two proper alternatives: to award the contract to the next lowest bidder who met the specifications, or to reject all bids and readvertise for new ones. The City exceeded its authority by allowing Gulf to bring its bid into conformity with the specifications and then accepting it.

Can a Public Entity Waive the Requirement for the Agent's Signature on the Bid as Informality?

Michael Menefee v. County of Fresno (163 Cal. App. 3d 1175 (Cal. Ct. App.1985)) involved the common issues of responsiveness and failure to sign a bid where required. Menefee Construction Co. was a general partnership and licensed contractor under California law. Brewer-Kalar was a joint venture also engaged in the construction business. Both Menefee Construction Co. and Brewer-Kalar submitted bid forms to Fresno County for a contract to construct water, sewer, drainage, and street improvements in a county service area.

The bids were opened April 29, 1982. Brewer-Kalar's bid was the lowest at $699,998, and Menefee Construction Co. was next lowest at $725,946. However, Brewer-Kalar failed to sign the appropriate line on the bid form. The bond accompanying the bid was properly signed.

The deputy county counsel who reviewed the documents for the board of supervisors concluded that Brewer-Kalar's failure to sign the bid's proposal sheet was a material irregularity that rendered the bid "non-responsive" and invalid. The county counsel advised the board not to accept the bid.

The board met June 1, 1982 and heard arguments by counsel for both Brewer-Kalar and Menefee. It then voted to accept the Brewer-Kalar bid and waive any irregularity caused by the absent signature on the bid form.

Menefee filed a petition for writ of mandate with the Superior Court to enjoin construction and compel the county to contract with Menefee. Relief was denied at trial and Menefee appealed.

To the appellate court, the issue was whether Brewer-Kalar would have been liable on the bond if they had attempted to back out of their bid after the board had accepted it. If the contractor would have been able to avoid forfeiture of the bond after their bid was accepted, then the deficiency of the bid would have given them an unfair advantage over other bidders and would have rendered the bid invalid.

The court considered other states' cases whose holdings went both ways. In this case, there were authorized signatures by Brewer-Kalar's principals at various locations within the bid documents, signifying its intention to be bound and making the bid binding as a matter of law. The court considered the failure to sign the bid in the required location as an irregularity that could be waived by the county.

In Those Cases Where the Bid Solicitation Requires a Bid Bond, Can a Public Entity Accept a Bid That Is Accompanied by a Form of Security That Is Different Than the Form Required by the Entity?

In the case of *Robinson Electric, Co. v. Dade County* (417 So.2d. 1032 (Fla. Dist. Ct. App. 1982)), the Dade County Board of County Commissioners' advertisement for bids in connection with a contract to renovate public housing required that a bid bond for 5% of the cost be submitted with the bid.

Robinson submitted the lowest bid of $10,368,515 along with a cashier's check for 5% of the designated cost as security. The second-lowest bidder also submitted a cashier's check. Marvin Markowitz, Inc., submitted the highest bid, $10,700,000; its bid included a bid bond in the correct amount. When the Director of Dade County Housing and Urban Development opened the bids and learned that the two lowest bidders had submitted cashier's checks instead of bid bonds, he asked the county attorney for his opinion. Upon receiving a recommendation that Robinson's bid be approved, the Board of County Commissioners awarded the contract to Robinson. Markowitz sued the Board, requesting injunctive relief. Robinson intervened in the lawsuit. Upon hearing testimony, the trial court found Robinson's bid to be non-responsive because it lacked the required form of security. The court vacated the award of the contract to Robinson and ordered the County to reissue an Invitation for Bids (IFB).

Robinson appealed the decision of the trial court. Robinson contended that the court erred in vacating an administrative decision that was not shown to be arbitrary or unreasonable. The Board, it contended, correctly waived the immaterial variance in the form of the security; the difference in the security did not affect the nature or purpose of competitive bidding. Furthermore, argued Robinson, the County reserved in the IFB the right to waive formalities. Markowitz, on the other hand, argued that since its bid met the qualifications, it should have been awarded the contract without reissuance of the IFB.

The court reasoned that although a bid containing a material variance is unacceptable, not every deviation from the invitation is material. In determining whether a specific noncompliance constitutes a substantial and, hence, non-waivable irregularity, the courts in Florida have applied two criteria: (1) whether the effect of a waiver would be to deprive the municipality of its assurance that the contract will be entered into, performed, and guaranteed according to its specified requirements; and (2) whether it is of such a nature that its waiver would adversely affect competitive bidding by placing a bidder in a position of advantage over other bidders or by otherwise undermining the necessary common standard of competition.

A bid may be rejected or disregarded if there is a material variance between the bid and the advertisement. In this case, the appeals court found that the variance was not material. The appeals court reversed the trial court and ordered the award be reinstated to Robinson.

When Can Matters of Responsibility Be Investigated?

Skyline Contractors, Inc. v. Spokane Housing Authority (289 P. 3d 690 (Wash. Ct. App. 2012)) is a case that highlights the relationship between responsibility inquiries and contract formation. In February 2010, the Spokane

Housing Authority issued an invitation for bids (IFB) for a federally funded project to furnish and install windows in homes. The IFB required window installers to have a minimum of five years of documented experience.

Skyline—who had been incorporated as a business for only three years—submitted a timely bid that was in line for award. But the housing authority refused to execute the contracts because Skyline did not satisfy the experience requirement. Skyline protested. Skyline pointed out that its bid identified a subcontractor with 20+ years of window installation experience. The housing authority granted Skyline's request for reevaluation.

During that reevaluation, the housing authority asked questions about how the work would be performed by Skyline and its subcontractors. In its responses, Skyline stated that it had "full intention of subcontracting all installation of the windows in the bid documents," and "Skyline . . . does not intend to self-perform installation of the windows. All contract documents will be followed as they were bid." After considering the additional information, the housing authority notified Skyline that it "shall be awarded the contract." The IFB instructions stated that written award to the successful bidder "shall result in a binding contract without further action by either party."

At the pre-construction meeting, the authority again asked Skyline about the subcontractors. The identity of the subcontractors remained unclear, so the authority asked to see the subcontracts. Skyline explained that because the owner-contractor agreement had not been executed, Skyline did not yet have subcontracts. Skyline further implied that the listed subcontractor might not be able to do all the work. Skyline maintained, however, that listing subcontractors on a bid proposal did not mean those subcontractors had to be used.

Apparently not satisfied, the housing authority's lawyer notified Skyline that its bid was "not responsive" to the invitation for bids. The authority awarded to the next bidder in line, and Skyline sued.

The appellate court found that, based on Washington judicial precedent, a contract existed at the time of the award notice.

What Discretion Exists When Deciding to Cancel a Solicitation?

In *A&A Industrial Piping, Inc. v. County of Passaic* (No. A-4902–10T4 (N.J. 2012)), the issue was whether the cancellation of a solicitation was lawful. In *A&A*, bids had been received for upgrades to the heating, ventilation, air conditioning, and fire protection systems for the county jail. A&A

protested the intended award to the low bidder on various grounds, including the fact that the apparent awardee was not prequalified by the county to perform structural steel or HVAC work. The county realized it had inadvertently omitted prequalification of contractors in the solicitation terms and conditions. The county cancelled the solicitation. A&A sued.

The court sustained the county's decision, agreeing with the trial court judge that the county did not abuse its discretion in determining that it needed to rebid the project to ensure that only prequalified contractors worked on the project. The court reasoned that the county's cancellation and resolicitation decision put potential bidders on an equal footing, ensuring that they had a common understanding of the qualification requirements. "[T]here can be no judicial declaration of invalidity in the absence of clear abuse of discretion," the court concluded.

Cases About Contract Administration

How Does the Termination for Convenience Clause Operate to Limit Damages for a Public Entity's Breach of Contract?

In *MB Oil Ltd. v. The City of Albuquerque* (382 P. 3d 975 (N.M. Ct. App. 2016)), a New Mexico court applied settled federal and state judicial precedent to give effect to a termination for convenience clause. MB Oil was a wholesale fuel distributor that contracted with the City of Albuquerque to be the primary supplier of certain fuels to the city's fleet management division. MB Oil promised to treat the city as a "preferred customer," agreeing to certain response times for delivering fuel. In exchange, the city agreed to make MB Oil its primary fuel provider, meaning it would satisfy requirements from MB Oil before going to alternate sources.

MB Oil had never bid on a government contract before. It was awarded the contract based on a bid that was one-sixth that of the second-lowest bidder. After performance began, there were various occasions when MB Oil could not deliver on-time, or at all. The city was forced to go to alternate suppliers.

The city informed MB Oil several times that it was not meeting fuel delivery obligations. One notice characterized MB Oil's performance as a default. The city finally terminated the contract both for default and convenience. MB Oil sued for breach of contract, alleging that the city misrepresented the amount and types of fuel that would be ordered. The complaint also alleged that the city breached its "covenant of good faith and fair dealing" in how it solicited bids and administered the contract—a common allegation in these kinds of cases.

The trial court found for MB Oil and awarded over $4 million in damages that included anticipatory profits. The court concluded that the city wrongfully terminated the contract for default because MB Oil's untimely and sometimes failed deliveries did not, in the trial court's judgment, constitute substantial impairment of the city's benefits under the contract.

The appellate court reversed, explaining that the termination for convenience clause permits termination without regard to whether there is a default or breach by the other party. The court noted that the clause is commonly used in contracts with the federal government and other states. The appellate court found that MB Oil's failure to meet city demands justified the termination for convenience. The court held that the city's termination was not a breach of the contract or the obligation of good faith and fair dealing. The appellate court thus reversed the judgment of the trial court, eliminating the award of breach of contract damages.

What Is the Effect of "Substantial Completion" in a Construction Contract?

In a New Jersey construction dispute involving takeover agreements after the original contractor defaulted, the "substantial performance" doctrine was an issue in litigation with the performance bond surety lasting almost 15 years (*American Motorists Ins. Co. v. N. Plainfield Bd. of Educ.* (No. A-4680–14T4 (N.J. Super. Ct. App., Oct. 20, 2016)).

The Plainfield New Jersey Board of Education (owner) executed takeover agreements with the surety after default by the original contractor. On the two projects at issue, the architect had issued substantial completion certificates.

Afterwards, the architect noted punch-list deficiencies and decertified the parking lot paving. The surety had executed payment bonds to cover the work completion, but the board learned that the United States Department of Treasury had terminated the surety's certificate of authority to qualify as an acceptable surety on federal bonds. The board stopped all payments on the troubled project, and the surety withdrew from the site without completing punch-list items or delivering project documentation.

The court determined that there was "substantial completion." The issuance of the architect's completion certificates and beneficial use of the schools established there was no material breach by the surety that would have entitled the board to stop paying. Once substantial performance was established, the contract permitted the board to reduce an amount for incomplete work. The owner, however, bears the burden of proof (not met in this case). Rejecting the board's breach argument, the court held that the contractor had not improperly abandoned performance; the board had stopped payment for some time with no legal justification.

Can a Termination for Default Be Based on a Failure to Satisfy a Service Level Agreement in an Information Technology Contract?

In *Charter Township of Shelby v. Technology Integration Group Services, Inc.* (No. 297190 (Mich. Ct. App. 2013), appeal application denied, 843 N.W.2d 139 (Mich. Supreme Court 2013)), the Township of Shelby, Michigan, contracted with Technology Integration Group Services (TIGS) for technology support services for a three-year period. TIGS had the previous contract for the services. The contract included a broad array of services including hardware, software, maintenance, and daily services. The contract included a Service Level Agreement to be used "as a benchmark for service goals." The contract further contained a procedure for TIGS to "provide a written report to the Township of the service level criteria and the actual results against those criteria." The township was authorized to request service level reviews each quarter or more frequently.

The contract had a procedure for addressing the township's dissatisfaction with any hardware or service. If a township employee deemed TIGS's service unsatisfactory, the employee was required to submit an incident report to TIGS within five days of the deficient service. TIGS was required to submit a response and take necessary corrective action.

Three days after contract execution, the president of TIGS and its sales manager (and liaison with the township) were both indicted on multiple federal charges related to alleged involvement in trade with Iraq during the United States' embargo against Iraq. The township supervisor testified that when he learned of the indictments, he decided almost immediately that the township should cease doing business with TIGS. The township board voted to discontinue its relationship with TIGS and to hire a different company. Following that vote, the supervisor publicly stated that the rescission of the contract had "nothing to do with performance."

TIGS personnel responsible for serving the township continued to report for work at the township offices. TIGS sued for breach of contract after the township refused to participate in mediation and advised TIGS that "no contract exists."

The township presented evidence at trial that TIGS's performance was inadequate, that on at least one occasion they were unable to promptly restore the township website after it crashed, and that TIGS did not immediately begin work on new services to be provided under the contract. However, the township never submitted a formal performance complaint.

At trial, both parties asserted that the other party was the first to materially breach the contract. The jury found for the township and awarded damages. TIGS appealed.

The court of appeals held that none of the township's allegations were sufficiently serious to justify the termination of the contract. TIGS did not cease serving the township until after the township stopped paying TIGS and brought in another firm to replace TIGS. The alleged failure by TIGS to timely restore the website or satisfactorily perform other services could eventually have allowed the township to terminate the contract without penalty, but the contract did not allow that as a first resort. Instead, the township was supposed to complain of any inadequacies in TIGS's service. The township made no attempt to address any performance issues and effectively repudiated the contract when it brought in a replacement for TIGS after ceasing all payments to TIGS.

The court of appeals held that the township breached the contract and was liable.

Can Consequential Damages Waiver Clauses Limit Damages for Data Breach in an Information Technology Contract?

A 2016 federal court of appeals decision created a firestorm of interest nationally in consequential damages exclusions and their application to damages from data breach (*Silverpop Systems, Inc. v. Leading Market Technologies, Inc.*, 641 F.App'x 849 (11th Cir. 2016)).

Silverpop Systems provides digital marketing services. Leading Market Technologies entered into a service contract with Silverpop to access its web-based e-marketing tool. Under the contract, Leading Market uploaded over 495,000 of its customer emails. The contract's confidentiality clause required Silverpop to safeguard the confidential information.

Someone hacked the Silverpop system and accessed Leading Market's emails. Although it was unclear whether the data was ever exported to any third parties, Leading Market sued Silverpop for contract breach, claiming that the market value of the emails (its customer list) was essentially reduced to zero by virtue of the data breach.

The contract contained a limitation of liability clause. Section 10.1 of the clause stated that "In no event will Silverpop be liable to the other party . . . for any consequential damages . . . in any way relating to this agreement." Subsection 10.2 of the clause set a maximum liability cap equal to fees received by Silverpop during the 12 months preceding a breach. The subsection 10.2 also stated that "This damages limitation shall not apply to a breach of [the confidentiality clause covering the data breach]."

The federal court analyzed whether the data breach damages were direct or consequential. Direct damages under the governing Georgia law "are such as arise naturally and according to the usual course of things from such breach." Consequential damages are "such as the parties contemplated when the contract was made as the probable result of the breach." The court held that service deficiencies caused by Silverpop's system would have been direct. Data breach damages, on the other hand, do not arise naturally according to the usual course of things in a service contract. Even though the contract had a confidentiality provision, the central object of the contract was not protection of data.

The subsection 10.2 exclusion of claims based on breach of confidentiality provisions did not help Leading Market. The court held that its placement in the clause showed that it operated only with respect to operation of the liability cap, not the exclusion of consequential damages, as Leading Market essentially had contracted away its right to recover data breach damages by agreeing to exclude consequential damages.

How Does the Indemnification Clause Shift the Risk of Loss in a Contract?

In the case of *R. Zoppo Co., Inc. v. City of Manchester* (453 A.2d 1311 (N.H. 1982)), the City of Manchester, New Hampshire, contracted with Zoppo Company for construction of an enclosure of a brook in the city. The city contracted with the architect for final plans, estimates of the cost of construction, specifications and contract documents for the project, as well as to provide consultation and advice to the city during construction.

The contract between the city and architect provided that the architect would hold the city harmless for all suits and claims arising out of, or in consequence of, the acts or failure to act of the architect-engineer.

An issue arose regarding the extent of the contractor's obligation on a project to build cofferdams. A cofferdam is a temporary, watertight enclosure from which the water is pumped to expose the bottom of a body of water and permit construction. Zoppo took the position that it was required to provide steel cofferdams only where the specification drawings indicated that they should be used. The architect and city, however, maintained that the entire brook enclosure must be built under the protection of a continuous steel cofferdam. Complete coffer-damming provides greater protection against storms and protects nearby residential buildings from settlement, reducing the city's exposure to suit from such hazards.

A master appointed by the trial court determined that Zoppo was misled by a deficiency in the plans and specification, and that the extra costs in performing in excess of the expected work were compensable. The master held that the architect should indemnify the city; the successful claim was attributable to the architect's failure in the preparation and content of the specifications.

The New Hampshire Supreme Court agreed. Considering the fact that the architect and city contracted to have the firm provide plans, specifications, and contract documents for the project, the court affirmed the holding that the architect was liable for the amounts the city paid to the contractor.

Applying the U.C.C. to Hypothetical Controversies

What Happens When Actual Damages Exceed the Allowances Specified for Liquidated Damages?

Under the contract signed by two firms, Owens Enterprises agreed to buy all of the citrus fruit of merchantable quality produced in the groves of Davis Fruit on or before February 19. The price specified was $1.25 a box, and the groves were expected to produce in excess of 20,000 boxes.

The contract also contained the following clause:

> The Buyer has this day advanced to the Seller the sum of $11,000, the receipt of which is hereby acknowledged by the Seller and which sum is an advance and part payment for said fruit at the price above stated. Should the Buyer fail to comply with the terms and conditions herein enumerated, this contract shall therefore become null and void, and the advance made to the Seller shall be retained by the Seller in full payment of liquidated damages.

Owens did fail to comply with the terms and conditions. After accepting 12,000 boxes of fruit and paying an additional $5,000 over and above the $11,000 advance, Owens lost a major customer and had no use for the remainder of Davis' production. Davis was unable to find another buyer and watched the equivalent of 9,500 boxes rot on the trees.

Does a buyer's unforeseen risk leave a citrus grower without payment for damages? The U.C.C. generally follows the common law rules governing liquidated damage provisions. Under U.C.C. (2)-718 (1), damages for the breach of a contract for the sale of goods by either party may be liquidated in the agreement, but only by an amount that is reasonable in the light of (1) the anticipated or actual harm caused by the breach, (2) the difficulties of proof of loss, and (3) the inconvenience or non-feasibility of otherwise obtaining an adequate remedy.

This provision concludes by stating that a term fixing unreasonably large liquidated damages is void as a penalty. An unreasonably small amount would be subject to similar criticism, and might be stricken under the section as unconscionable.

Simply stated, the law, as a matter of public policy, opposes the use of liquidated damage provisions to set damages that are viewed as "penal" in character. This includes agreements for damages unreasonably disproportionate to the anticipated losses. The probable reason for the opposition to penalty clauses stems from the belief that one should be free to breach one's contract upon payment of the actual damages the breach causes and that certain breaches maximize economic resources.

Further, penalty clauses contradict the basic rule of contractual damages, which is based on the notion that the non-breaching party should only recover damages that cover the "benefit of the bargain" and no more. Whatever the reasons, the rule is well accepted that liquidated damage clauses are valid and enforceable, while penalty clauses are not.

In this case, Owens, the buyer, contends that the grower/seller should be limited to the recovery of the $11,000 liquidated damages specified in the contractual provision and that the grower/seller has already collected a sum in excess of that amount. Davis, the grower/seller, argues that the parties contracted for the sale of all of the fruit of merchantable quality from the seller's orchards. Although the buyer has paid the seller a total of $16,000 on the contract, he has left 9,500 boxes of merchantable fruit unpurchased that would have earned the grower/seller an additional amount of approximately $12,000 if the buyer had fully complied with his agreement. The grower/seller contends that to enforce the liquidated damage provision would constitute a penalty against him because it is an unreasonably small amount and, therefore, would be unconscionable.

If the court as a matter of law finds the contract or any clause of the contract to have been unconscionable at the time it was made, the court may refuse to enforce the contract. Alternatively, it may enforce the remainder of the contract without the unconscionable clause, or it may so limit the application of any unconscionable clause as to avoid any unconscionable result.

While most cases on liquidated damages occur when the stipulated sum is unreasonably high, there are some decisions in which the complaining party demonstrated that the liquidated figure was so inadequate as to justify the court permitting him to recover his actual damages. Here then, the grower/seller would be entitled to a further recovery if he can prove that the amount is too small and, therefore, unconscionable.

Absent a finding of unconscionability, the grower/seller may still find relief in U.C.C. Section 2–719(2), which provides: "Where circumstances cause an exclusive or limited remedy to fail of its essential purpose, remedy may be had as provided in this code."

There may have been good reason to enforce the liquidated damages provision in this case had the buyer utterly failed to perform the contract. However, the buyer had already taken delivery of enough fruit to use up the deposit. If the grower/seller's recovery is limited to the amount of the deposit, he will be entitled to no damages whatsoever for the buyer's failure to pick the remaining 9,500 boxes. This could easily be a case in which the circumstances have caused an exclusive remedy—the liquidated damage provision—to fail its essential purpose of permitting the grower/seller to pursue other remedies provided by the Code.

When Does the "Indefiniteness" of a Contract Still Constitute an Enforceable Contract?

Company President Steve Janelle claims that the loose ends of a contract will nullify the agreement to purchase computer chips from a supplier named MicroChips. The contract did not specify when or where delivery will take place, and the price was whatever the market would bear when the chips were delivered. Although Janelle's company had accepted delivery on that premise, the market changed within the next two months, and Steve Janelle had found another supplier willing to confirm time and place of delivery as well as a good price. When MicroChips attempted to perform under the first contract a week later, Janelle refused, arguing that he "didn't have a contract because the important terms had been left open."

Janelle Computers argues that the alleged contract with MicroChips, Inc., failed for indefiniteness due to its numerous "open terms," such as time and place of delivery. In addition, Janelle argues that the price term for the memory chips (i.e., "market price at time of delivery") is too indefinite to allow enforcement of the contract. Although Janelle's argument might have had some merit under common law/pre-U.C.C. cases, when all essential terms to a contract had to be included or the contract would fail, this argument has no chance of success on the facts under the provisions of the U.C.C.

The controlling section in this regard is U.C.C. Section 2–204(3), which provides as follows: "Even though one or more terms are left open, a contract for sale does not fail for indefiniteness if the parties have intended to make a contract and there is a reasonably certain basis for giving an appropriate remedy." It appears from the facts that at least the following terms were agreed upon by the two parties:

- The type of memory chips ordered;
- The quantity ordered;
- The price to be paid for the quantity ordered (market price at time of delivery); and
- The approximate delivery date.

The facts as presented put to rest any argument as to whether, under the first prong of the test in Section 2–204(3), the parties intended to make a contract. Similarly, these terms, if in fact entered into, would also provide a reasonably certain basis for giving an appropriate remedy.

Thus, the legal question posed by the second prong of Section 2–204(3) must also be answered in the affirmative. The alleged contract clearly delineates a promise to sell identifiable goods of a specified type and quantity at a specified or reasonably determinable price and time.

Accordingly, even though the contract contains several open terms, the contract does not fail for indefiniteness, because the U.C.C.'s "gap filler" provisions may supplement such open terms. For instance, time and place of delivery are dealt with in Sections 2–308 and 2–309, which provide that in the absence of a specified place and time in the contract for delivery, the place for delivery is the seller's place of business and the specific time for delivery shall be a reasonable time.

Moreover, the more traditionally difficult issue of a market-based open price term is expressly recognized by the Code as an acceptable contract under Section 2–305(1)(c):

> The parties if they so intend can conclude a contract for sale even though the price is not settled. In such a case the price is a reasonable price at the time of delivery if . . . (c) the price is to be fixed in terms of some agreed market or other standard

Accordingly, Janelle's argument that the terms of this contract are indefinite is without merit.

When Do Additional Terms on a Purchase Order Represent an Unenforceable, Material Change to the Contractual Relationship Between Buyer and Seller?

When the Simpson School complex was destroyed by fire, the cause was identified immediately. Children playing under the building had ignited exposed polystyrene insulation. School officials launched a suit against the manufacturer, Dominion Insulfoam.

Dominion explained in court that it formed Insulfoam by expanding and molding polystyrene beads supplied to it by SWANCO. The company argued that if it was to be held liable for fire damage to the school and its contents, it was entitled to indemnification from SWANCO as the negligent manufacturer of the polystyrene beads. SWANCO, however, pointed to the indemnity provision on the reverse side of purchase order confirmations it routinely sent to Dominion after Dominion had placed an order but before the beads were shipped. The indemnity provision states:

> INDEMNIFICATION—Buyer (Dominion) agrees to defend, indemnify, and save harmless Seller (SWANCO) from any and all claims of whatsoever nature, including but not limited to injuries to Buyer's or Seller's employees or to third parties (including death), or for damages to the property of Seller, or to the property of Buyer, or of third parties, caused by, arising directly or indirectly from, or occurring on a) any handling of said materials, including but not limited to unloading railroad cars, tank cars, trucks, tank trucks, or barges, or in handling containers of materials sold, and b) any use of said materials.

Arguably, this express indemnity provision shielded SWANCO from Dominion's implied indemnity claim. Nevertheless, Dominion claimed that the hold-harmless indemnification provision was a "material alteration" of the parties' agreement and, thus, is not a term of the contract under the U.C.C.

The key issue here is whether the indemnification clause contained in SWANCO's confirmation form was incorporated into the parties' purchase agreement under U.C.C. Section 2–207 and whether the indemnity provision constituted a "material alteration" of the parties' agreement and, as such, did not become a term of the parties' contract.

Section 2–207 of the U.C.C. states:

1. A definite and reasonable expression of acceptance or a written confirmation, which is sent within a reasonable time, operates as

an acceptance even though it states terms additional to or different from those offered or agreed upon, unless acceptance is expressly made conditional on assent to the additional or different terms.

2. The additional terms are to be construed as proposals for addition to the contract. Between merchants such terms become part of the contract unless (a) the offer expressly limits acceptance to the terms of the offer; (b) they materially alter it; or (c) notification of objection to them has already been given or is given within a reasonable time after notice of them is received.

One must first determine whether the small proviso contained on the back of SWANCO's confirmation form converts an otherwise valid acceptance into a de facto rejection and counteroffer. That is, if SWANCO's purchase order confirmation form operates as an acceptance, then the indemnification clause becomes incorporated only if it is not a "material alteration" of the parties' contract under Section 2–207(2)(b). Confirmations such as SWANCO's are routinely held by a majority of the courts to operate as acceptances, rather than counteroffers, and contested clauses thus incorporated only if deemed immaterial under 2–2007(2)(b).

Consequently, the express indemnity clause contained on SWANCO's purchase order confirmation form is enforceable only if it does not constitute a material alteration of the parties' purchase contract. Generally, materiality is a question of fact. U.C.C. Section 2–207 provides that the test for materiality is whether the newly introduced clause would result in surprise or hardship to the non-assenting party.

Generally, warranty disclaimers are routinely deemed material as a matter of law. Similarly, courts commonly hold that indemnification clauses like SWANCO's are "material" as a matter of law. These factors lead us to predict that courts would hold that SWANCO's indemnity clause was a material alteration of the parties' purchase contract under Section 2–207(2) (b) of the U.C.C.; and, therefore, the clause is unenforceable as a matter of law.

When Can a Buyer Rely on Skill and Judgment of the Supplier to Invoke a Warranty of Fitness for a Particular Purpose Under the U.C.C.?

Tropic Construction was contracted to install multiple pipelines between several Caribbean islands for their local governments. Tropic decided that it needed a certain type of pipe that did not alter the delicate underwater ecosystem of the Caribbean.

Tropic contacted a leading pipe supplier, Coated Pipe Company, and spoke to a materials representative regarding the Coated Pipe Company's expertise with the type of pipe that will support coral reefs and underwater ecology. Tropic discussed its project needs, requirements, and objectives with Coated Pipe and subsequently executed and sent a purchase order to Coated Pipe. In the purchase order, the quantity, price, and shipping terms were listed. In addition, the purchase order specified that the pipe was to be "coal tar enamel-lined." Coated Pipe accepted the order and shipped the goods according to specifications.

Upon installation, Tropic discovered that the lining was not compatible with the coral reef environment and that the pipeline had to be replaced. Tropic sued Coated Pipe for breach of contract, arguing that Tropic had relied on Coated Pipe's expertise in pipes when they ordered the specified pipes for this job. Coated Pipe contended that it did nothing wrong.

The U.C.C. provides for several types of implied warranties—warranties included in the sales contract even though not specifically agreed to by the parties. Tropic is seeking recovery under the "breach of an implied warranty of fitness for a particular purpose."

The circumstances under which an implied warranty of fitness for a particular purpose will arise are specified in U.C.C. Section 2–315:

> Where the seller at the time of contracting has reason to know any particular purpose for which the goods are required and that the buyer is relying on the seller's skill or judgment to select or furnish suitable goods there is, unless excluded or modified under the next section, an implied warranty that the goods shall be fit for such purpose.

By the terms of U.C.C. Section 2–315, an implied warranty of fitness will not arise unless the buyer "is relying on the seller's skill or judgment to select or furnish suitable goods." It is essential, therefore, that the buyer proves that his or her organization relied upon the judgment and skill of the seller for the actual selection of the goods purchased. Courts recognize that buyers may rely upon a seller to "furnish" goods suitable for a particular purpose, even though the individual unit purchased is selected by the buyer.

The seller must have reason to know two things: (1) the particular purpose for which the buyer requires the goods and (2) the buyer is relying on the seller's skill of judgment to select or furnish suitable goods.

Both these requirements must exist before the warranty will be implied. It is not enough that the seller has reason to know the use to which the buyer intends to put the goods unless the seller also has reason to know that the buyer is relying on the seller's skill or judgment to select or furnish suitable goods.

The reliance factors, however, are in the disjunctive; the second requirement is satisfied based on the seller's skill or judgment to select or furnish suitable goods. The seller need not both select and furnish; either will suffice. Accordingly, the fact that the buyer selected the goods he or she wanted does not preclude reliance on the seller to furnish pipe suitable for the known application.

In this case, Tropic chose the pipe but informed Coated Pipe of the pipe's intended application. One can presume that Tropic wanted Coated Pipe's expertise in the selection of the requisite pipe, or at least the benefit of Coated Pipe's experience regarding the specified application. Arguably, Tropic did not expect Coated Pipe to stand silent as to any possible problems and merely ship the pipe. Consequently, Tropic has a good case against Coated Pipe. Tropic advised for what the pipe was to be used and arguably relied on Coated Pipe's expertise even though Tropic picked the specific pipe.

Does a Buyer Have to Comply With Volume Purchase Commitments and Low-Cost Supplier Provisions?

In July of 1996, Freemen, Inc., entered into a purchase agreement with Justin Foundry. This agreement incorporated two key provisions. The first was a "volume purchase commitment" under which Freeman "committed to purchase yearly an amount of 300,000 pounds of aluminum castings and 990,000 pounds of brass castings" from Justin.

This commitment was "predicated upon a continuation of a business sales level of Freeman products that requires the amount of aluminum and brass castings specified above on a yearly basis." No fixed period or termination date for this commitment was specified.

The other provision was what the parties termed the "low-cost supplier clause." The purchase agreement states:

> In situations where the cost per pound does not permit Justin to be the low-cost supplier of castings, Freeman will provide Justin with the opportunity to make every attempt to become the low-cost supplier of castings for Freeman. This opportunity to discuss individual price requirements that differ from competitive cost schedules is intended to be a mutually beneficial agreement to allow Justin the opportunity to compete to be the low-cost supplier in all situations and to also maximize Freeman's ability to remain cost-competitive in the marketplace.

Freeman never met the annual purchase commitments for brass and aluminum castings, and a year after signing the agreements was not even soliciting bids from Justin on additional work. By the fall of 1997, Freeman had completely terminated Justin as a supplier.

Because Freeman was Justin's major customer, this termination had dire consequences on the foundry. In December of 1997, Justin ceased operations and filed a petition for bankruptcy. Justin also filed an adversary proceeding in the bankruptcy court, alleging that Freeman breached its contract by failing to comply with the volume purchase commitment and low-cost supplier clause.

Does Justin have a case? Yes, Freeman may have some liability under the volume purchase commitment, but not under the low-cost supplier clause. Article 2 of the U.C.C. governs the resolution of Justin's claims under the "volume purchase commitment" concept.

As noted, Freeman committed to purchase 300,000 pounds of brass castings from Justin, predicated "upon a continuation of a business sales level of Freeman products that require the amount of aluminum and brass castings specified above on a yearly basis." The volume purchase commitment is a "requirements contract." Such contracts are governed by U.C.C. Section 2–306, which states that:

> term which measures the quantity by the . . . requirements of the buyer means such actual . . . requirements as may occur in good faith, except that no quantity unreasonably disproportionate to any such estimate . . . may be tendered or demanded.

The volume purchase commitment expressly conditioned the quantities of aluminum and brass castings to be purchased on Freeman's requirements.

Thus, although Freeman never purchased the stated amount of brass castings in the years 1996–1997, and also failed to purchase the stated amount of aluminum castings in 1997, these failures constitute a breach only to the extent that Freeman, in good faith, had a requirement for such castings but refused to purchase them from Justin.

Accordingly, the bankruptcy court should determine whether in the years 1996–1997 Freeman had a good-faith requirement for up to 990,000 pounds of brass castings, and whether in the year 1998 Freeman had a good-faith requirement for up to 300,000 pounds of aluminum castings. To the extent that Freeman may have had good-faith requirements for castings up to the quantities set forth in the contract but failed to purchase them from Justin, Freeman would have breached its purchase commitment and would be responsible to Justin for damages, including but not limited to lost profits.

As previously mentioned, the agreement also included the low-cost supplier clause. According to the agreement, Justin would provide castings "should (Freeman) desire" that it do so. The agreement then states that Freeman will provide Justin "the opportunity to make every attempt to become the low-cost supplier of castings," the "opportunity to compete" for all casting orders, and the "opportunity to discuss individual price requirements."

This is not a language of obligation and does not create a contractual duty on the part of Freeman to purchase castings from Justin; it merely sets forth a willingness to consider bids to fill additional orders by Justin. Clearly, this clause did not obligate Freeman to purchase any additional castings from Justin, and any failure by Freeman to purchase such additional castings was not a breach of contract.

Appendix A NIGP Code of Ethics

The Institute believes, and it is a condition of membership, that the following ethical principles should govern the conduct of every person employed by a public sector procurement or materials management organization:" See https://www.nigp.org/home/about-nigp/code-of-ethics

- Seeks or accepts a position as head (or employee) only when fully in accord with the professional principles applicable thereto and when confident of possessing the qualifications to serve under those principles to the advantage of the employing organization.
- Believes in the dignity and worth of the service rendered by the organization, and the societal responsibilities assumed as a trusted public servant.
- Is governed by the highest ideals of honor and integrity in all public and personal relationships in order to merit the respect and inspire the confidence of the organization and the public being served.
- Believes that personal aggrandizement or personal profit obtained through misuse of public or personal relationships is dishonest and not tolerable.
- Identifies and eliminates participation of any individual in operational situations where a conflict of interest may be involved.
- Believes that members of the Institute and its staff should at no time, or under any circumstances, accept directly or indirectly, gifts, gratuities, or other things of value from suppliers, which might influence or appear to influence purchasing decisions.
- Keeps the governmental organization informed, through appropriate channels, on problems and progress of applicable operations by emphasizing the importance of the facts.

- Resists encroachment on control of personnel in order to preserve integrity as a professional manager.
- Handles all personnel matters on a merit basis, and in compliance with applicable laws prohibiting discrimination in employment on the basis of politics, religion, color, national origin, disability, gender, age, pregnancy and other protected characteristics.
- Seeks or dispenses no personal favors. Handles each administrative problem objectively and empathetically, without discrimination.
- Subscribes to and supports the professional aims and objectives of NIGP—The Institute for Public Procurement.

Appendix B
UPPCC Code of Ethics

All applicants and certified professionals shall subscribe to and be bound by the following Code of Ethics & Professional Conduct:

- I shall only seek or accept a position of employment when fully in accord with the professional principles applicable thereto, and when confident of possessing the qualifications to serve under those principles to the advantage of my employer.
- I shall endeavor to keep myself knowledgeable and current on the practices and issues related to my profession.
- I shall conduct myself in a professional manner that reflects the dignity and worth of the services rendered by my employment and the societal responsibilities assumed as a trusted public servant.
- I shall be governed by the highest ideals of honor and integrity in all public and personal relationships in order to merit the respect and inspire the confidence of my employer and the public served.
- I shall neither seek nor accept any form of personal aggrandizement or profit through misuse of public or personal relationships.
- I shall identify and eliminate participation of any individual in operational situations where a conflict of interest may be involved.
- I shall not at any time or under any circumstances accept directly or indirectly, gifts, gratuities or other things of value from suppliers, which might influence or appear to influence the performance of my professional duties.
- I shall keep my governmental organization informed, through appropriate channels, on problems and progress of applicable operations by emphasizing the importance of the facts.
- I shall handle all personnel matters on a merit basis.

- I shall neither seek or dispense personal favors that are in conflict with my professional duties.
- I shall handle each administrative problem objectively and empathetically without discrimination.
- I shall subscribe to and support the professional aims and objectives of the Universal Public Procurement Certification Council.

Prohibited Acts

Individuals currently certified by the UPPCC, certified in a retired status or applying for UPPCC certification may be subject to review and appropriate action including revocation or denial of certification for conduct detrimental to the dignity and respect for their position, including, but not limited to, the commission of any of the following Prohibited Acts:

- A material misstatement or misrepresentation or fraud on application materials for certification or recertification.
- Willful violation of examination procedures, confidentiality or security.
- Failure to report or concealing knowledge of potentially illegal activity by any staff, volunteer or vendor related to his or her job or professional activities.
- Failure to pay certification or recertification fees in a timely manner.
- Misrepresentation or improper use of the CPPO, the CPPB or any other professional credential.
- Conviction for or entry of a plea of nolo contendere to any crime involving an individual's professional practice in the field of public procurement including but not limited to matters of conduct related to his or her employment and conduct related to professional associations and other professional activities.
- Failure to comply with the Code of Ethics & Professional Conduct provisions listed here or other behavior that may bring discredit to the profession.

Appendix C Organizational Conflicts of Interest—Consultants

[The Purchasing Office] suggests that consultants not participate in the development of the RFP and specifications unless the consultant has executed an "organizational conflict of interest" agreement or otherwise is limited in its ability to subsequently participate in developing a proposal in response to the solicitation.

Although the State of Colorado has statutes addressing conflicts by state employees, issues involving consultant involvement in procurements are not easily resolved using those standards. One technique is negotiation of an "organizational conflict of interest" agreement that limits the ability of the company providing the consulting expertise from participating in the proposal development or, in some cases, subsequent contract performance. The provision should also highlight the requirement that the consultant treat procurement-sensitive information as "confidential" and insure that only authorized employees of its organization have access to drafts and other procurement sensitive information.

The clause that follows is an example of an organizational conflict of interest provision:

> WHEREAS the Consultant [Company Name], is providing the following services to the Department of [Department] in connection with the acquisition and implementation of the billing, docketing, and case management system:
>
> - Project Management
> - Project Communications (including Web Pages)
> - Verification of Common Requirements

- Identification of unique requirements of sections within the department.
- Obtaining and coordinating information to/from Suppliers
- Creating updates and changes to the RFP issued as a result of this procurement
- Other procurement assistance on an as-needed basis

Because Consultant will be retained to define requirements and draft portions of the solicitation, including the scope of work and evaluation criteria, and otherwise make recommendations related to this solicitation, consultant agrees that it will not participate in development of proposals in response to this solicitation, or serve as a Consultant or subcontractor (at any tier) to any offeror who is awarded this contract until completion of the implementation phase of any contract awarded as a result of the solicitation.

This retention will involve disclosure of official information and possible supplier commercial information not publicly known. Consultant agrees to not disclose any information gained during the course of this engagement to any person, except to other State employees or authorized consultants who may in the normal course of State business have a need for such information.

Reference

Colorado State Purchasing Office Procurement Pearl 2000–3, Organizational Conflicts of Interest, reprinted in Appendix G, McKenna Long & Aldridge LLP. *Colorado Procurement Handbook.* Eagen, MN: West Publishing, 2010.

Index